PRESSURE

DES WILSON

DES WILSON is probably Britain's best-
known and most experienced and effective
campaigner.

In this book he draws on nearly 20 years' experience as a leader of British
charities and pressure groups, as a journalist, and as a politician, to offer a
practical guide to how to campaign for change in Britain. He explains why
extra-parliamentary pressure is necessary, and defines the role of the 'caring
revolutionary'.

Des Wilson, who was born in New Zealand and came to Britain in 1960, left
school at 15 to be a journalist and first achieved prominence as Director of
Shelter, the National Campaign for the Homeless (1966–71), and is now a
member of its Board. He was in the Sixties also a member of the National
Executive of the Child Poverty Action Group, and in the early Seventies of the
National Executive of the National Council for Civil Liberties.

In January 1982 he launched CLEAR, The Campaign for Lead-free Air, and
within 15 months had achieved its major objective of a Ministerial decision to
phase lead out of petrol. In that capacity he continues to campaign for the
elimination of lead pollution. In 1982 he was also elected Chairman of Friends
of the Earth (UK) and has played a major part in the revival of that campaign
over the last two years. He is also Chairman of the 1984 Committee for Freedom
of Information.

He has political experience as a member of the Liberal Party for the past ten
years and was parliamentary candidate at the Hove by-election in 1973 and a
subsequent general election in 1974. He is currently on the Party Council.

As a journalist he has written a weekly column for *The Guardian* (1968–71)
and *The Observer* (1971–75) and has contributed to many other newspapers and
magazines, notably *The Times*, *The London Evening Standard*, *The New
Statesman*, and *Illustrated London News*, for whom he has been a contributor for
12 years and was Deputy Editor from 1979 to 1981. He was the Editor of *Social
Work Today*, Britain's leading weekly social services magazine from 1976 to
1979.

DES WILSON

**FOREWORD BY
RALPH NADER**

PRESSURE

THE
A TO Z
OF
CAMPAIGNING IN
BRITAIN

HEINEMANN
LONDON · EXETER (NEW HAMPSHIRE)

*To my special friends
Sam and Kathy Smith
in Washington DC*

HEINEMANN EDUCATIONAL BOOKS LTD
22 Bedford Square, London WC1B 3HH

HEINEMANN EDUCATIONAL BOOKS INC
4 Front Street, Exeter, New Hampshire 03833

First published 1984

ISBN 0 435 83941 1
ISBN 0 435 83942 X Pbk

Typeset and printed in Great Britain by
Biddles Ltd, Guildford, Surrey

CONTENTS

PRESSURE IN PRACTICE

ACKNOWLEDGEMENTS

MY THANKS to Tony Smythe for his invaluable advice, and Susan Dibb and Patricia Simms for their practical assistance and good-humoured support.

I thank all the authors and publishers whose works I have quoted, and my own publishers, especially David Hill, Robin Frampton, and Joe Smith, for their confidence and help.

Above all, I owe thanks to Godfrey Bradman whose support for my work with CLEAR, Friends of the Earth, and the 1984 Campaign for Freedom of Information has been so generous, loyal, and inspirational.

DES WILSON
May 1984

The author (right) with Ralph Nader at a press conference to launch their three-day environmental campaign in Britain in April 1983

FOREWORD BY RALPH NADER

DES WILSON is a New Zealand-born campaigner living in Britain, who loves his adopted country so much that he wants to make it more lovable. This book is his latest contribution to a labour of love that he calls being a citizen activist. Distilled in these pages are the experiences of Des Wilson and others who have learned the programs and strategies which get a society moving to a higher plane of justice. The knowledge imparted to you, the reader, flows from both successes and failures because the author has learned from both. He led the campaign to aid the homeless with imagination and verve. He led the campaign against lead in petrol and soon that scourge will be diminishing, as it is diminishing in the US with the growing use of lead-free petrol. Now he is deep in the critical campaign to enact an effective freedom of information law in the United Kingdom through one of the broadest coalitions of public-spirited organizations ever brought together in Britain. Information, after all, is the currency of democracy, and secrecy its Achilles heel.

Some observers may look at this book and say that all it does is describe the kind of democratic activity that Britain has known for many generations. But a closer look will reveal an important distinction. Wilson is writing of a civic culture *outside* formal political parties to work *on* those parties and *on* governmental and corporate institutions to change their behavior in the direction of respecting broader human values than even most pressure groups recognize.

In recent years, the strains on parliamentary systems brought about by citizen demands have not been accommodated with much dispatch or substance by either the ruling or the opposition political parties. As large corporations converge with governmental authorities and as the differences, in terms of operating theories of power and grass-roots organizations, between the major parties – drawn toward electronic campaigning – become narrower, a momentum builds up for citizen campaigns. Furthermore, a certain staleness of ideas has seized the parties of the western world notwithstanding the presence of enormous technological, economic and environmental changes. This dichotomy may appear paradoxical, but more likely it can be understood as a product of both concentration and bureaucratization of power that freezes a society's or a culture's ability to respond. People need elbow room and fresh starts in such a constricting though changing period. That means developing the will and the levers of citizen campaigning so diffused and so deeply-rooted as to comprise a new civic culture, a new and engaging experience for millions of people assuming more responsibility for their democracy.

Certainly the headlines of the day are not obscuring any need for people to acquire the skills of campaigning which this book advises in such practical and specific ways. Conflicts over nuclear power, inadequate housing and mass transit, pollution of drinking water, toxic waste dumps, poverty, the arms race, consumer fraud, unemployment, deterioration of social services, together with a feeling by too many good bystanders that little or nothing can be done about these social ills, were some of the news items and impressions conveyed to me on a recent visit to Britain.

So this manual represents the civic energy that can be reproduced all over the United Kingdom to confront and dissolve these and other nagging problems and abuses. What the full-time citizen, Des Wilson, is asking of you is that you spend a *regular* portion of your waking hours on your citizen duties, as you define them, to make the country work better. Once you decide to do this – whether you wish to specialize on Parliament, a particular governmental department or a local condition – it will not be difficult to develop talents that will astound you with their impact for constructive change. After all, consider how few forebears it took to initiate the progress that contemporary Britons have inherited.

Citizen participation is not only a precondition of deep democracy; it is also pleasurable, fulfilling of one's potential and provides purpose to one's life view. Most certainly there is little pleasure in going through each day feeling powerless, alienated and disengaged from counting as a human being who is making a difference.

A good way to read this book is to first think of three or four conditions in your country that *you* would like to help change. Then watch the pages come alive with relevance for your own civic wishes.

Ralph Nader
Washington DC
May 1984

PREFACE

THIS BOOK has its origins in three separate incidents in April 1983. Early in the month two women came to ask me for help in tackling an injustice. For some considerable time they had worked to establish a nationwide network for those who had difficulty in obtaining just compensation after accidents. Theirs was a story of innumerable mistakes costing them time, money and heartache. Their attempts to encourage suitable legislation had failed. They had also been poorly advised about charitable status.

I was later telephoned by an acquaintance who was trying to organise her own community to stop a major nationalised industry from causing a local environmental hazard. She, too, needed help and advice.

On both occasions I was extremely busy with my own campaigns and, although I made a few practical suggestions, I was conscious of how much more I could have done if I had had the time. I was also made aware of how much knowledge I had accumulated over the years which simply isn't available to the ordinary citizen who is suddenly confronted by an urgent need to influence the powers-that-be.

Then one memorable evening at the end of April, I shared a platform at the Green Rally organised by Friends of the Earth at the Central Hall, Westminster, with the American consumer and environmental campaigner, Ralph Nader. In the course of his speech, Nader called for more citizen action to combat the power of centralised bureaucracies, both governmental and in multinational companies, and said, in effect, that we should all become individual pressure groups, leaders for change. I was struck by one particular remark: *'The duty of leaders is to help create more leaders – not more followers.'*

But how? I decided that one contribution I could make would be to share as widely as possible the experience and knowledge I had accumulated over nearly 20 years. Hence this book. . . .

For Whom?

This, then, is a 'How to do it' book (albeit with introductory chapters on the role and nature of pressure groups). But for whom?

The images we attach to words originate in our own backgrounds and experiences. When workers for CLEAR, or Friends of the Earth, or Shelter, talk about pressure groups we really mean *our kind of pressure group*, the kind that campaigns for relief of need and disadvantage, for civil liberties, for environmental protection, for peace, and for other interrelated causes linked by a common desire for a fairer, healthier, safer world. If required to describe them in one word or sentence, what would we all say? Pressure groups for social change? Radical pressure groups?

Specific concerns may differ, but these pressure groups would see themselves as of the same breed, and generally feel sympathetic to and supportive of one another. Many people are members of more than one group. On the whole, their cause is furthered by public exposure and advanced by public goodwill. This characteristic distinguishes them from the vested interests who prefer and often need to achieve their ends behind the scenes.

Because when we talk of pressure groups we mean *our kind*, we speak of pressure groups approvingly and positively, as I do in my explanation of their role in Chapter 1. The fact is, however, that we are only one kind of pressure group and often we are the least effective. For it is not only the poor who have pressure groups – so do the rich; not only the environmentalists and conservationists – so do the polluters and the squanderers of resources; not only the civil libertarians – so do the forces of authoritarianism. Thus it is necessary from the beginning to understand there are two kinds of pressure groups – those whose motivation is a concern for the health and wellbeing of the community, and who usually campaign to change or improve priorities or policies, and those with vested interests, whose cause is usually maintenance of the status quo, or furtherance of policies beneficial to them, irrespective of the implications for the community.

Students of pressure groups have tried to find words to describe the categories. Some have described pressure groups for the community as '*fors*' and pressure groups of vested interests as '*ofs*'. Some have called the former '*idea pressure groups*' and the latter '*interest pressure groups*'. Some have described the former as '*problematic or promotional*' and the latter as '*sectional*'. Some have divided them as '*do-good*' and '*selfish*'. Some have defined the first as '*campaigning*' and the second as '*spokesmen*'. Others, who argue that pressure groups should be classified in terms of their access to decision-makers, see the former as '*outsiders*' and the latter as '*insiders*', arguing that the 'outsiders' threaten 'the system' itself, whereas the 'insiders' are more likely to wish to strengthen the status quo.

One writer divided pressure groups into three 'worlds':

The first world . . . includes groups, whether interests or promotional, whose access to the decision-makers is continuous, resources impressive, legitimacy established, and whose demands are considered to be mainly routine. Some can, and do, impose commanding constraints but when acting as pressure groups it is in their interests to maintain rather than to disturb the balance of power. . . .

For second world groups, access is more or less accepted, although it is likely to be intermittent. Resources are varied yet limited relative to first world groups. They tend to be issue-orientated and engender opposition, but the balance of power is only marginally affected. Second world groups accept and further consensus. Some are social reform groups . . . some of the groups establish sponsor-client relations and more properly belong in the first world while others mobilise support at the parliamentary level. Considerable attention has been devoted to these groups which may be less important politically than some of those in the third world.

The third world . . . is more amorphous. The degree to which these groups are recognised varies widely and access is likely to be sporadic. At the same time the groups tend to be highly active and at different levels of the political system. Many cannot meet the requisites of legitimacy and even when they do they remain suspect . . . it is not just a matter of issue recognition, but of establishing its priority and promoting its resolution. Since the ultimate satisfaction of their demands may involve a radical restructuring of society and the reordering of priorities, they challenge or threaten the balance of power.[1]

The power of the vested-interest lobbies is enormous. Take the case of transport: There was a time when British Rail provided a service the nation could be proud of and the people were happy to use. Yet in the past 30 years the number of people travelling by rail in Britain has fallen from around 20 per cent of the population to around five per cent, while the number travelling by private car has increased from around 45 per cent to over 90 per cent. The motor car has become overwhelmingly the dominant form of transport. An appalling price has been paid for this.

- In road casualties. During the 32 years from 1946 to 1978, we killed nearly 210,000 people, seriously injured 2,427,000 and slightly injured nearly 10,000,000 in road accidents. These figures are staggering. In one year, 1980, over 6,000 people were killed on the roads, 79,400 seriously injured, and 243,300 slightly injured. One researcher estimated that in the lifetime of any one driver we have a one in 59 chance of killing someone, including ourselves; a one in five chance of seriously injuring someone, including ourselves; and a one in 1.5 chance of slightly injuring someone, including ourselves. If these accidents occurred in one catastrophe in one day in one place, it would achieve worldwide attention as a human disaster of unbelievable proportions.

- In pollution: between 1970 and 1980, air pollution from all road vehicles increased by 33 per cent, with carbon monoxide showing a 40 per cent increase. Of all man-made processes, road traffic contributes 90 per cent of carbon monoxide, 90 per cent of lead in the air, 41 per cent of hydrocarbons, and 26 per cent of nitrogen oxide. In 1980, the Noise Advisory Council estimated that six million people – one-ninth of the UK population – lived in houses and flats exposed to traffic noise in excess of the acceptable levels in the noise insulation regulations.

- In energy consumption: Petroleum consumption increased by 27 per cent during the past decade for all transport uses; by 42 per cent for cars. The motor car is devouring huge quantities of oil every day.
- In economics: One economist has assessed congestion costs as being 2.6 and 3.1 per cent of the GNP in EEC countries. Assuming the lowest rate for Britain, that gives a congestion cost of £3 billion.
- In environmental blight: I could write endlessly about agricultural land lost, attractive countryside ruined, homes destroyed, and urban centres split by multi-lane highways, flyovers, underpasses, subways, roundabouts, and the huge streams of largely unnecessary traffic they carry.

This is the price we pay for domination by the car of transport in the UK. You would think that responsible authorities would have done all within their power to control our love affair with the car and maintain a high level of efficient, inexpensive public transport. Yet the opposite has been the case. The majority of cars on the road are company cars, heavily subsidised by the tax system. The whole of the community pays for the roads, although 40 per cent of households do not have a car. The motorist is not called upon to pay the real price to make vehicles safer and pollution-free. Traffic laws and implementation are relatively weak (our speed limit of 70 mph is 15 mph faster than allowed on the huge motorways crossing the open spaces of the US). The whole system is prejudiced towards the motor car.

At the same time we have allowed public transport to become steadily weaker. Our subsidies don't compare with other developed countries – on the latest figures, Holland subsidises public transport 70 per cent, Belgium 69 per cent, France 56 per cent, USA 46 per cent, Australia 45 per cent, Sweden 45 per cent, but the UK figure is only 29 per cent. The result, of course, has been the curtailing of rail and bus services, higher prices, less dependability, and inevitably a further move towards the road rather than rail. In 1963 there were nearly 17,000 miles of railway, but by 1983 over 6,000 miles had been closed. In 1963 British Rail had 4,200 stations; it now has only 2,400.

The lunacy of what has happened is reflected by one statistic: of all the people who work in central London and travel by road, about 40 per cent travel by bus and 60 per cent by car, yet these people are carried by only 3,000 buses and over 130,000 cars.

Finally, let me emphasise that this cannot even be defended on the grounds that everyone has the option of either car or public transport.

One writer explains:

> Firstly, only a limited number of people in the household can drive. Children, and teenagers under the age limit cannot. They are forced to depend on public transport, cycling or walking. As the number of cars on the roads has grown, so these members of our society have lost mobility or independence – or both. Furthermore, they are high on the list of those injured or killed by cars. Second, very few old people have car licences. They were born in an age before widespread car ownership and many never learned to drive and most of them never will. Many others are now beyond driving. They, too, have lost much mobility and independence. Thirdly, a substantial number of adults can't drive. Roughly six out of ten adults with a driving licence are men, and many women are unable to drive the 'family car'.[2]

How can this have happened? The answer can be summed up in three words: *The car lobby*. The car lobby represents the other side of the pressure group equation.

The car lobby is as powerful as any in Britain. First, it consists of the car manufacturers themselves, and their trade unions. They have a vested interest in the production and sale of more and more cars and thus a vested interest in first class facilities for cars and in poor public transport. Second, a huge sum of governmental money has been poured into the British car manufacturing industry and thus government itself has a considerable vested interest in recouping that investment. Because it is also held responsible for unemployment, as so many workers are dependent on the car manufacturing industry, government's vested interest is political as well as economic. Then, of course, there is the petroleum industry, itself hugely powerful, dependent on a big motoring market for sales of petrol and oil. There are the car retailers, the car repairers, the tool and parts manufacturers, and, of course, the petrol retailers. There are the advertising and marketing and public relations businesses and others who feed on major industries. There is a massive road haulage industry. And finally, there are two of the most powerful 'member' pressure groups in the country – the Automobile Association and the Royal Automobile Club. The AA alone has a membership of about 5½ million and an income from subscriptions and commercial activities of near to £100 million. That money buys a lot of influence.

Opposed to this massive lobby is British Rail, restricted in the extent it can campaign to combat governmental policies by dependence on government sympathy for adequate subsidies. There are the rail unions, but they are weakened by the collapse of their industry and have little bargaining power. And there are a number of small consumer pressure groups, or groups like Transport 2000, ten years old with two full-time workers and a tiny budget.

The pro-car pressure groups have no need to argue their case in the court of public opinion. They negotiate with government at the highest levels, and employ economic pressure; they join together to achieve their aims; and so far no government has been able to resist and do other than proceed on the lamentable course to a transport system that is the least safe, the most expensive, the most energy-consuming, the most polluting, the most environmentally-damaging, and the most socially divisive.

Let's take, more briefly, another case: *the farming lobby*. It was said about the time of the 1983 election that the National Farmers' Union had been spending about £2 million a year on public relations and political lobbying. In financial terms alone this represents a huge advantage over the combined conservation and countryside pressure groups. But the power of the farmers is far greater than that. While they have succeeded in retaining public goodwill, they have been able to cause devastation to much of the countryside, destroying wildlife habitats, ripping out hedgerows, eliminating medieval meadows, old woods, and so much that is beautiful and irreplaceable. They have contaminated the soil with pesticides. They have emptied the country-side of people at work; from 1948 to 1979 farm workers left the land at over 7,000 a year, falling in total from 563,000 to 133,000. And their use of energy has been colossal.

One writer has stated that:

> . . . despite winning the press debate almost handsdown, it came as little surprise when the conservation lobby failed to make much impact on the Wildlife and Countryside Bill which became an Act very much in line with the wishes of the National Farmers' Union and the Country Landowners' Association. Environmentalists were up against a political and propaganda machine which has been described by one ex-minister as 'the most powerful lobby in Britain, probably in Europe', and was credited as long ago as 1962 as having a relationship with government 'unique in its range and intensity'. So effective is the NFU lobbying machine that it was used as a model by the Confederation of British Industry when it wished to increase its influence over Labour MPs.
>
> During the passage of the Bill the NFU's lobbying was by far the most extensive and detailed of any of the groups involved. In all it issued 13 parliamentary briefing papers. The list of recipients in the House of Lords was 150 and in the Commons 354. These lists are computerised, carefully amended as necessary, and any MP who shows an interest of concern to the NFU can be supplied with additional background material, tapes and interview facilities. . . . The NFU, with three representatives from the Land Use Division working full-time on the Bill, were the only group with the resources to be present at all stages of the Bill's passage through both houses.[3]

So powerful is the agricultural industry that it has actually obtained its own Ministry. That Ministry deals daily with the NFU and with the farming and landowning lobby, and mixes on both a professional and social basis in such a way that it is automatically assumed by conservationists to be committed to the farmers' point of view. As if that isn't enough, some of the most powerful political figures are themselves farmers and landowners. Until recently several of the most senior members of the cabinet were big landowners; two or three still are.

Most industries create associations or 'research organisations' that are, in fact, public relations fronts. Their sole role is to act as pressure groups for these industries. For instance, CLEAR, The Campaign for Lead-free Air, in its endeavours to rid the air of lead in petrol, found it impossible to deal with individual companies, but rather had to communicate with the UK Petroleum Industry Association and the Society of Motor Manufacturers and Traders whose role was to hold the party line rather than to engage in any kind of worthwhile discussion. These organisations actually speak disparagingly of the 'undue influence of pressure groups', referring, of course, to pressure groups like CLEAR, as if these were the only pressure groups around. If one points out that their organisation is also a pressure group, they look pained. After all, they are in business; they have a rightful and responsible place and an acceptable function! 'Pressure groups' (i.e. not their kind) are, on the other hand, irresponsible!

Often these industrial and economic pressure groups make considerable efforts to pretend they are otherwise. In the 1960s an organisation emerged called 'The London Foundation for Marriage Education', a trust dedicated to the promotion of contraceptives other than the pill, including those made of rubber. Another organisation, 'The Genetic Study Unit', specifically campaigned in opposition to the pill. They denied it at the time, but it subsequently emerged that they were both the creations of London Rubber Industries, Britain's number one manufacturer of rubber contraceptives, who in an effort to maintain their share of the contraceptive market in the face of the increasing popularity of the pill, had set up pressure groups intended to look morally-virtuous or scientific in nature.

How these other pressure groups operate and the extent of their influence will emerge in more detail in my story of the CLEAR campaign in Chapter 6. As this book is not intended for them, and yet it is necessary for the reader to be aware of their existence and relative strength, I have dealt with them at some length here. The advantage, in terms of money, economic and relative strength, is heavily weighted to the powerful pressure groups. As a result, the pressure groups for whom this book is intended – those of and for the community – are more often than not the 'Davids' involved in an unequal fight with industrial or governmental 'Goliaths'.

How do I describe the Davids? No all-embracing term is satisfactory, but I have chosen to call them *community/cause pressure groups* – groups that exist for the benefit of the whole community, or to further minority causes that will make the community a better place to live in, groups who need to become effective advocates to protect themselves, to protect their towns and countryside, and ultimately to protect the planet itself. On the whole they have no inherent resources. They have to combat big money with hard work; behind-the-scenes influence with mobilisation of community concern; and cynical manipulation of 'the system' with idealistic campaigning aimed at public conscience.

The object of this book is not just to help community/cause pressure groups to win, for even they may sometimes not deserve to. My aim is to help them to be effective with the resources at their disposal, and help them to be heard, so that their case is properly presented in the court of public opinion. In that way, we, the jury – the public, the community as a whole – can reach a fair verdict on the issue.

Why Me?

For the main section of the book, *The A to Z of Campaigning in Britain*, I have drawn on my own experience and can therefore say that the majority of my ideas and suggestions have been tried and tested. I have been fortunate because my experience has covered the three inter-related areas of the media, politics, and charities/pressure groups. Perhaps I should briefly detail it. . . .

I was born in a small town in New Zealand in 1941. The population of Oamaru was about 10,000 and remained static for many years. This was unusual, for although New Zealand is best known for its farm produce and its scenery, the vast majority of New Zealanders live in towns and cities, and they have steadily grown in size throughout the century. The reason Oamaru did not was because it was one of the few places in the Southern Hemisphere that had prohibition. A coastal town with a harbour, it had suffered from the excesses of sailors from overseas, and in 1905 voted to ban liquor. Every three or four years the town had the opportunity to vote for the restoration of 'the licence' but up until the late 1950s this never seemed likely to happen.

It was in Oamaru in the Fifties that I saw pressure groups in action for the first time. Inevitably it was over prohibition. I was a reporter on the local newspaper and it was clear that at this particular poll there was a real chance 'the licence' would finally be restored. Both sides formed pressure groups. The breweries, who clearly stood to gain financially, sent down a public relations man from the North Island who joined with some locals to form the Restoration Committee. A local Presbyterian clergyman chaired the No Licence Committee.

No holds were barred. There was no local radio station, nor did New Zealand have television at that time, so the battle took place at public meetings and in the local newspaper, although I do recall that the No

Licence Committee paid for slides on the screen at the local cinema showing a drunk lying in a gutter, or throwing up over a garden fence, with the message 'Would you like a pub next to your home?'. I also learned for the first time what some will do to influence the media when the clergyman who was so passionately opposed to restoration of 'The Licence' came to our office and offered a bottle of Scotch to each of the reporters if his campaign was generously covered!

Both campaigns had a theme. The Restoration Committee argued that the economic and population growth of Oamaru was curtailed by prohibition. 'Even travelling salesmen bypass the town', they claimed. Furthermore, they argued, heavy quantities of drink were imported into the town and consumed in homes. Surely it was better that men should drink in pubs, rather than in front of their own children, they said.

The No Licence Committee emphasised how fortunate Oamaru was to be able to raise its children in such a clean town, and held out the prospect of drunks in the streets, old women being attacked, and young women suffering a fate worse than death.

The high spot of the campaign was a public meeting, chaired by the Mayor. One of the speakers, a Boar War veteran called George Cutriss, the local billiard saloon proprietor, who hoped to be able to have a bar in his saloon if 'The Licence' was restored, upset the Mayor by rising to speak a second time when the Mayor had ruled that no-one could speak twice. When upbraided, he protested 'But I understood it was permissible to ask a question, Mr Mayor'. The Mayor apologised. Of course George could ask a question. George then proceeded to make point after point to enhance his case. The Mayor rose. 'I am coming to my question now, Mr Mayor', George reassured him. He then continued to hammer home his argument, until, seeing the Mayor getting impatiently to his feet, he cried 'And my question, Mr Mayor, is this . . .'. There was an expectant silence. 'Does this meeting or does it not agree with what I have been saying for the last ten minutes?' He sat down amid uproar.

In the years I have been away the town has at last voted 'The Licence' back.

It was in Oamaru that I had my first experience of publicity activity. One of my passions in those days was the theatre, and Oamaru had a level of theatrical activity that was remarkable in both quantity and quality. As I could not act my way out of a paper bag, but had the advantage of being a reporter on the local paper, I became the publicity officer for virtually every production. I fed both my newspaper and its rival with stories. I booked advertising, distributed posters, and generally publicised the shows as if they were a Broadway opening. The theatres were packed. I would like to claim this was entirely due to the publicity but the reader should understand that apart from two films a week in the local cinema, there was little else to do in Oamaru! (This relatively brief passage in my life was to have an extraordinary sequel, for in 1974 I took on a two-year contract as Head of Public Affairs with the Royal Shakespeare Company, and from publicising the productions of the Oamaru Repertory Society with a budget of £50 or so, I found myself with the Royal Shakespeare Theatre in Stratford-on-Avon and the Aldwych Theatre in London with part-responsibility to fill them every night of the year, and with a considerable budget to do it.)

Undoubtedly this feeling for the theatre has helped me a little in pressure group activities, in the sense that I have always insisted that press conferences, public meetings, or symposia, should be well-staged, with professional presentation and good timing. On the principle that one should always seek to achieve the highest standards, I think this has been beneficial. Undoubtedly one lesson I learned from the theatre was the importance of attention to every detail, which in the RSC is remarkable.

In 1959 I left New Zealand for Melbourne, Australia, and worked on the *Melbourne Sun* for nearly a year before travelling to Britain. I arrived on June 10, 1960, and after some freelance work, and two relatively short spells on local newspapers and a trade magazine, became press officer in an advertising agency, where I had to learn to write more selectively to present clients and products favourably. I hated the work. The attitudes, priorities and politics of advertising people were not mine. I say that without criticism or rancour – it was simply a fact of my life that I could not tune into theirs. At the same time, I learnt all I could about how advertising agencies worked, what the basic techniques of public relations were, and how to plan and budget a campaign.

My inability to conform with the views of colleagues in advertising had much to do with the fact that I had become politically conscious. I had in the early Sixties been one of the millions all over the world who had been captivated by the Presidency of John F. Kennedy. I can still remember watching on television in a basement room in Earls Court the broadcast of his 'Don't ask what your country can do for you, but what you can do for your country' inaugural speech in January 1961. As a result I turned to politics and joined the Labour Party of Hugh Gaitskell and then Harold Wilson. My front room was a local ward election headquarters in 1964 and 1966. I became ward secretary, constituency press officer, and a council candidate. Yet I never felt at ease. I liked my friends in the Labour Party but found that many were locked into attitudes and slogans that were both inflexible and out-of-date. I found myself in a minority of one on many occasions. What was worse, I was frustrated by the lack of practical action. This was a Conservative-dominated constituency so there was little opportunity for involvement in council work. As a result the Party seemed to me to be all talk and self-indulgence. At the same time, the Wilson administration was the cause of much disillusion. Thus it was that when I saw a television programme about the work of charitable housing trusts I was particularly struck by the fact that these people were not only concerned about the homeless but actually *acted*. They may not have housed a lot of families, but by buying up older properties, improving them, and letting them at cost rents, they were doing a lot more than I was achieving as a participant in earnest discussions about housing legislation at ward meetings attended by ten or 12 people.

I contacted the Notting Hill Housing Trust whose members, I discovered, were engaged in talks with other housing associations about the possibility of a major national campaign to both raise money for housing trusts and campaign on behalf of the homeless. 'What we need', one of them said, 'is an Oxfam on the homefront'. The idea captured my imagination. I offered to leave the advertising agency and become the campaign's first full-time worker and I did this in June 1966. On December 1 of that year Shelter was launched. I was then campaign director and was appointed director by the Trustees in May 1967. I will tell the Shelter story in full in Chapter 5, but suffice to say that it became one of Britain's best known charities. By 1970 our income was £1 million a year, we had 350 local fund raising groups, fed money into 40 local housing trusts, backed a number of housing aid centres, and had made a considerable impact on housing legislation. During this period I also spent a year on the Executive Committee of the Child Poverty Action Group. Shelter was both a charity and a pressure group, and CPAG was strictly a pressure group. Over the four-and-a-half-years I was with Shelter I had to learn a lot, often by mistakes, and often because we were entering pressure group territory that had not been explored before.

While I was with Shelter I wrote a weekly column for *The Guardian* for three years and *The Observer* in 1971 engaged me full-time to campaign on behalf of minorities in its columns. I found myself dealing on a daily basis with pressure groups and was able to campaign for gypsies, the elderly, the disabled, the homeless, the poor at home and the poor abroad, and on almost every kind of minority issue. One of the insights I gained was that different pressure groups varied greatly in their ability to seize the opportunities provided by a column like mine.

At the same time, I worked with a number of voluntary organisations, and was on the Executive Committee of the National Council for Civil Liberties. By then my disenchantment with the Labour Party was complete, and I left to join the Liberals. I was rather quickly pushed into a parliamentary by-election in Hove in November 1973, and now added to my experience the unique one of fighting a major by-election under the full glare of the national political spotlight. I polled over 17,000 votes, reducing the Conservative majority substantially, and forcing Labour to lose its deposit. I went back at the General Election in February 1974 and increased my vote by a further 1,000. It was then suggested to me by the local constituency that if 'a radical like you can do so well, a more moderate candidate could win'. I took the hint and made way for another candidate. There was a further election in November 1974 and the Liberal vote fell by 6,000. (The moral of the story, I hasten to add, is not that I was worth more votes than the other candidate, but that the Liberals in the constituency had failed to realise that the voters were actually *responding* to a radical message.)

From *The Observer*, I was tempted to my non-acting engagement with the Royal Shakespeare Company. Although the attraction to me was the complete change from what I had done before, and, of course, my years in the theatre in New Zealand, the highlight of my RSC experience did not occur in the theatre at all. Relations between the Royal Shakespeare Theatre and the citizens of Stratford-on-Avon were appalling. The fault lay on both sides. The theatre made little attempt to communicate with, and integrate itself with the town. The towns-people, on the other hand, were happy to capitalise on the tourists drawn to the town by the theatre, but tended to carp and criticise at all that the theatre people did. I made it a high priority, therefore, to tackle this problem.

First, I arranged to speak to a number of local organisations such as the Rotary Club to explain some of the theatre's problems and why theatre people behaved as they did, and also to urge greater co-operation between town and theatre. Second, I arranged to have a monthly column in the local newspaper in order to tell townspeople of the company's plans so that they felt more involved. Then I set up a town advisory committee, with the role of improving communication, and arranging shared events. For me the high spot was when the theatre celebrated its centenary, and I persuaded the townspeople to join with the actors and theatre administrators in organising a huge Elizabethan fair in the parkland across the river from the theatre. We attracted 20,000 people for an event that lasted 15 hours including a joust, a fireworks display, and the whole of the Warwickshire Symphony Orchestra floating down the River Avon on a barge, prior to an Elizabethan gun battle on the water outside the theatre at midnight. To make it work, we had to involve every organisation in the town. The Council even set up a special sub-committee to liaise with the fair committee. The response was amazing and I have never experienced an occasion when a whole town came together to organise an event quite like it. I don't think there was a single local organisation that was not involved in one way or another. On the eve of the fair, we had to use the company's smaller theatre, The Other Place, for a meeting of all those involved, and it was packed. Even the weather co-operated, and we made over £10,000 profit for the appeal. But the real achievement was the town spirit that was created.

From Stratford-on-Avon, I returned to journalism and spent three-and-a-half years as editor of the weekly magazine for the social services, *Social Work Today*. Throughout the Seventies I wrote for *Illustrated London News*, a magazine I had always read in the public library back in Oamaru in the early Fifties, and when the offer came in 1979 to be its Deputy Editor, I found this irresistible. Unpredictably, it was to lead me back into campaigning.

In 1981 I decided to explore the problem of lead pollution for an article for *ILN*. As a result I came into contact with the different personalities involved in the anti-lead movement and in particular with Godfrey Bradman, a wealthy businessman who had become sufficiently concerned about the problem to move his home out of London. So determined was he to end this form of pollution that he decided to make available a sum of money for an effective campaign to achieve an objective of a ban on lead in petrol. He had gathered together anti-lead campaigners of the past and had already set out to find a campaign manager when I came on the scene and was persuaded to put my name forward. Ultimately I became its executive chairman.

About the same time, Neil MacIntosh, the Director of Shelter, suggested it was time I joined the organisation's Board, and shortly afterwards I also joined the Board of Friends of the Earth. In December of 1982 the Board of FoE elected me Chairman and I found myself engaged on a wide variety of campaigns concerned with conservation of resources and all forms of environmental protection, including the fight to protect public transport, to save the countryside and wildlife, to prevent the introduction of the pressurised water reactor at Sizewell, to achieve controls on the use of pesticides, and to force the authorities to introduce greater freedom of information.

Arising out of Friends of the Earth, came the Freedom of Information Campaign and its 1984 Committee of which I am also Chairman.

This, then, briefly outlines my experience. If the emphasis of this book is on anecdotes from the Shelter days, from CLEAR and from Friends of the Earth, that is how it should be because that is where I have both made my mistakes and achieved my successes. I would like to stress that if I tell a story of a success, it is not to boast. It is simply to illustrate what can be done. Over all of these years I have also made many mistakes, and these too form part of my experience. I would also like to stress that my experience has been more in national campaigning than in local campaigning, although I have tried in this book to advise on local issues as well. I am well aware that not all of my experience or suggestions can be applied to other situations, but some can, and many more can be adapted, and I hope others may spark off alternative ideas in the reader's mind.

Above all, I hope this book will represent a message of encouragement and hope. As I wrote in my record of the work of Shelter back in the

Sixties, the work of effective pressure groups is a source of hope. I have learned from my experience that it is possible for the individual to work with others to make an impact even on the most powerful institutions, if we believe in the cause, are prepared to fight with persistence, perspective and professionalism, and if we have the benefit of a little know-how.

PRESSURE POINTS

1 WHO GUARDS THE GUARDS? – THE ROLE OF PRESSURE GROUPS

COMMUNITY/CAUSE pressure groups, as defined in my preface, are not a modern phenomenon. They have predecessors as far back as the nineteenth century. Those who these days criticise charities for '*Victorian* attitudes of paternalism and philanthropy' fail to acknowledge, as Francis Gladstone has written, that pressure for social reform was in Victorian days often linked to charity:

> Many recognised that charitable service-giving would have had only a superficial impact if the underlying causes of social misery remained untouched. Beginning with the anti-slavery campaign, the reformists tirelessly pressed for legislation to end the exploitation of child labour and improve conditions in factories, to humanise the appalling harsh criminal law, and to end the squalor of the prisons and to remedy a host of other social evils.[4]

The emergence of the trade union movement and the Labour Party provided in the earlier part of this century an alternative vehicle for social campaigning. Throughout the 1950s, however, Britain's two major political parties developed what was virtually a policy consensus. Those who were dissatisfied with the performance of this consensus began to express their concern outside of the political parties, first on the issue of peace with CND and the Committee of 100, and then on a variety of other social problems.

Involvement in pressure group activity increased as a result of a convergence of the idealistic spirit of the Sixties with widespread disenchantment with Harold Wilson's Labour administration. I know I was only one of many who enthusiastically assisted the Labour Party in the early Sixties and then sadly abandoned it for pressure group activity as I became increasingly disillusioned with its failure to match its promise on social issues. The Child Poverty Action Group was born of the frustration of Socialists with their own government. Socialist academics like Richard Titmuss, Peter Townsend, and Brian Abel-Smith, assumed, as Frank Field, later Director of CPAG, was to acknowledge, that 'the mere presentation of facts would lead to action'. Instead, as Field records:

> . . . right to the end of the 1964–70 government's life, the Wilson Administration would fail to even develop an effective strategy against poverty, let alone begin to implement one. Indeed, while the Child Poverty Action Group's initial belief was that the Labour Government would act swiftly once it was presented with evidence, its early activities and its Christmas 1965 meeting with the Prime Minister does not even rate a single line mention in Wilson's own record of the period. Nor is there a single entry on poverty, or child poverty, in the index.[5]

At the same time as this was occurring in Britain, there was inspiration from across the Atlantic in the non-party-political campaigning of Martin Luther King and others over racial discrimination and in the huge protest movements about the Vietnam war.

All of these factors contributed to the mushrooming of pressure group activities in the 1960s and subsequently. However, another factor was the attraction of involvement in the pressure groups themselves. In particular, Shelter captured the imagination of the public in the Sixties in a way that was virtually unique and became one of the most popular and widely-supported pressure groups (or pressure group-cum-charities) ever. Even today a considerable number of pressure group leaders in Britain can trace their careers back to the early days of Shelter. Pressure groups operating more in the corridors of power, such as the CPAG, then managed by Tony Lynes, and the National Council for Civil Liberties, led by Tony Smythe, were also seen to be pioneering fresh approaches, in particular by combining detailed negotiations with Whitehall and Westminster with exploitation of the media to force politicians and civil servants to take them seriously.

Such was the impact of the community/cause pressure groups that there were attempts at a backlash. *The Daily Telegraph* complained that 'the land is alive with pressure groups' and later Ronald Butt wrote in *The Times* that pressure groups had 'power without responsibility'. He claimed that the Abortion Act of 1967 and the Divorce Reform Bill of 1969 were 'pushed through parliament as Private Member's Bills under the steam of a minority pressure group while Ministers stood safely on the sidelines, but gave them a helping hand with parliamentary time'. He argued that 'it is not right that they should be hustled through a thinly-attended parliament, without proper amendment, by the will of a pressure group without the government taking any responsibility for what is being done'. In 1983, Butt, now an influential *Sunday Times* columnist, wrote of the Sixties and subsequent decades that 'in sector after sector of public life, the pressure group has mattered most'. These, he claimed, flouted common opinion instead of reflecting it, and led to political decisions that reflected the influence of vocal minorities rather than the public desire as a whole. As the re-emergence of CND before the 1983 election led to an all-out war between it and the newly-appointed Secretary of State for Defence, Michael Heseltine, *The Times* published a leader thundering at the influence of single-issue pressure groups. One former Prime Minister, James Callaghan, described pressure groups to me as 'a nuisance, if not a menace'. He stated that his role as Prime Minister and that of his colleagues was to tackle the problems of the nation as a whole, putting each in its proper perspective, and that 'shrill, single-minded pressure groups' made the country more difficult to govern. 'He who makes the loudest noise tends to win, irrespective of where the justice of the case lies', he said, looking, I felt, rather accusingly at me.

Callaghan, of course, was the classic wheeler-dealer of politics, a man of the so-called 'smoke-filled rooms'. The less public debate on any issue the better. The country should go about its business and leave it to him, benevolent Jim, to do what was right. Nevertheless, he did articulate the one substantial criticism that can be made of community/ cause pressure groups. It does not worry me that pressure groups make the country more difficult to govern. I think the country *should* be difficult to govern if the alternative is easy-going acquiescence with the exercise of centralised power. Countries easy to govern are easy to misgovern. A country that is difficult to govern in the sense that Callaghan meant, and in the sense that I address here, is a country in which those in power can never take that power for granted and have to be convincing in their defence of their policies, and respond to public opinion. Where the critics of community/cause pressure groups are on stronger ground, however, is when they charge that these groups are uneven in terms of financial resources, influential friends, or talented campaigners, and can project an issue into the forefront of public attention out of all proportion to its importance, and often at the expense of others. Undoubtedly the CLEAR campaign illustrated what is possible when you have a combination of an emotive case, substantial resources, experienced campaigners and friends of influence. I don't wish this to be misunderstood; I believe the CLEAR campaign was fully justified and vindicated by events. Nevertheless, there were other issues that deserved at least equal, if not greater media attention and higher political priority. In this case, fortunately, our achievement was not at the expense of these other issues. On the contrary, good was done and no harm. But I can see that in many circumstances it could have been different. I can see that if a Minister with limited resources is confronted with a number of competing pressure groups, the most emotive, most muscular, best-equipped could win the day and force a weak or politically vulnerable Secretary of State to spend more on one section of the community at the expense of another than might, in fact, have been justified.

So what is the answer to this? I believe it is to remind ourselves what pressure groups are. They are not decision-makers. They have no power, other than their ability to mobilise support and to seek to influence decisions. Decision-makers can keep the pressure groups in perspective simply by accepting a responsibility to argue their case just as the pressure groups do. Instead of refusing to debate with pressure groups, and often attempting to brush them aside with arrogance, and instead of trying to steam-roller policies by ruthless use of power and by expansive use of the governmental propaganda machine, they should evolve their policies after greater consultation with individuals and organisations, and they should be prepared to argue their case, as pressure groups do, in the court of public opinion. That is what pressure groups are – they are advocates in the court of public opinion. They present their evidence to the court either on their own behalf or on behalf of their cause, seek to undermine the evidence of the opposition, and hope that the jury of their peers, the public, will become convinced that their case is just. If pressure groups are particularly influential in the court of public opinion it is partly because those in power often choose not to be represented or even present their own case.

(It is well known within media, political and pressure group circles that, with very few exceptions, Ministers of both major parties have for nearly 20 years refused point blank to confront lobbyists in television discussions. They are advised by their PR men in Whitehall that this 'reduces them in stature'. However, this is not the only reason. What civil servants are more concerned about is that their Ministers have an inadequate grasp of the issue and are likely to be defeated in the debate. Furthermore, the civil servants try desperately to keep pressure group leaders away from Ministers, or at least to keep them from meeting alone. The thought that a Minister and a lobbyist may have to spend half an hour over a drink in the 'green room' of a television studio strikes fear into the heart of any civil servant who has carefully presented to his Minister only what he wants the Minister to know. Usually the media cringes before the Minister, allowing him to dictate the terms and appear alone. Thus, genuine debate does not take place. Without debate between equals, the television appearance is usually complacent, lacks balance, and has little impact. Even if the Minister's policy is right, this is not the way to capture people's attention and convince them. The most he will achieve is to defuse the issue until the pressure group strikes again. If the Minister is on top of the issue, and appears to debate it fully with the lobbyists on television, he should, if he is in the right, have at least an equal chance of winning public opinion.)

The criticism that pressure groups distort decision-making also arises where a decision has to be made between a number of alternatives in a situation where someone is bound to suffer. Take, for instance, the never-ending debate over a third London airport. A number of sites have now been chosen only to be rejected after massive local pressure activity. Here, the outstanding priority of the different local pressure groups has been to avoid the third London airport being sited on their patch. Anthony Crosland, a past Minister responsible for the issue, said of one local residents' association that it was 'in danger of giving the impression that it does not care twopence for anyone else's noise and environment'.

Frankly, one cannot have too much sympathy for those in power who find decision-making difficult. Did they think it would be easy? Did they think that they could put airports wherever they wished, and that local communities would just like it or lump it? It is up to the decision-makers to legitimise their decisions by the consultation process, by the comprehensive nature and objectivity of public debate or inquiries, and by the assembly and availability to the public of all the relevant facts.

Pressure groups must, however, also accept the need to prove their case fairly and fully. One of the diseases that can afflict the lobbyist is to become excessively self-righteous or closed to reason. I will argue in Chapter 2 that perspective is crucial for pressure groups. One way that the pressure group must reflect that perspective is to argue its case reasonably and responsibly, to argue it in its proper context, to fully accept the rights of others to argue their case, and to encourage the same kind of open debate that it demands of those in power.

Pressure groups should also try to avoid furthering the cause of one disadvantaged group by undermining others. When I was Director of Shelter people would often say 'I believe charity begins at home. I would rather donate to Shelter than Oxfam or one of the overseas aid charities'. We always replied by saying that poverty was an adverse human condition that should be tackled everywhere, and that we could not put boundaries around it and say 'our concern stops here'. We therefore urged those who supported Shelter to also support Oxfam and other Third-World charities, and to tackle poverty as an unacceptable human condition rather than a local problem. Also while I was Director of Shelter, we received a number of gifts of money marked 'for whites only'. In every case we returned the money, advising the donor that we could not possibly assist one unjustly-treated group at the expense of another. We housed families irrespective of colour, and were not prepared to channel funds in one direction and thus endorse racialism.

Most of the justification for community/cause pressure groups lies in the nature and exercise of power itself. I am a firm believer that power corrupts, and also that our institutions fail to reflect the ideals of the majority of citizens. Ideals like peace, justice, liberty, equality, are not clichés to ordinary people – they are actually the ideals of the vast majority. Why, then, are they promoted by what are seen to be minority pressure groups? The answer is that the majority assume that their institutions exist to further those ideals, whereas those institutions often undermine and palpably fail to reflect them. Take three of the outstanding issues on the human agenda – war, poverty, and the environmental crisis.

Somehow, because the worst – a full-scale nuclear war – has been avoided, those in power have persuaded the people that we live in peace. In fact, more people have died in wars since 1945 than died in the First and Second World Wars combined. Violence on a colossal scale continues. In Britain we are told that our deterrent policy has helped to avoid nuclear war. Yet we live permanently in a war-like situation, in fear of the devastation of nuclear war, bearing the financial costs of nuclear war, seeing social priorities distorted by the need to hold our own in a nuclear war. Our institutions have totally failed to achieve the ideal of genuine peace. The response by the majority of people to emergency appeals at time of famine, severe drought, or other disasters in the Third World, reflects their ideal that people should not have to suffer if it is within the capacity of others to help. Institutions that genuinely reflect human ideals would communicate to people in developed countries that those emergencies are occurring on a daily basis, that the vast majority of their fellow critizens on this planet suffer appalling misery, hunger and disease, and that this will always be so until there is a radical change in the organisation of the world economy. The institutions do not convey that message. On the contrary, they perpetuate the inequalities between the north and south of our planet. Our institutions refuse to respond to the known facts about the environmental crisis and continue to allow squandering of the world's resources. They know that if we live on a planet, forever devouring and squandering its resources, forever exploiting its every advantage to satisfy our immediate appetites, forever polluting its air, soil, and water, forever assuming that all other living species exist only to serve our needs and wants, then one day that planet will become uninhabitable. Yet they defend and perpetuate the practices that guarantee massive problems for the generations to come.

It is in these and other failures by our institutions, failures rooted in a deep bias towards the status quo, and vested interest in power and wealth, that we find the outstanding argument for pressure groups.

That said, I would list seven other key justifications for the existence of community/cause pressure groups in our society:

1. *There is more to democracy than the occasional vote.*
   Democracy, said Abraham Lincoln, is government 'of the people, by the people and for the people'. This is not achieved by a vote every four or five years and then blind faith that all will be well. This may well be government 'of the people' and sometimes may even be government 'for the people', but it is not government *by* the people. At best it is government by the people's representatives. Even then, these are representatives of a minority of the people (the Thatcher Administration was elected in June 1983 by roughly two in five voters).

   This point apart, it is not a healthy or even genuine democracy in which the individual takes responsibility for a decision once every four or five years. To be healthy, a democracy has to be participatory at every level, offering the maximum number of opportunities for the maximum number of people to influence the maximum number of decisions. Pressure groups are one way whereby people can exercise their right to know and comment on what is happening, and to argue for different policies and priorities throughout a government's term of office. It could be said, of course, that the opposition parties meet this need. The opposition parties, however, are themselves part of the governing system. They too have a vested interest in maintaining many existing practices, and are also partly restricted within the strait-jacket of party dogma. In any case, government is much more than just 'the government' or the sum of the activities of the political parties; '*the government*' is transitory, whereas *government* (i.e. the bureaucracy, the interrelated power bases in our society, often described as 'the system') is permanent. Often specialist pressure groups are more effective than all-issue political parties in opposing 'the system'.

   Politicians of all parties who argue that charities or pressure groups 'should not be political' are in effect saying that politics is entirely the preserve of the political parties. This should not be so, for the basis of a free society is choice, and pressure groups, together with other forms of voluntary organisation, offer people a choice of how they can be involved in the running of their communities. If the only form of expression on many issues was via political parties, then in fact we would have very limited access and limited influence.

   There is more to democracy than the occasional vote, and there is more to democracy than political parties. Pressure groups, offering an alternative form of expression, are a healthy component of genuine democracy.

2. *Pressure groups counter-balance two inherent weaknesses in democracy.*

There are two fundamental weaknesses inherent in the democratic system.

The first is that democracy does *not* work for *all* people. It is obvious that if leaders are elected by the majority and if they hope to be re-elected, they have to satisfy that majority. Thus minorities in the community have little bargaining power.

The majority itself may break up into many different groups and sets of attitudes and interests, but all of its members share in the basic standard of living of the country and most of its opportunities – there are no special factors that automatically cut them off from the same opportunities as their fellows, and while their quality of life may vary widely, their lives are not a constant struggle for survival. Politicians necessarily define their priorities and policies to appeal to the appetites or needs of this majority. The majority can insist upon the protection of its interests; minorities, however, are dependent upon the majority for compassion, generosity, or tolerance.

Pressure groups offer a chance for minorities and disadvantaged groups to argue their case. Thus we have the Disability Alliance, the Council for One-Parent Families, the Gypsy Council, Shelter – the National Campaign for the Homeless, the Child Poverty Action Group, and so on.

The second inherent weakness in parliamentary democracy is that politicians need to obtain votes by popular support at very frequent intervals and thus short-term political considerations tend to prevail over the long-term interests of the country. One would like to think this was not so, but it is the reality. Those who have power never willingly relinquish it, and there is overwhelming evidence of sell-outs of long-term interests of the community by politicians driven by what they perceive as the need for self-preservation.

Thus politicians of all parties often follow policies even when they know them to be wrong. Pressure groups can be left as lone voices pointing out the desirable long-term alternative approach. One classic case is that of tax relief on mortgages. This, in its present form, is completely distorting the financing of housing so that those who can afford to buy their homes, and in particular the most expensive homes, receive the highest form of public subsidy It has an inflationary effect on house prices as well as being socially unfair. But the fact remains that more than 50 per cent of the electorate live in their own homes and although all of the major parties know that they should radically revise their tax relief there is little likelihood that they will risk the loss of votes involved.

Yes, this is democracy. It is government responding to the will of the majority, for undoubtedly home owners do wish to keep the tax relief on mortgages. But the test of real leadership in a democracy is the ability to educate people to the stupidities and injustices of what they perceive to be in their self-interest and to lead them to a more enlightened view.

Sometimes these two weaknesses in democracy combine, for majority rule also allows politicians to bully minorities for short-term gain. Typical of this was the way in which the Home Secretary, Leon Brittan, at the Conservative Party Conference in 1983, purchased a safe ride from the law-and-order mob by announcing draconian prison sentences that his own officials, the prison service, and almost anyone else concerned with penal policy, knew would ultimately be counter-productive.

The community/cause pressure groups, because they are not motivated by a need to pander to the majority instinct, have therefore a crucial contribution to make in exposing the tragic waste of opportunity and the injustice of many short-term policies and the need for the right, longer-term approach.

3. *Pressure groups improve surveillance of government.*

MPs in Britain are appallingly equipped, given the enormous centralised bureaucracy and power base over which they are supposed to maintain surveillance on behalf of the citizen. It is not unusual for US Senators and Congressmen to have a dozen or more researchers, in addition to other administrative staff. In Britain, however, most MPs have a secretary or a share of a secretary, and some have one researcher. As a result they tend to be appallingly briefed on most of the matters that come before parliament, even those on which they have some record of concern. Ministers whose resources are considerable, are usually able to sidestep awkward questions or bulldoze policies through the House simply because there is literally nobody on either side who is sufficiently well-equipped with information to be able to mount an effective challenge. Pressure groups therefore have begun to play a crucial role in acting as unofficial researchers and briefers to MPs.

Few people in Whitehall or within local authorities or other big corporate bodies have any vested interest in freedom of information. Secrecy covers up inadequacies, failures, compromises and corruption. Another function of pressure groups is the exposure of information. They tend to know what information exists even if they do not actually possess it themselves. Often, too, they can establish contacts within government who will use the pressure groups to leak information in the public interest. Another way government covers up is by simply not undertaking research where it would be helpful. Pressure groups often undertake the research and thus do for the public what public 'servants' prefer not to do.

Ministers, too, can find pressure groups of assistance. As they become increasingly dependent on the options and back-up information provided by civil servants, they cannot be certain that they are receiving *all* of the options or *all* the information. Pressure groups often warn Ministers that there are other aspects to the question than those being placed before them. The late Richard Crossman once told me that when he was Minister for Housing, and later Secretary of State for Social Services, he found pressure groups invaluable as an early warning system of possible mistakes caused by over-reliance on briefs from the civil service. He also argued that Shelter and other social service pressure groups were crucial in enabling him to argue for the necessary resources when Cabinet had to make tough choices on expenditure.

Thus, wise and sensitive MPs or Ministers do not automatically treat the pressure group as a menace, but rather as an essential resource and aid to their efficiency as a representative of the people.

4. *Pressure groups combat other pressure groups.*
It is ironic that one of the crucial roles of pressure groups – community/cause pressure groups – is to combat other pressure groups.

In the preface to this book, I stressed that there are many kinds of pressure group, and that a fundamental difference between community/cause pressure groups and their opposition, is that the latter usually do not rely on public opinion. They exercise their enormous power behind the scenes. One of the roles of community/cause pressure groups is to balance or reduce the influence of these huge vested interests.

I should make it clear that I accept the right of these pressure groups to exist. No-one – no matter how powerful, as well as no matter how weak – should be denied their day in court. My objection to them, apart from the fact that they are so often acting against the public interest, is that they seek to achieve their objectives in non-democratic ways, in what have become known as the 'corridors of power', without proper public debate, and that their resources are not the resources of community support but rather of sheer money and on occasions corruptive power.

5. *Pressure groups give causes their 'stamina'.*
One of the manifold weaknesses of the media is its tendency to pick up issues, then drop them. Another crucial role of the pressure group, therefore, is to maintain the momentum and to put the stamina into an issue. Its persistence, its ingenuity in finding fresh ways of promoting its cause and keeping the issue in the forefront of public and political attention, is necessary if 'the system' is not simply to 'ride out' unfavourable publicity or public pressure in the hope that

both media and the public will lose interest.

This was the problem in the past with lead in petrol. It was good for one feature article in a newspaper, and would arouse temporary concern, but given the other national and international issues with greater political potency, how could it be maintained in the forefront of public attention long enough to become an embarrassment? The commercial companies – the car manufacturers, the lead additive manufacturers, the petroleum industry – did not believe it could, and that complacency was to cost them dear. Government, too, believed that the CLEAR campaign would be a one-week wonder. The fact that CLEAR was one of the few organisations to crack the 'resolute approach' of the Thatcher Adminstration was due to its ability to put stamina into the issue.

6. *Community/cause pressure groups offer people the weapons to fight on their own behalf.*
Many community/cause pressure groups are quite simply the providers of weapons with which individuals can unite in their own defence, and sometimes literally fight for survival. Those weapons are organisation, skills and talents, money and the like. Pressure groups are necessary so that individuals can have confidence in numbers, can share their abilities, and can create a platform on which they can express their desires and needs. Pressure groups are, in the final analysis, collections of individuals, most of whom could not achieve their objectives on their own but who seek strength in unity.

7. *Pressure groups relieve frustration.*
Imagine if there were no community/cause pressure groups – if all minorities, if all those who think there is a better way to run our community, if all those with a cause have only one option, and that is to knock on the door of the political parties. If they are rejected, or if it is clear that they will never be listened to, what do they become? An embittered, defeated, crushed and frustrated minority. Community/cause pressure groups may not enable them to achieve all their objectives, but they do create an outlet for their frustration, an opportunity for them to argue their case and fight for what they believe in, and a sense of hope.

It can be seen from the above seven points that pressure groups are not a threat to a genuine democracy, but a vital contributor. Probably most politicians, and even civil servants, would pay lip service to the case I have made for community/cause pressure groups. They would no doubt find less acceptable, however, my additional view that 'the system' by which we are governed in Britain – in which power is concentrated in Westminster, Whitehall and in such institutions as the City – is, if not the enemy of the people, at least not necessarily their servant. Whitehall civil servants, who are so little answerable to democracy and have so much power, are not only secure in their employment but have obtained for themselves guaranteed advantages in society that no other section has secured. The bureaucracy has an enormous vested interest in maintaining these advantages and powers. It protects itself with excessive confidentiality and with the enormous dampening influence of bureaucratic hold-up. Politicians, the moment they reach Westminster, are seduced by its privileges. Ministers change overnight and begin to talk a different language and to adopt a different perspective. The whole British governmental system is held together because all new entrants are immediately endowed with comforts and privileges and protective layers that draw them in.

Furthermore, there are influences upon decision-making that go far beyond the democratic will of the people – above all, multinational companies. For instance, as explained in the Preface, the Ministry of Agriculture exists entirely to relate to a particular industry. While we would like to believe that it is there to represent the people in dealing with the farmers, the reality of the lives the civil servants lead, the way they work, and the contacts they make, is that the Ministry of Agriculture exists to serve the farmers alone. In a recent book on the poisonous pesticide 2,4,5-T the point is made that 'for those who have been involved in the debate it has often proved difficult to distinguish between the voices of the spokesmen for the agro-chemicals industry and those of the Ministry of Agriculture'.[6] Likewise, anti-lead campaigners would say that the language of Whitehall spokesmen was the language of the motor car industry and the petroleum industry, not the language of public servants genuinely serving the public interest.

What it adds up to is that government's priorities are self-serving ones. At the end of the day, the main function of community/cause pressure groups as a contributor to democratic activity is to be an extra-parliamentary opposition – to represent the public to, and where necessary, against its own government.

If the government are the guards, who guards the guards? Answer: the pressure groups.

2 THE CARING REVOLUTIONARY – THE PRINCIPLES OF PRESSURE

COMMUNITY/CAUSE pressure groups fall within three main categories:

(a) *Single-issue pressure groups*
These have one objective, or seek to further one particular cause. CLEAR is a single-issue pressure group – its sole aim is to reduce and if possible eliminate lead pollution.

(b) *Issues-in-context pressure groups*
These pursue a number of objectives or issues, but within an overall context. Such a pressure group is Friends of the Earth, contesting the expansion of nuclear energy, fighting for decent transport policies, campaigning for countryside and wildlife protection, exposing pollution, but all within the overall context of a campaign for conservation and environmental protection. Another such pressure group would be the National Council for Civil Liberties, campaigning to protect personal privacy, achieve adequate rights for the accused and for prisoners, defend freedom of speech, but all within the context of the overall cause of civil liberties.

(c) *Practice-based pressure groups*
These may well be single-issue pressure groups, or 'issues-in-context' pressure groups, but they are not solely pressure groups – they also have an element of aid or direct service in their make-up. They form a link between the expression of principles and the practice of those principles. The charity-cum-pressure groups fit into this group, one such being Shelter. It has provided direct assistance to the homeless by financing housing programmes or housing aid centres, and by other activities, but it is also a pressure group calling for specific housing policies and greater priority for housing.

All of these pressure groups at some point or another have to decide whether they are campaigning for fundamental social change or piecemeal reform. Or to put it more bluntly – are they revolutionaries or reformists? When I was Director of Shelter I would frequently be confronted with comments like this:

> At the most you can only help a few homeless families a year. But there are thousands who are homeless. They are there because of the failure of the economic and political system. You, by helping a few, are actually dealing with the symptoms instead of the real cause. You are applying a band-aid to a national disease, and thus contributing to its perpetuation. Your reforms are not the answer – what we need is a political and economic revolution. Why don't you press for that?

Of course they have a valid argument. Of course the problem will never be solved without the proper economic and political policies, and without fundamental changes. Of course these objectives have to be pursued politically, and I hope everyone will do so. However, we don't live in a revolutionary situation. Fundamental change inspired by the majority is possible where the majority are homeless, or poor, or suffering injustice, but where the majority are well-housed and reasonably affluent and do not feel themselves to be the victims of mass injustice, and when the problem is that of a minority, albeit a substantial minority, 'revolution' is hardly likely.

I prefer the third alternative: what I call the *'caring revolutionary'*. The caring revolutionary *does* understand the need to tackle root causes instead of symptoms alone. However, the caring revolutionary also cares about people and will not ignore suffering if practical steps can be taken to relieve it. The caring revolutionary *does not* use and even create human need to foster discontent and fuel the fire of change. The caring revolutionary builds a platform of achievement in tackling problems upon which he or she earns a respectful audience for the call for peaceful and positive change.

Shelter, for instance, has always based its activities on two principles: first, that we should campaign for fundamental change to eliminate the conditions that lead to homeless families; second, *until that change comes about, we should do all in our power to help those who are in desperate need.* I believe that most Friends of the Earth are caring revolutionaries because they not only argue for a complete change in the way that society is organised, but seek to begin with their own lives, to put forward positive alternatives that will not undermine the quality of people's lives but rather enhance them, and to campaign with humour and friendship and lack of personal hostility to the opposition.

In this chapter I wish to suggest seven principles that I believe should be applied to the activities of community/cause pressure groups. I begin with the three P's of pressure group activity – persistence, professionalism, and perspective:

1. *Persistence*

To achieve any change in Britain takes time. Don't begin unless you are prepared for a battle that could possibly take years, and unless you are willing to give it high priority in your life. If you don't devote sufficient time to it, you will fail. If you make a promising start but run out of steam you will fail. 'The system' counts on having more stamina than you – more resources, more time on its side, and unlimited capacity for delay. Thus one of its responses to your campaign will be to test your persistence.

What you must remember is that every failure makes a fresh initiative in the same area more difficult. Every failure strengthens the opposition in its belief that there is no real concern about the issue and no need to respond. Thus anyone who undertakes a campaign has a responsibility to do it properly and try to see it through. In the planning of your campaign, you should not only prepare for a long fight, but reserve some of your fire power. A slow start and a steady build-up over a two or three year plan is far better than a great drive that loses momentum after going for three or four months.

By persistence I don't just mean 'keep going' – I also mean that you have to keep working. Campaigning is about attention to detail, chasing every option and opportunity, raising money, rallying support, research, and a hundred and one other things. It is hard, hard work. Although the CLEAR campaign took only 15 months to achieve its primary objective – the decision to move to lead-free petrol – it seemed like an age, for usual working hours were from seven in the morning until 11 at night. And those hours were always insufficient.

Persistence is when journalist number 999 telephones you and asks the same questions the other 998 have asked and you still reply with enthusiasm and energy and with all the information they need. I remember during the Shelter campaign two different women journalists coming to interview me and asking the same questions about the homeless that I had answered for four years. They had not done any background research, not been to our press office and obtained the basic information about Shelter and the homeless to save my time, and that was thoughtless of them. But that is a reflection on them; I couldn't change them, nor was it my responsibility to try. I had to accept them as they were. I should have patiently answered all of these banal questions. I didn't. I showed my impatience. I was brusque and unhelpful and rid myself of their company as quickly as possible. No story appeared in either newspaper. Who was the loser? It was the homeless and it was Shelter. I had lost some of my persistence, some of my stamina, and the cause had suffered. It was about that time that I decided it was time to make way for someone else.

2. *Professionalism*

It isn't, however, enough to work. You have to work well. You have to be professional. It is the height of irresponsibility to take on a cause that may affect the well-being of others, and then not do it properly. I believe in the highest standards, and that begins with the way the telephone is answered, continues through the quality of design and print material, and should be reflected in every activity of the campaign. If a campaign is incompetently or carelessly run, it will be assumed by others to be of no consequence.

You don't need money to be professional – just care and attention to detail. One way to be professional is to involve professionals. Seek volunteers with skills – an accountant who will agree to do the books, a lawyer who will agree to do the legal work, a designer who will design your print material, and so on. It is surprising how few professionals are approached by pressure groups or campaigns and asked for their professional skills, yet many would actually like the opportunity to exercise them in unusual or worthwhile ways.

I will return to this theme of professionalism frequently in Chapter 4 for it is of critical importance.

3. *Perspective*

It is essential that you keep a sense of perspective. Everybody who runs a campaign tends to believe their cause is the most vital and urgent. For instance, some anti-lead campaigners believe lead pollution to be the biggest threat to mankind short of nuclear war. Some have actually said this. My own view is that lead pollution is one of a number of serious environmental health hazards that should be eliminated. This should be done as soon as is practicable. It is a hazard to health and that is all that need be said. There is no need to exaggerate the issue.

The effective campaigner avoids at all costs becoming a fanatic. The dangers are manifold: first, a complete inability to see the wood for the trees, so that every action he or she takes is given equal weight; second, a tendency to paranoia, so that anyone who is even sceptical, let alone arguing the opposite side, is automatically assumed to have sinister motives, and often is criticised or condemned, with no evidence whatsoever, in a way that discredits the campaigners; third, misapplication of persistence to the point where they are written off as cranks, and although they may be completely right in their diagnosis of the problem, or in their proposed reforms, they have undermined the cause. Finally, perspective is necessary to preserve your own sanity. To be excessively committed is to risk obsession – it is a fine balance – and this in turn can cause a distorted personality.

To sum up, the object should be to make the strongest possible case for the earliest possible action consistent with not raising serious doubts in the minds of others as to whether your judgement can be trusted. A sense of perspective enhances credibility; lack of perspective will leave you talking to yourself.

4. *Reflect in your behaviour as a pressure group your broader ideals*
It is hard to see how you can convince others if you do not reflect in
your own behaviour the ideals you proclaim.

Thus, if we wish to live in a non-violent society, we must ourselves be
non-violent. If we wish to live in a more caring and sharing society, we
must ourselves care and share. If we wish to live in a conserving,
ecologically-based society, we must begin to alter our own lifestyles
to show it can be done. If we wish to live in a more democratic,
participatory society, then the structure we ourselves set up should be
democratic and participatory.

As one writer has said:

> New structures in society reflect groups which bring them about. If the
> group is doctrinaire, élitist or middle class, then any new structure it
> brings into being is likely to be doctrinaire, élitist or middle class. For an
> élite to take power in the name of the people is usually a hoax; all that is
> accomplished is the replacement of one set of rules by another. A movement
> for change in society towards greater democracy, local control and less
> hierarchy must also be open and participatory. This means developing
> means for collective decision-making, encouraging participation by all
> interested people, and making all policies open and without secrecy.[7]

None of the organisations I have been involved with have yet met these
standards, although some have been more effective than others. I think,
for instance, of Friends of the Earth, Birmingham, who genuinely run
as a collective, with decision-making by the group, with no hierarchies,
and genuine equality between men and women. It is also non-violent.
Its work is for conservation and it seeks to apply ecological principles to
its lifestyle. Yet it is a constructive contributor to the community. It
has, for instance, insulated over 3,000 homes of old folk, the disabled,
and one-parent families. Not a bad beginning.

No-one suggests that this should be the model for every kind of
pressure group. A pressure group in a local town whose objective is to
get a by-pass, and whose membership is entirely voluntary, won't
operate in that way. But the more individuals and representatives of the
community you get involved, and the more that responsibilities are
spread around as many people as possible, the more you will reflect
both the kind of participatory community that is desirable and at the
same time be effective – for the more people involved in a campaign,
the greater the chance of success.

This is not to say that there should not be personalities to front the
campaign if that is desirable in particular circumstances. Personalities
can often take the message on to radio and television programmes or
into quarters where it would otherwise not be heard. It is, however,
advantageous to have more than one and the more the better.

My advice is to encourage and train as many spokesmen for the
campaign as possible and share out the appearances, using local radio

and television appearances, and smaller audience programmes, to give experience and build up the confidence of others in the campaign.

On the question of violence, I can think of no cause in Britain that justifies its use.

> Violence as a means for obtaining social change has several severe flaws: it often causes suffering; it abdicates moral superiority and alienates potential support; it requires secrecy and hence leads to undemocratic decision-making; and, if successful, it tends to lead towards a violent and authoritarian new ruling élite. Non-violent action as a policy and as a technique avoids these problems; its means reflect its ends. With non-violent action, energy is aimed at policies or structures, and not their supporters.[8]

Organisations trying to further their cause with violence are usually admitting that they have no hope of success, perhaps because the cause will not survive close examination. If this is the case it deserves to fail.

Martin Luther King and his non-violent civil rights movement showed what could be done in the United States. The trade union movement in the early part of this century showed what could be achieved without violence to relieve conditions of the working classes. Of course these were fairly big minorities, but the non-violent options for action are many and varied, as I hope we will see in this book, and I doubt if many groups in Britain could demonstrate that they have exhausted them all.

There is, however, a big difference between violent protest and direct action. If a farmer is about to demolish a rare wildlife habitat with bulldozers, and environmentalists need to buy time and achieve official protection for it, then they are, in my view, justified in taking direct action. *Violence* would be to pull the farmer off his machine and restrain him forcibly – possibly to throw stones at him or even tie him up. *Non-violent direct action* would be for the conservationists to sit in a circle around the habitat and defy the farmer to run them down with the bulldozer. Of course, there is a possibility that he will do so. That is the risk the non-violent protester has to take and it is one that he or she *must* be prepared to take, because unfortunately, for non-violent protestors to be ultimately effective, they must demonstrate that even in the face of violence they will (a) not retreat, and (b) not resort to violence themselves. To retreat is to confirm in the violent that violence will always win. To reply with violence is to lose the moral advantage. What has frequently moved communities to be sympathetic to protesters has been the sight of their dignified, peaceful and brave resistance, in the face of the violence of their opponents, or even the police or armed forces, or others.

Direct action can, therefore, be justified in many circumstances although it becomes less effective the more it is employed and the earlier it is employed. It should always follow every possible effort to persuade by reason. It must be demonstrated to fair-minded people that the direct action is a genuine expression of total frustration at the obstinacy, unfairness, and possibly the brutality of 'the system', rather than a self-indulgent expression of the impatience of protesters.

Direct action, to be defensible, should always relate to the cause itself, and wherever possible, the only victims of it should be the perpetrators of the injustice. This is not always possible, but that should be the aim. Thus, I have no sympathy with the protestors who destroyed a test match cricket pitch in order to draw attention to a man they felt to have been unjustly imprisoned. The test cricketers, the cricket authorities, and cricket followers not only had no jurisdiction over whether the man should have been imprisoned, but probably had not heard of him. Once they did – because they found their test match ruined – their sympathy was hardly likely to be engaged. The perpetrators of the damage would no doubt argue that it achieved massive publicity and that ultimately their man was released. My reply would be that they could have achieved the same objective by some other form of direct action more related to the police, the court, and the law generally.

Wherever possible, therefore, the direct action should be devised and planned so that it contains a number of ingredients:

- if possible it should be relevant to the injustice so that a clear message emerges from the action;
- it should have imagination and humour;
- it should enlist the sympathy of people, not alienate them;
- it should be non-violent;
- it should be seen to be an expression of genuine injustice, and not the first but rather the last resort;
- wherever possible it should be within the spirit of the law.

This last point brings me to a key question: is it permissible to break the law? We had a lengthy debate on this subject at Friends of the Earth. Mike Smyth, a lawyer, who is one of our Board members, prepared a paper on law and demonstrations. Mike explained that the law relating to demonstrations is complex and obscure. In many cases it is also extremely old. In a memo to FoE Board I wrote:

> I suspect it works rather well for the authorities in the sense that there is considerable flexibility for them but little flexibility for would-be demonstrators.
> My own view is that the difficulty in discussing whether we should act 'within the law' is that it is a blanket phrase, and obscures the fact that in some areas the law is 100 per cent sound, and in other areas highly questionable. It is further implied that the law is an expression of the democratic will of the people in terms of the rules and regulations they wish applied to the organisation of society, when many laws are, in fact,

inflicted without a mandate, probably highly unpopular, and in many cases, unnecessary. Thus the assumption by some people that 'the law' is automatically good and right and should or can be inflexibly obeyed at all times is a naive one.

On the other hand, they would no doubt argue and have a point, that the alternative – that we pick and choose the laws we obey – is a recipe for anarchy. Can we choose some laws and say of those laws 'this one is an ass and we choose to disobey it' and then object if someone else chooses another law and says the same thing, even if that law is one prohibiting robbery or violence?

I then went on to argue that FoE has always recognised that an element of social organisation was required and that this involved laws. Indeed it is often campaigning for laws. Currently it is campaigning for a Countryside Act that would impose laws. We would like to restrict the polluting activities of many companies by law. Thus, we have chosen to work within a society that has and needs laws and 'in my view, of the two options, either picking and choosing laws to obey, or obeying (in principle) all laws, the latter is the one we reluctantly have to accept as the only rational option'. This does not, of course, preclude opposing silly or restrictive laws or seeking to have them changed.

However, I reminded the FoE Board of the flexibility the authorities themselves have when it came to laws on demonstrations. 'The fact is that police themselves tend to interpret the law differently on different occasions. In other words, at their best, they seek to act "within the *spirit* of the law".'

I argued that we should do the same. Take the law of trespass: If you or I camp or picnic on a piece of farming land without the farmer's permission, and possibly do damage to the farm, we are trespassing on his land. We have no reason to be there except self-indulgence. We should have asked permission. We are trespassing. Further, if we proceed on his land with destructive intent – to damage or steal or for some other destructive reason – we are trespassing. He has the right to engage the law. But if he is proceeding with tractors, etc., to destroy a Site of Special Scientific Interest, either in defiance of laws and regulations himself or because he knows that steps will be taken to use those laws and regulations to stop him from proceeding, and if we proceed on his land to sit in front of the tractors and stop him from doing so, we are, in my view, trespassing with reason, 'within the spirit of the law'.

I advised FoE:

I accept there is no legal basis for this, but I believe a moral case can be made. We may ultimately be evicted and even charged with trespass, but while we may have broken the letter of the law, I do not believe we will bring on ourselves much anger from the public at large. Indeed, it seems to me that is the real test of whether one breaks the law while observing 'the spirit of the law' – what will the public reaction be?

Crude this may be, but the moment we move into the phrases like 'spirit of the law' we move into flexible interpretations and of course everybody will reach a conclusion according to their prejudices. In other words, there is no way the farmer will support our position. Ultimately the police and the courts may not be able to either. But then presumably we have decided we are prepared to face any legal penalty and the real test of the matter has been whether the public will feel there is justification 'within the spirit of the law'.

I accept this is hardly a sophisticated line of argument, and it is undoubtedly a controversial one, but it is relevant to say that as it is the same authorities who are often the perpetrators of the injustice or the wrong that the pressure group aims to change, there can be a further injustice in that the obstacles to campaigning effectively to change the policy of the authorities are the authorities' own laws.

I do believe that the crude test I suggested to FoE – the likely public response to the activity – is in fact a sound one, both because the aim must be to retain public sympathy, and because the public sense of fair play will be an invaluable guide to whether in fact it is a fair (i.e. justified) form of direct action.

A classic piece of direct action was the Friends of the Earth demonstration in opposition to the policy of the Schweppes Company of producing non-returnable bottles. Friends of the Earth supporters all over the country collected Schweppes bottles and one day they were dumped in a colossal pile on the front doorstep of the Schweppes office. This attracted considerable publicity, and met most of the requirements of direct action – it was 'within the spirit of the law', it was an act that only affected the perpetrator of the bad policy (Schweppes), it was imaginative, and good humoured, it was undoubtedly an effective media event, and it did not alienate the public at large.

Let me quote another case where I believe that direct action would be justified. For some years I lived in the lovely Worcestershire town of Bewdley. Because of the weakness of the local Conservative MP, and the indifference of the Conservative County Council, Bewdley was always missing from the list of towns to be given a by-pass. Yet its narrow streets were the main thoroughfare from the West Midlands to Wales and huge lorries and heavy traffic thundered down the main street shaking the foundations of historic old houses, and both spoiling and endangering a remarkable piece of historic heritage.

In my view the authorities will continue to ignore the urgent case for a by-pass until such time as the people of the town take direct action as a reflection of their lack of confidence in their representatives and as a demand to be heard. The only way into the town is over a relatively narrow bridge across the River Severn. In my view townsfolk should be organised to sit on that bridge in such numbers (and to regroup themselves every time they are removed) so that they become a substantial obstacle. The police would have to continuously man the bridge not by just one or two policemen, but by a battalion. Determined and sustained blocking of the bridge by the townspeople for a week, fully covered by the media, if it were well organised, good humouredly carried out, but determined and persistent, would win the day.

5. *Be positive*

Seek to be 'for' rather than just 'against'. Be positive. A proposal for constructive action is always more attractive and more likely to obtain support than solely negative thinking.

Thus, Shelter is called the National Campaign *for* the Homeless, and not the Campaign *against* Bad Housing. CLEAR is called the National Campaign *for* Lead-free Air, not the Campaign *against* Lead Pollution. It is of importance to hold out the prospect of better circumstances and to define the ultimate objective. The ultimate objective is not to destroy or defeat but rather to create and improve.

FoE always seeks to offer positive alternatives. We oppose the building of a PWR at Sizewell and the growth of the nuclear energy industry, but in the context of being *for* the positive alternative of renewable energy sources; we oppose domination by the motor car, but in the context of being *for* an efficient, safe, economic, environmentally clean public transport system; we oppose indiscriminate use of pesticides, but in the context of being *for* controlled use or integrated pest management.

Pressure groups demanding improved services or changed policies should always acknowledge the good in the other side. This was a point made in a recent radio interview by David Ennals, who has been on both sides of the fence, in the sense that he was once the Director of MIND, and thus a lobbyist, but became Secretary of State for the Social Services, and thus a senior political decision-maker.

> I think that if a pressure group has had some success in a campaign it must show some appreciation of what the authorities have done. As a Minister, I sometimes found that I had gone a considerable way towards what a voluntary organisation had asked for, but it didn't say thank you. It just jumped that hurdle and said 'right, Minister, the next thing you are going to do is this'. Now that can be very irritating because it is the Minister who actually takes the decision. And part of the whole process is to get the Minister in the receptive mood, not only to accept part of what you say, but to go on later and finally accept all of what you say.

Surely it is better to approach someone you wish to persuade on the basis of 'I admire what you have done . . . I broadly support your policies . . . but I would like to propose that a positive next step would be such and such . . .'. Surely this is better than to approach on the lines of 'What is wrong with you? Why don't you do such and such? Are we the only people who care?' I am not advocating a show of weakness, or unnecessary flattery . . . just that one should be positive about what they have done as well as critical of what they have not.

6. *Remember who the enemy is*

It is rarely that an organisation's objectives are furthered by the use of one second of time, one penny of money, or one ounce of energy, trying to compete with, undermine, or negate the activities of organisations on the same side. Such behaviour suggests a complete lack of perspective, and lack of genuine concern for the issue.

One of the worst aspects of voluntary activity in Britain is the lack of co-operation and sometimes downright hostility between different groups. Wasted energy and emotion in rivalries between organisations, and wasted resources in duplication of effort and lack of co-operation, are unforgivable.

I have always tried to create coalitions of organisations and it is always exciting and reassuring when organisations sit around a table and agree to co-operate to deal with a particular problem. Remember who the real enemy is; don't waste your ammunition firing on your own side.

7. *Where you can, meet needs as you go along*

The pressure groups I feel most comfortable with are those where the campaign has emerged from the experience of caring – from dealing with the 'consumers' and from actually working in the field. MIND is a campaign for the mentally ill based on the provision of services over many years by its parent, The National Association for Mental Health. Shelter was a campaign for the homeless based on its rescue operation for homeless families. Such pressure groups, many of them charity-cum-pressure groups, are enormously strengthened in two ways: first, by actually dealing with need where it confronts it, and positively trying to help, the organisation builds the moral platform upon which it has the right to demand the attention of society as a whole; second, from its day-by-day experience of the problem, the organisation develops a unique knowledge of its causes and solutions.

When Shelter went to talk to Housing Ministers about landlord–tenant relationships, or about housing rehabilitation, or about the kind of people comprising Britain's homeless, we did so as an organisation actually involved in landlord–tenant relations, actually rehabilitating old property, actually dealing with the homeless on a day-by-day basis.

The day-by-day confrontation with victims of injustice also helps you to maintain a sense of urgency and to remember what the priorities are. Above all, it is direct expression of concern in action. The relief work impresses the public. It is beyond criticism. And this in itself wins attention and sympathy.

In summary, most community/cause pressure groups have an objective and an ideal. The *objective* is the achievement of your particular aim – a change of policy, increased priority for a particular group, the end of an injustice, or whatever. The *ideal* varies from group to group and from individual to individual, but nevertheless is a generally-shared vision of the kind of caring, participatory, just and equal society we would like to live in. If possible the achievement of the individual goal should be linked to changes in society as a whole, and this can be achieved in three ways:

First, as I have argued, by operating in the way that you would like society to operate. In a non-hierarchical, open, honest, and democratic, non-violent, caring way.

Second, by relating the individual problem to the underlying causes. For instance, as it became obvious that CLEAR's campaign would achieve its objective of lead-free petrol, we increasingly used the opportunities of articles and speeches on the subject to point out that lead pollution was but *one* environmental issue, and that all had the same basic causes and needed to be approached in the same way. By so doing we were able to make this particular defeat for polluters and the authorities just one nail in what we hope will become a coffin of eliminated health hazards.

Third, it is crucial at every stage to involve as many people as possible, not only in order to be effective in the short-term, but in order that as many people as possible can experience the faults in 'the system' and the need for wider change.

Community/cause pressure groups should be determined, single-minded, highly efficient, and professional, but also caring and reasonable. It is a revolution we seek, but a revolution by evolution . . . rapid evolution by all means, but evolution with the support of the people as a whole.

Such is the approach of the caring revolutionary.

3 AN UNCHARITABLE VIEW OF CHARITY LAW – THE PENALTY ON PRESSURE GROUPS

THE OFFICIAL British approach to voluntary activity or, as officialdom likes to call it, 'the voluntary sector' (i.e. non-governmental community or public activity), discriminates between those who relieve some of the symptoms of human need and those who wish to tackle the underlying causes. The relief of symptoms is respectable. Organisations that do this can register as charities. To tackle the underlying causes is dangerous, because it is likely to threaten vested interests. Organisations that seek to do this are therefore denied the advantages of charitable status.

Thus we have charities and pressure groups, but charities are not supposed to be pressure groups and pressure groups are not allowed to be charities.

Although the rules are vague, haphazardly applied, and often part-circumvented by both charities and pressure groups, charity law is one way whereby 'the system' can effectively undermine pressure groups, and that is why demands for reform have so far been ignored.

Why does it matter?

First, because there are considerable tax concessions available to charities which are not available to pressure groups. If the funds are applied for 'charitable purposes', charities are exempt from most taxes, including income tax, corporation tax, capital transfer and capital gains tax. They can claim a 50 per cent reduction in rates. They don't have to pay stamp duty on the employer's national insurance surcharge. In addition, bequests and donations to charities are untaxed as far as the donor is concerned; thus charities benefit enormously from being able to recoup tax on covenanted donations. It is said that the tax benefits to charities are alone worth over £200 million a year. Secondly, it affects income in two ways: first, charitable foundations can normally only make grants to other charitable organisations, or organisations that intend to spend the money in furtherance of a charitable purpose. Thus the number of foundations that pressure groups can apply to for grants is strictly limited to those that are not charitable foundations and there are few of them. Second, companies and many members of the public prefer to donate money to charities in the belief (albeit often without justification) that they are better administered and therefore the money will be more usefully spent.

Voluntary organisations, including charities, have a remarkable record of contribution to policy-making, mainly by experimental activity in welfare, but in post-war years tended to concentrate much more on the relief of immediate need rather than the advocacy of policy which would reduce the need for charities altogether. Shelter was one of the first of the major charities to abandon this approach in the Sixties. First, we were able (to our surprise) to register the name 'National *Campaign* for the Homeless' instead of 'National *Charity* for the Homeless'. The Charity Commissioners were either unaware of the intent or not sufficiently imaginative to anticipate what would follow. Shelter did begin with a heavy emphasis on relief of need, and on fund-raising for its voluntary housing trusts. But within a year of the launch we had strengthened our pressure group activities and by the late Sixties were a substantial thorn in Whitehall's side. We campaigned vigorously for greater financial priority for housing, for reform of the Rent Act, and for changes in local authority treatment of the homeless. We were outspoken in our criticisms of politicians. We held fringe meetings at party conferences, issued 'shock reports', and even encouraged our local Shelter groups to become involved in campaigning at local level. Although one Conservative Member of Parliament, Evelyn King, launched a series of attacks on Shelter for what he described as its 'political motivation', the majority of people seemed unperturbed by its dual role.

Not so the Charity Commissioners. Disturbed by the activities of Shelter and other charities who were increasingly undertaking pressure group activities, they in 1969 devoted a section of their Annual Report to their 'concern' at the increasing desire of voluntary organisations for 'involvement' in the causes with which their work is connected. (In the whole history of mindless bureaucracy, this phrase must be one of the most mindless. Were they really suggesting that people should not be *involved* in the causes with which their work was connected? That those who helped the homeless should not feel *involved* with the homeless? That those who worked for the relief of 'world poverty' should not be *involved* with the issue of world poverty? It was absurd.)

'Many organisations,' they wrote, 'now feel that it is not sufficient simply to alleviate distress arising from particular social conditions or even to go further and collect and disseminate information about the problems they encounter. They feel compelled also to draw attention as forcibly as possible to the needs that they think are not being met, to arouse the conscience of the public to demand action, and to press for effective, official provision to be made to meet those needs. As a result "pressure groups", "action groups", or "lobbies" come into being. But when a voluntary organisation which is a charity seeks to develop such activities it nearly always runs into difficulties by going beyond its declared purposes and powers.'

They then went on to argue that 'it is a well established principle of charity law that a trust for the attainment of a political object is not a valid charitable trust and that any purpose with the objective of influencing the legislator is a political purpose. Thus no organisation can be a charity and at the same time include among its purposes the object of bringing influence to bear directly or indirectly on parliament to change the general law of the land. If the governing instrument of an organisation were to give it power, other than in a way merely ancillary to some charitable purpose, to play a part in bringing political pressure to bear, that by itself would throw serious doubts on the organisation's claim to be a charity. Thus it is very unlikely that it will lie within any charity's purposes and powers to sponsor action groups or bring pressure to bear on the government or adopt or alter a particular line of action'.

They defined three areas where it was 'proper' for a charity to be involved in semi-political activities:

First, where officialdom itself sought advice and information. 'By publishing a Green or White Paper the Government may impliedly invite comments from the public generally, and a charity may justifiably avail itself of such an invitation to make any comments which may appear to be useful. Again when a Parliamentary Bill has been published a charity will be justified in supplying relevant information to a member of either House and such arguments to be used in debate as it believes will assist the furtherance of its purposes'.

Second, 'it is probably unobjectionable for a charity to present to a government a reasoned memorandum advocating changes in the law provided that in doing so a charity is acting in furtherance of its purposes. On the other hand, a charity can only spend its funds on the promotion of public general legislation if in doing so it is exercising power that is merely ancillary to its charitable purposes'.

Third, a charity could encourage legislation which directly affected itself.

What was clear was that the Charity Commissioners accepted that organisations *would* become 'involved' in their cause, in the sense of wishing to make available their knowledge and expertise and views, but it was the *way* in which they did it that concerned them. A 'reasoned memorandum' was OK; presumably a public meeting or a powerfully-argued press release was not.

It is fair to say that this report of the Charity Commissioners was largely ignored. Just the same the restraints came to be seen to be increasingly absurd. Because they dared to speak for the least advantaged, organisations like the United Nations Association, Amnesty International, The National Council for Civil Liberties, The Child Poverty Action Group, and others, including Friends of the Earth, which clearly exist for the benefit of the community as a whole, were denied charitable status, while public schools for the wealthy, like Eton or Harrow or Winchester, could actually register as charities and receive all the financial benefits.

The determination of many charities to do what they felt was right was reflected in an article in *The Observer* the following year. It said:

> Charities used to be anxious to keep out of politics for fear that their fund-raising may slacken or dry up. Many are still very careful. One of the four voluntary agencies in famine relief, Save The Children Fund, under Royal patronage, still tries to keep its nose clean. It refused to join in the current (political) campaign, Action For World Development. The three that did join in, Oxfam, Christian Aid, and War On Want, felt it essential to educate as well as beg; in other words, to educate individuals to give but also to demand similar action of the government.

Of Shelter, *The Observer* article said:

> Shelter, which raises nearly £1,000,000 a year, is even more vulnerable to attack because the housing shortage is bound to be the stuff of domestic politics. But Des Wilson, its Director, is adamant that he will not separate the two sides of Shelter's work. 'If Shelter has to be the charity which goes to the wall in order to change the role of charities in this country, we will be that charity', he says.

The Observer story ended like this:

> If controversy has the effect of drying up the funds, can it be afforded, or must political opposition come to be accepted? In an open society it should be hoped that people will give even in the teeth of argument and that politicians will be big enough to welcome the work of bodies like Shelter, even though on one point or another they disagree with it.

Over ten years later, in 1981, the Charity Commissioners returned to the point once more. Quoting a variety of court judgements that charities should not pursue political objects, they offered a number of guidelines, including:

> . . . its governing instruments should not include power to exert political pressure except in a way that is merely ancillary to a charitable purpose. . . .
> The powers and purposes of a charity should not include the power to bring pressure to bear on the government to adopt, alter, maintain a particular line of action. It is permissible for a charity, in furtherance of its

purposes, to help the government to reach a decision on a particular issue by providing information and argument, but the emphasis must be on rational persuasion. . . . A charity can spend its funds on the promotion of public general legislation only if in doing so it is exercising a power which is ancillary to and in furtherance of its charitable objects. . . . If a charity's objects include the advancement of education, care should be taken not to overstep the boundary between education and propaganda in promoting that object: for example, the distribution of literature urging the government to take a particular course, or urging sympathisers to apply pressure to MPs for that purpose, would not be education in the charitable sense. . . . A charity which includes the conduct of research as one of its objects must aim for objectivity and balance in the method of conducting research projects; and in publishing the results of the research must aim to inform and educate the public rather than to influence political attitudes or inculcate a particular attitude of mind. . . .

They then went on to suggest what a charity could freely engage in including:

Where the Government or governmental agency is considering or proposing changes in the law and invites comments or suggestions from charities, they can properly respond . . . perhaps to a Green or White Paper . . . or publication of a Parliamentary Bill. . . . Where a Bill would give a charity wide powers to carry out its purposes, it can quite properly support the passage of the Bill . . . Where such action is in furtherance of its purposes, a charity may present to a government department a reasoned memorandum advocating changes in the law.

I have conveyed the Charity Commissioners' view at length for two reasons: first, because those who seek guidance in organising pressure group activity from this book need to know the position; second, because I think it illustrates the inconsistencies of the present position, and the absurdities, and the unfairness.

It is quite clear that most of the major charities in the country are not operating according to these guidelines. The reason is simple enough: many of the problems that such organisations face are of such size, and the human need is so considerable, that they would feel it both irresponsible and morally wrong not to share their concern with the public as a whole and not to argue for the kind of priorities and policies that would reduce the need. Indeed, they would feel if they were not speaking out strongly that they were contributing to the perpetuation of the problems – 'letting the authorities or society off the hook' – by creating the incorrect impression that their work was sufficient answer to the need. Second, by their day-by-day experience in the field, charities learn exactly how distorted priorities are, how inadequate policies can be, and how unfair is the system that deals with its 'consumers'. They feel that they have a responsibility to point this out. If 'reasoned memorandum' means documents and research reports that the authorities can file away and ignore, then most charities feel this simply won't do.

While charities handle the problems caused by charity law as best they can, pressure groups have simply had to decide from the start that there is no point in attempting to register. This has not, as we have discovered in Chapter 1, stopped the formation of pressure groups, but it has penalised them financially.

The authorities like to play all this down. The Chief Charity Commissioner is quoted in *Voluntary Action* magazine in 1982 saying 'I don't think that the argument that there are great political restrictions is really a runner. I know it's a very strongly held view, but I think by a small minority of charities.' If he means that out of 140,000 registered charities, only one hundred or so major ones complain, he may be correct, but those hundred charities probably raise about 90 per cent of all charitable money and are major national organisations.

The fact is that charities *are restricted and inhibited* by charity law, and pressure groups are *financially penalised* by not being able to register as charities. This is more than 'an argument', as a Charity Commissioner puts it; it is a fact. It is noticeable, too, that he refers to the effect of the law on charities but appears indifferent to the fact that many worthwhile campaigns cannot become charities in the first place.

Fortunately, the National Council for Voluntary Organisations, representative of the majority of charities and service organisations, is now engaged in a campaign for reform. One of its key staff members, Francis Gladstone, has written a splendid book on the subject, and the organisation has published a consultation document 'Charity Law – A Case for Change'. It points out that:

> the rapid social and economic changes Britain is going through have created an urgent need for new forms of voluntary organisations. There is no lack of energetic people, ready to take up this challenge. But charity law can be a serious obstacle to new initiatives. Charity law is a complex, ramshackle . edifice built on foundations dating back to 1601.

It explains that 'although unemployment is the foremost social evil of our time', it is not lawfully a charitable purpose to help the unemployed. It argues for relaxation of controls on the work of information and advice centres, and for other activities that are presently not seen as charitable – the achievement of racial harmony, maintenance of human rights, improvement of international relations – to be allowed to be so.

On the question of advocacy by charities, it states that:

> . . . many charities work on the ground, day by day, with disadvantged and vulnerable people. They have valuable first-hand experience of how existing policies and administrative practices are generally affecting those they serve. They know that the help they can offer is only part of the solution to such people's needs. Changes in the law and in administrative

practices are often equally important. Charities, we believe, must be free
to argue their case for such changes.

It condemns the Charity Commissioners' guidelines on advocacy as
'ill-founded and un-warranted; they should be withdrawn and revised
guidelines prepared in consultation with the volunteer sector'.
   It argues that:

> decisions about whether or not an activity is charitable should be based on
> the following simple and objective test: that 'politics' is essentially about
> the retention and transference of government power. Hence, in the present
> context, 'political activity' includes only activity which aims – overtly or
> covertly – to influence the electoral process in favour of (or against) any
> person or party. On that basis, contributing to debates on public policy
> and administration does not constitute political activity.

So far, first class. Then we come to the point where I feel the NCVO falls
short. It continues:

> It is well established at law that no charity may seek to advance any party
> political cause or other electorally motivated purpose; nor may a charity's
> *ultimate* purposes include securing or preventing a change in the law or
> administrative policy in practice. *We do not think there is much prospect of
> removing these restrictions nor do we believe that to remove them would
> necessarily be desirable.* [my italics]

It is at this point that the NCVO appears to contradict itself. It has
defined, with respect to charity law, politics as 'essentially about the
retention and transference of government power . . . political activity
includes only activity which aims . . . to influence the electoral process.'
This seems to me an admirable definition. Once it is accepted, why
then argue, as the NCVO, that charities should be prohibited from
engaging in all the other pressure activity which is usually and carelessly
described as 'political' and which is in no way intended to further the
cause of any one political party or political ideal? And why support a
system that stops a pressure group not concerned with party politics
from becoming a charity? The NCVO seems to miss the point that by not
allowing a charity's 'ultimate' purposes to be a change in the law or
administrative policy, 'the system' stops pressure groups being
registered as charities and thus penalises them.
   Some causes that are charitable in all but law cannot offer a service or
directly meet human need because it is not the nature of the problem.
For instance, Amnesty. Why should they be denied charitable status?
In any event, the final decision whether to financially support an
organisation lies with the public. Surely tax relief should be available
proportionate to public support, and that is effectively what would
happen if tax advantages were extended to all.
   As it is, the law *is* geared to controlling charities and voluntary
organisations and making sure that their accumulated knowledge and

expertise does not become an embarrassment or threat to the status quo. It emphasises the fact that while society has little to fear from community/cause pressure groups, the authorities clearly feel that they do.

In the meantime, the classic British compromise, based to some extent upon hypocrisy, has come into existence: what has happened is that pressure groups have had to form two organisations. One is a non-charitable pressure group, and the other a charitable trust. The first undertakes the normal pressure group activity. The second undertakes that activity which could be termed educational or research and which is consistent with the charitable definition of such.

If you intend to launch a pressure group, it is therefore possible to list all of the activities you intend to undertake, and place them under headings of 'pressure group' or 'charity' depending on whether they fit within the definition of charitable activity. Education and research can be charitable objects. Of course, you need to meet the Charity Commissioners' qualification that 'conduct of research as one of its objects must aim for objectivity and balance in the method of conducting research projects; and in publishing the results of the research must aim to inform and educate the public, rather than to influence political attitudes or inculpate a particular attitude of mind'.

It is, however, more than likely that you will wish to undertake such activities. For instance, in addition to CLEAR, The Campaign for Lead-free Air, there is the CLEAR Charitable Trust. This organises seminars, symposia, and the commissioning and publishing of research, all of it done independently and objectively.

On the whole there is a limit to the amount of charitable funding that CLEAR or other pressure groups would be able to attract in any event, and thus it is normally possible to reconcile charitable income with acceptable charitable spending. It is absurd, however, that pressure groups have to go to this length. The main beneficiaries are lawyers. The Chief Charity Commissioner in the interview quoted above said 'I know people criticise the setting up of separate companies for campaigning purposes as artificial, but it works.' The question is for whom?

Now charities have their own pressure group, in the form of the NCVO Charity Law Working Group. Unfortunately, although they are a pressure group, they fall short of advocating policies that will benefit pressure groups as well as charities. That is a pity. Perhaps we need a pressure group to press the pressure group set up by the NCVO!

In the meantime, the injustice remains. Let the last word on the subject be with the NCVO's own Francis Gladstone, who wrote:

> While it may be true that even the best laws and the widest of civil liberties cannot achieve a full just and free society, bad laws and the suppression of civil liberties are obstacles to charities' wider aspirations. And time and

again the small, still voice of conscience has compelled protest, however dangerous, however inconvenient to those in positions of power and authority. For the spirit of charity cannot be muzzled – it will always spontaneously cry out against injustice and oppression. . . . Whatever judges may rule that 'charity' means within the letter of the law, the spirit of charity (shorn, if need be of tax concessions) will retain its concern for social justice and the improvement of the human condition. . . . Charity – romantic but unsentimental concern for the fate of every fellow human being, equal and unconditional love of every neighbour – cannot sit back quietly in the face of misery, suffering and violence. The spirit of charity rebels. . . .

THE
A TO Z
OF
CAMPAIGNING IN BRITAIN

4 HOW TO CAMPAIGN EFFECTIVELY – A PRACTICAL GUIDE

AIMS

A SO YOU want to launch a campaign. The first essential is to determine your aims or objectives. This should be done with clarity and a sense of reality. You would be surprised how many campaigns or organisations fail because they have never been clear about what they wish to achieve, or because they have fixed unrealistic objectives that predetermine failure.

The first question is:
what do we want to achieve?

The second question is:
what part of that objective is actually achievable?

Then follows:
how? when? at what cost?

Getting the answers right is the best possible start to your campaign.

Let's take the CLEAR campaign to illustrate the point:

What was our objective? Answer: it was to persuade or force the government to ban lead from petrol.

What was possible? This is where the answers differed from one section of the anti-lead movement to another. At one extreme, there were those who said it could be banned within a matter of weeks. It didn't matter what the cost was – the threat to children justified action.

In determining *our* objectives, however, we took a number of factors into account:

(a) We could not demonstrate that a near-overnight ban was technically possible. The countries which had introduced lead-free petrol had phased the lead out over a generation of cars (i.e. insisted that new cars be made to run on lead-free petrol, and that lead-free petrol be available for them, whilst old cars could end their lives on leaded fuel).

(b) We knew that the petroleum and car manufacturing industries would fight an immediate ban far more vigorously than they would contest a phasing out.

(c) We were well aware that many influential individuals and organisations had maintained their distance from anti-lead campaigners for fear of becoming involved in what they cautiously believed to be an over-emotive or unrealistic campaign. To obtain their support we knew we had to be seen to be medically and scientifically sound, and also to be fair and reasonable about the practical problems of a move to lead-free petrol. It was essential that what we asked for should be acknowledged by everybody as attainable. While the industries did not want a phasing out of lead in petrol, they acknowledged that it could be done. Thus this demand could not be condemned as impractical.

We defined our objectives as follows:

● To demand that as soon as possible, and in any event by early 1985, all new cars sold on the UK market be required to run on lead-free petrol.

● To demand that as soon as possible, and in any event by early 1985, all petrol stations be required to have lead-free petrol available for sale to the public.

● To urge that taxation on the sale of petrol should be imposed to create a price advantage to motorists purchasing lead-free petrol.

Thus we had established clear and realistic objectives. We came in for criticism from the more extreme wing of the anti-lead movement for what they saw as an unacceptable compromise, but I believe our realism helped win the final decision to move to lead-free petrol.

If your objective is to have a by-pass for your town, then your objectives can be simply stated to the public as:

> The . . . by-pass committee seeks to have a by-pass built at . . . within three years because of the environmental damage caused to historic buildings, and the road safety hazard caused by heavy traffic on crowded streets, several of them with schools.

This brief statement still succeeds in being comprehensive and straight-forward. No one can be in any doubt what you exist to do and why. You want a by-pass. You want it in a reasonable time. And you want it because your children are in danger and your lovely town is being spoilt. It also sounds so reasonable that your listener's sympathy will automatically be aroused.

ANNIVERSARIES

WHEN YOU do your research, note all the significant dates to do with the issue. Anniversaries create good opportunities for publicity or other campaign activities or special events. For instance, Friends of the Earth on the third anniversary of the near-accident at Three Mile Island, made a birthday cake in the shape of a nuclear power station, and got Glenda Jackson to blow out the candles. A simple enough exercise, but the photograph made a number of newspapers and contributed to keeping people aware of the hazards of nuclear energy. Centenaries, fiftieth anniversaries, one-year-afters, etc., all create the opportunity for demonstrations, receptions, or other activities.

I once worked on a magazine and the editor/publisher drew my attention to the fact that the *Spectator* had just attracted a lot of advertising and publicity for its 2,000th issue. 'We can do that too,' he said, 'We must have our 5,000th issue coming up shortly.' We both turned to the magazine, and checked the number of the most recent issue. It was number 5,000! Oh well, you don't win them all.

ADVERTISING

AT THE time Shelter was launched in the mid-Sixties it was possible to obtain a worthwhile return – often as much as £4–£5 for every £1 spent – from advertising in newspapers such as *The Guardian, The Times, The Observer*, etc., as well as in religious newspapers, such as the *Catholic Herald* or the *Church of England Newspaper* or *Church Times.* Unfortunately, the cost of advertising has risen astronomically, and yet the sum of money that donors send in response to advertising has remained more or less the same. Inflation has not affected charity donations. The person who gave £5 to charity in 1966 probably would still give £5 in 1983. Thus advertising for funds is rarely any longer a profitable exercise.

This does not rule out advertising altogether, however, for there are still occasions when it can have value:

First, if it is timed to exploit an opportunity, such as a major television documentary on the subject of your campaign, or some other event that is likely to attract a higher response than you would normally expect.

Or if you are having a 'week' (i.e. Mental Handicap Week, or Shelter Week, or whatever) where local groups all over the country are undertaking activities, and some shrewdly positioned advertising will reinforce their efforts and contribute to the success of the week.

Or if your campaign is planning a major drive and you feel the best way to convey your message to the most people is by a well-timed ad in a magazine like the *New Statesman*, or *The Spectator*, or a specialist magazine.

CLEAR took the exceptional step of booking a full-page ad in *The Observer* to climax the launch of its campaign early in 1982. The ad was intended to hammer home the message of the campaign. We emphasised in it that we hoped readers would contribute to its cost, and in fact the immediate return, plus the return from a second appeal to the same people later in the year, did more than cover the cost of the ad. Of greater importance it meant a revival of interest by radio and television programmes, and thousands of pounds of additional free publicity.

It was, however, a gamble, albeit one that paid off, and I would not necessarily recommend such an action.

The Police Federation achieved a major coup with an ad at a time when they were having difficulty over a pay rise. They placed advertising in the national newspapers showing policemen injured in riots, or maimed by criminals, with the headline 'One way to earn £40 per week!'. The effect was considerable and the advertising helped them win a higher pay award.

If you plan advertising, you should consider the possibility of persuading a number of supporters to contribute to the cost of it. An 'open letter' with a lengthy list of signatories, each contributing a proportion of the cost, can also be effective.

BEGINNING

B ONE OF the most frequent questions I am asked by those who plan to launch a campaign or pressure group is 'how do we begin?'. As I have stated, the first step is to *establish clear and realistic objectives*. Having done that, you have to *determine the correct strategy and tactics*.

I cannot over-state the importance of planning and preparation for a campaign. We began the research and planning for the Shelter campaign in June 1966 and it was five months later that it was launched. We began planning the CLEAR campaign in July 1981 and it was the end of January 1982 before it was launched. At Friends of the Earth we began with other organisations to plan a pesticides campaign early in the new year of 1982, but it was not launched for 12 months. A campaign I am currently engaged in for freedom of information went into the planning stage in April 1983 but it was not launched until January 1984. You need this time to:

● research the problem
● settle your objectives
● put together your organisation
● undertake the legal work if you register as a company, or as a charity
● prepare your initial print material, and your case
● brief in advance those journalists, politicians and other organisations who are likely to support you

A crucial part of this planning process is to *determine the route to the decision you wish taken*. Where does the decision lie? Is it with the local authority? Is it with government? If with government, with which ministry? Is it with a nationalised industry? Or a commercial company? Or a health authority or school board of governors? Wherever the final decision lies, that is your *target*.

Having fixed your target, you then ask: *what is most likely to influence that target?* In other words, where is the vulnerability?

You also have to decide whether there are other subsidiary targets. For instance, while the Government was the main target for CLEAR, the petroleum and car manufacturing industries were subsidiary targets, for by undermining their resolution, we would undoubtedly also reduce the government's.

One of the key questions to ask is whether it should be a 'corridors of power' campaign or a public campaign.

A *'corridors of power' campaign* will be chosen where there is a possibility of achieving your objective by behind-the-scenes persuasion, by pulling strings, or by getting the right people to lean on the right people.

A *public campaign* is necessary where it is clear that the normal negotiating channels need to be by-passed and politicians or companies reached at the point where they are most vulnerable – where they might lose votes in the case of the former, or money in the case of the latter.

In the case of the CLEAR campaign, we considered these two options. We decided that as the government had only a matter of months before it decided on its policy of a reduction to 0.15 grams per litre, but not lead-free petrol, there was no possibility of changing their minds behind the scenes. Furthermore, we had little influence behind the scenes, whereas the power of the petroleum and car manufacturing industries was enormous. If we tried to win by persuasion in the 'corridors of power' we would be delayed, patronised, and ultimately rejected. There was no doubt in our mind that the only way to proceed was to create such a public head of steam that those in the 'corridors' were forced to find a way to change their policy.

So, to begin, you proceed logically from step to step, answering these questions:

- What are our objectives?
- Who are the decision-makers – who is the target? How should we approach them: should it be a 'corridors of power' campaign or 'public' campaign?
- Whose help do we need to achieve our objectives?
- What research do we have to undertake?
- In what form are we going to present our case? What resources of money and skills do we need to undertake the campaign, and where can we find them?
- When is the best time to launch and where and how?
- What are the various activities we intend to undertake, over what period of time, in what order, and with what objectives?

Only when all these questions are satisfactorily answered, and all the preparatory work done, are you in a position to begin.

BARNSTORMING

ONE TECHNIQUE that I picked up from studying American political campaigning is that of barnstorming. What this means is to *hit a given area to the maximum possible effect in the shortest possible time*. Just as leading politicians at election-time try to achieve as much as possible in a town or city as quickly as possible before moving on to the next, we developed barnstorming at Shelter to a point where we could achieve considerable results, and we repeated the technique when we had the provincial launches of CLEAR. What we would do was to choose a city and plan a 24-hour campaign to achieve as much publicity as possible and to leave the city with a thriving Shelter group. A public meeting would be fixed for 8.00 pm. We would arrive in town about 4.00 pm. The schedule could then consist of:

4.00 pm: interview with local morning newspaper for the next day
4.30 pm: interview with local evening newspaper for the following night

(Note the order – the morning newspaper will be published first and therefore its deadline is nearer; this attention to detail is critical.)

5.00 pm: record interview to go out on the local radio stations' local news programme at 6.00 pm
5.30 pm: record television interview with one of the two local stations in order that at . . .
6.00 pm: . . . we can appear 'live' on the other

(They will both begin by saying that they either have you 'live' or not at all, but once you have made your decision as to which one is going to get you, the other – unless it is a busy news day – will normally cave in.)

7.00 pm: meet potential leaders of local group, local personalities, ideally the MP, leader of the council, etc. at small reception
8.00 pm: public meeting (which should have been extremely well prepared and is therefore well attended – see section on public meetings)
10.00 pm: follow-up drinks or reception for those who have attended the meeting and want to remain to sign up for a local group
11.30 pm: appearance on local radio late night chat show

The following morning
8.00 am: possibly another local radio appearance
8.30 am: breakfast in hotel with some influential local people – perhaps a newspaper editor, leader of council, local church leader, or whoever
9.00 am: address assembly of most important local school

(I have often done two school assemblies in a dash by car in one morning.)

10.00 am: special period with the 6th formers of the school
11.00 am: address meeting of a local women's organisation
12.00 noon: attend lunch and address the local Rotary Club.

By then the town has been 'hit' and the local group should be well launched. (See also G for Groups on pages 69–73.)

COALITIONS

C GIVEN THE strength of the opposition you are likely to encounter, one of the first steps in any campaign is to recruit as much support as possible. Before seeking the support of the public, politicians, or the media, it makes sense to *accumulate as much support as you can from other organisations*. These bring with them their own memberships, branches, contacts, and influence. Thus it is possible to build up a considerable constituency of support by negotiations with a relatively small number of people or organisations.

A case in point was the CLEAR campaign. Well before it was launched we had personal meetings or correspondence with a variety of organisations we anticipated would be sympathetic. Obviously the first step was to talk to those campaigns that had already been concerned with lead in petrol, the Conservation Society with its own Working Party on the subject and Friends of the Earth. In addition we recruited the support of the Association of Community Health Councils for England and Wales, Transport 2000, The Association of Directors of Social Services, The Advisory Centre for Education, the Association of Neighbourhood Councils, and the Health Visitors Association. The invitation to the opening press conference went out in the names of all these organisations and this helped to alert the media to the potential strength of the campaign. In addition, these organisations included the CLEAR print material in their mailings and this guaranteed a wider circulation than otherwise would have been the case. They also strengthened our hand in approaching others, and eventually CLEAR was supported by 20 major organisations, all invited to nominate a member to the Campaign's Advisory Committee.

One of the effects of the coalition was to help counter the suggestion we knew our industrial opponents would make – namely that the anti-lead-in-petrol people were, as they often said, 'a small bunch of nutters'. Clearly a coalition of well-known organisations could not be brushed aside in such cavalier fashion.

Shelter also was launched by five organisations for the homeless, and this too added credence to the launch of the campaign and established it as the major organisation in its field.

The 1984 Campaign for Freedom of Information has now developed the idea of coalitions even further. At the first meeting of organisations to discuss the campaign, we laid down a number of requirements for supporting organisations: they had to contribute money; they had to be represented on one of the campaign's major committees and had to allocate a staff member with sufficient time to contribute to the campaign; they had to undertake campaigning on the same subject during 1984; and we looked to them to feed into the main campaign their knowledge and experience of confidentiality in their own field. The intention was to build up a coalition that offered more than just support and sympathy, but also a practical working force. The effect, we hoped, would not only be one major campaign, well-financed and supported by other national organisations, but also a series of mini-campaigns running in concert with the main one.

This coalition approach in no way undermines either the separate identities or the work of individual pressure groups, but it does help to get pressure groups working together and creates a situation where each pressure group helps and strengthens others.

The coalition approach can be used at both national and local level. I can think of virtually no cause that cannot benefit from it.

Having quoted the case of a town needing a by-pass let's stick with it to see how a coalition could be built for a local campaign. Let's assume the moving force is a small group of townspeople who have become frustrated at the failure of their MP and the local authority. The townspeople should list the number of organisations that could be concerned: local conservation and environmental organisations, organisations concerned with children such as parent-teachers, an organisation, if one exists, of residents on the streets directly affected, etc. All the organisations should be called to a meeting to settle on a plan, nominate representatives to a central committee, but also be invited to run a separate campaign themselves. Thus, the local authority, county council, and ultimately the local MP, will not find themselves dealing with only one, albeit powerful, committee on behalf of the town, although this is essential, but also with correspondence and deputations and approaches from a variety of other organisations as well. The local authority and MP should be shamed by all this activity into action by being made to feel as ineffectual as they have probably been.

Remember: strength comes in numbers. *Every organisation you can involve gives your campaign greater credibility, greater influence, and greater resources.*

This is of such importance that you should approach it properly. If you write letters, they must be well-presented, well-argued, and give all the reasons (a) why other organisations should support the campaign, (b) why you believe you will succeed, and (c) what you expect of them.

Far better, however, is to meet with the key figure in the organisation and discuss it fully so as to recruit their individual support within their own organisation; far better that when your letter arrives at an Executive Meeting of the organisation, its Chairman or Secretary can explain fully what the background is and argue the case.

This can take a lot of time, but the rewards are considerable.

CHURCH

THE CHURCH may not be the influential force in the community that it once was, but it is still a major institution with both local and national influence. Its members are, or are supposed to be, a caring and compassionate group within the community. *It is, therefore, worth considering whether your cause is one likely to have the sympathy of the church,* and if so approaching church leaders.

Because we knew the churches would have a lot of sympathy with the poor and the homeless, Shelter sought to involve the church both at national and local level. Representatives of the Quakers, the Church of England, the Catholic Church, and others were on the Board of Trustees. We advertised in church newspapers, and provided articles for them. We did mailings to clergymen encouraging collections and church fund-raising efforts. The result is that churches have probably contributed about £1 million to Shelter since it was launched in 1966 in one way or another – either by collections, fundraising events, or by producing people who became Shelter group leaders.

Clergymen tend to be influential figures in their local community. Even other community leaders who are not themselves religious find it difficult to brush aside an approach from local clergy.

Clergymen vary in their attitude to pressure groups. Some clergymen take the view that the church should play a full and active part in the community and seek to reflect Christian ideals in all local community affairs. Others prefer to concentrate on a traditional charity role – relief of poverty and distress. In any event, don't forget the church. It can be a valuable ally.

CONTACTS

THE OLD saying 'It doesn't matter what you know but who you know' is, like all cliches, not entirely the truth. Nevertheless *contacts with the people with the right skills* or people with *influence in the right places* are crucial to any campaign. Thus an early step is to list every contact that your group has – politicians, civil servants, industrialists, churchmen, leaders of other organisations, show business people, journalists – anybody at all who could be an asset.

Once you have that list, how you approach and seek to deploy those contacts is critical. Perhaps a far more useful saying would be *'It doesn't only matter who you know, but how you approach them'*. *Never* approach a contact until you know exactly what it is you wish them to do. *Always* approach them with a clear request, making it as simple as possible for them.

I have often been approached by organisations who have told me of their campaign or problem. 'What do you want me to do?' I have asked them. Most times they have no answer. They have not thought of that. They have simply thought 'Des Wilson would be useful'. This simply won't do. Most people who rate being on a list of valuable contacts are there because they are busy, and effective in their fields. They may well be prepared to help but they haven't the time to think for themselves how they should help. The correct answer should be 'Well, we know you don't have a lot of time but it would be tremendously useful if you could . . .'. As always, you should show perspective – you should make a request that is clear and realistic, given the likely time-availability of your contact. It should be a request that is actually within their capacity to grant with the minimum inconvenience.

In approaching a contact, it is crucial that you engage their sympathy quickly, and this is not always done just by telling them of the problem. Often they are more impressed by what you are doing about it. Thus it is better to say 'We are deeply concerned about the lack of facilities for the handicapped in the community. We are already raising money and have provided a mini-bus for day trips. In addition, we have persuaded the local shopping centre to create ramps for wheelchairs. Now we wondered if you could help us by . . .'. In a few brief words you have conveyed the problem you are concerned about, but also that you are a positive force for good. It is more difficult, therefore, for the contact to refuse to help, particularly if the request is a relatively simple one.

Second, if you believe a contact has a lot to offer, it is sometimes best to approach with one or two minor requests that are easily fulfilled. Once a contact has delivered the goods, you are then able to respond with genuine thanks, and also by telling him or her the effect of what they have done. This makes them feel good and worthwhile and useful, and thus more receptive to a fresh approach. 'We were tremendously grateful for what you did on . . . occasion and the results have been invaluable. We wondered if you could possible spare a little more time to. . . .'

It is often a good idea to ask contacts whether they can be listed as 'sponsors' of your campaign. The initial approach should stress what you are *not* asking. 'We know you have a record of sympathy for the disabled, and other needy and wondered if you would lend your name as a sponsor of our campaign for better facilities for the disabled in our community. This does *not* call for financial sponsorship, although of course we welcome any donations, but rather allows us to include your name among a list of public figures who we believe will encourage the community at large to become involved. I can assure you the campaign will be responsibly administered and run, and some of the key figures involved are. . . .'

It is important to remember that if contacts are valuable to you, they are probably valuable to others. Thus they receive many approaches and many pressures on their time. The easier you make it for them to help you, the more likely they are to repeat the help.

DESIGN

D CRUCIAL TO the success of a campaign is the image that you create for it, and in particular the design of print material. If you are a national organisation, likely to produce a lot of print material, money spent on a clever designer to create the best possible image for your campaign, is money extemely well spent. If you are a local organisation, or a small one without funds, then try to find a designer who cares sufficiently about your cause to donate their services.

Often your letterhead, your poster, or your leaflet is the first contact that others will have with your campaign. It should:

● show that you are a campaign of substance
● show that you are professional
● convey a feel for the campaign

I believe the designs that the professional Peter Davenport created for CLEAR and for the 1984 Committee met all of these objectives.

The CLEAR symbol

The CLEAR symbol conveyed the image of children and pollution and motor vehicles, all within the traditional symbol for a warning on the roads. All this in one simple symbol was a real achievement. The strength and clean look of the typefaces and the layout of the various pieces of print material helped to make the campaign look professional. When taken together, our print material was designed to make the campaign look substantial.

I never cease to be amazed at the poor quality of the design of many major organisations. They almost seem afraid of appearing too professional.

DEMONSTRATIONS

IN ANY word-association test 'pressure groups' would probably be linked with 'demonstrations' more than with any other word. Yet over the years that I have been involved with pressure groups I have hardly ever organised a demonstration. In fact I can number them on the fingers of one hand. Two were really 'rallies'. At least the first was intended to be a rally – we booked Trafalgar Square in United Nations Human Rights Year, for a rally on the theme 'Housing is a Human Right' but that day London was hit by a torrential downpour that turned roads into rivers and Trafalgar Square into a lake. Because we had issued press releases, each of the speakers made their contributions, albeit brief, to an audience that consisted of a number of soaked pigeons and a reporter from *The Guardian* who dutifully covered the 'rally' the following day. Shelter subsequently held its own rally in Trafalgar Square. These two occasions achieved their objective of newspaper publicity but could hardly be called demonstrations.

On two occasions as Chairman of the London branch of the New Zealand organisation HART (Halt All Racial Tourists) I was involved in mini-demos when the New Zealand rugby team was in Britain prior to a planned tour of South Africa. After all attempts to meet the team and put our point of view failed, we sat down in their hotel foyer, and later obstructed their bus on the way to the International at Twickenham. The former demo won a few paragraphs in the New Zealand newspapers, and the latter made the ITV news.

That is the sum of my demo experience. We never had one for CLEAR. This is not to say that I am opposed to demonstrations. They are a useful weapon in the pressure group's armoury. However, I do believe that demonstrations should be organised sparingly, and only when there is no alternative. The more demonstrations there are, the less they will be a noteworthy event, and the less the media will cover them. Furthermore, they become devalued and in the end an irritant rather than an eye-catcher. Finally, in terms of influence on officialdom, demonstrations are of little value and can be counter-productive unless related to a variety of well-argued and more responsible activities as well.

The point is: anyone can demonstrate, but few can assemble a well-researched and well-presented argument and sustain it in more conventional ways.

When is a demonstration appropriate?
First, when a special opportunity arises that is directly related to the cause and where a demonstration can be seen to be relevant and justified.

For instance, when the International Whaling Federation met in Brighton in 1983, Friends of the Earth and other wildlife organisations arranged a number of eye-catching demonstrations outside the hall. This was calculated to remind the delegates and the media of widespread conservation concern, and calculated to back up those who were lobbying inside the conference. The opportunity only arises once a year and this is an entirely appropriate and peaceful demonstration.

On another occasion, the Environment Secretary, Tom King, was due to meet farmers to discuss the necessity for conservation measures for some land in his constituency which Friends of the Earth were particularly anxious to protect. A FoE demonstration was staged outside the hall where the meeting took place. Inside the hall King was heard to urge the farmers to accept conservation proposals and to draw their attention to the demonstration outside. 'That is but a small indication of public opinion', he was heard to say. This was an occasion where a Minister actually used a demonstration to reinforce his argument that the farmers could not act with indifference to public opinion. While the demonstration was not intended to alter the policy that King advocated, it helped him to sell it to the farmers, and thus was a worthwhile exercise.

Second, demonstration is valid where all other attempts to persuade the target to listen have failed, and the demonstrators can justify their actions on the basis of legitimate frustration. (The justification for our demos when the All Blacks were in Britain was that we had sought a private and unpublicised meeting to put our points of view and had been consistently rejected. We were finally forced to draw the All Blacks attention to ourselves in more direct ways. We would have much preferred the former.)

The key to effective demonstrations is imagination and humour; these are some organised by FoE over the years

Third, a demonstration is valid where, unless it takes place, more moderate action will be too late. (If, for instance, a farmer intends to destroy a valuable wildlife habitat on a Saturday morning, and the pressure group hears about it a few hours before, a well-reasoned letter to the authorities is not likely to arrive let alone be considered. A demonstration may just awaken the farmer to the seriousness of his action and force him to give it second thought.)

The rules for demonstrations should be much the same as those for direct action:

- They should be non-violent;
- They should be imaginative and where possible good-humoured;
- They should be relevant to the cause and to the target;
- They should seek to win sympathy and support, and not to alienate.
- They should where possible involve public or 'respectable' personalities whose presence underlines the seriousness of the cause and makes it more difficult for opponents to say that 'they are just a bunch of trouble-makers'.

A useful test of the validity of an exercise is to ask yourself 'What is different about this event that – given the number of demonstrations that take place, and given all the other potential news stories of the day – will convince a news editor that he should devote a reporter to yours?' It is not enough to say 'Because our message is important'. That's what they all say. You have to have a convincing answer.

Let's say the necessary conditions exist for a demonstration, and you have a good idea. Don't forget the following:

- *Involve disciplined people.* Demonstrations can be ruined by over-excitable or uncontrollable people, who, confronted by police, or your opponents, get out of hand. Many a carefully-planned and well-organised demonstration has ended up with pictures in the newspapers of one demonstrator being carted off by the police for an undisciplined violent act. You've made the papers alright, but not with your message. Indeed, the whole event could have been counter-productive.
- If it involves banners or placards, they should all convey, good humouredly if possible, your clear message, and if possible the name of the pressure group. I have seen many photographs of demonstrations in newspapers and been unable to work out from the placards what the demo is about, or who organised it. Not everyone stops to read the caption. If possible, the photographs of your demonstration should convey the message in themselves, and that is less the photographer's responsibility than yours.
- *Don't forget to invite the appropriate media.* Also, try to have your own photographer there, so that if the media don't attend, you can quickly circulate photographs of the event.

- Consider whether it is appropriate to invite the police. The police have become accustomed to demonstrations and are not always negative. Sometimes the presence of police adds to the sense of occasion. The police can be bit-actors in the dramas.
- *Maximise the potential of the demonstration*. Don't make it just a media event. Have brief and well-written leaflets (not excessively indignant, but rather informative) for passers-by and spectators. Have at least one or two senior spokesmen available to take part in a private briefing if the demonstration leads to officialdom trying to diffuse the situation by calling in your representatives. (Imagine, for instance, you have a demonstration outside a Ministry, and the Minister decides to invite a spokesman in and you have no-one there who can adequately represent the case. The Minister will become all the more convinced that you don't deserve attention.)
- If at all possible try to organise a demonstration that does not alienate or inconvenience people who are not directly involved.

EFFICIENCY

IT CAN'T be repeated too often:

E

- be professional;
- work hard;
- and be efficient.

If there is one way to kill off support it is when people write for information or offer help, and they don't receive a reply. Or if someone telephones for information or to offer help, and the person who answers the phone simply doesn't know where the information is, or what the potential supporter can do. It is taken for granted in commercial practice that the telephone switchboard operator is a key staff member, and that the way in which the telephone is answered can affect the whole business. Why do so many pressure groups and voluntary organisations think they are any different?

The public, as most voluntary organisations know, tend to be ultra-critical of the administration of organisations they donate to. This is sometimes unreasonable, but it is a fact of life and should be recognised. In the setting up of any organisation, make sure that you have adequate administration. There is no point in being creative and exciting and having dynamic campaigners, if when the public response comes, your administration simply cannot handle it. Telephone calls should be efficiently dealt with. Letters should be answered quickly and well. Donations should receive a receipt and follow-up material very quickly. All donors and potential supporters should be recorded and up-to-date lists kept.

One way to achieve efficient administration with minimal resources is to anticipate every kind of enquiry, and have standard approaches. For instance, there were only three of us in the CLEAR office, and it was obvious that we could not send individual letters to everybody. We therefore anticipated every kind of enquiry or offer of help that we would get and prepared standard letters. We made it our target to respond to every day's post on the same day.

If you have an office, and an information system, start as you intend to go on – have it well organised and keep it up-to-date. Good administration takes no time at all; bad administration is unbelievably time consuming. If you deal with the post every day, if you keep the filing up-to-date by filing every bit of material every day, you avoid huge backlogs, piles of material all over the office, and the hours you spend trying to find letters or pieces of paper when you need them.

This efficiency should be reflected in all you do. If you have a press conference the media who attend should be impressed by the efficiency of its organisation. The way letters are written and information is provided is crucial. If Members of Parliament, for instance, write for information, they should receive it by return of post and it should be as clearly and easily presented as possible, with one sheet of paper on the top summarising what has been sent to them and where they can find what they want. This efficiency achieves two results: first, it gives the MPs what they need, and that should hopefully contribute to the campaign. Second, the efficiency impresses them with the organisation itself, and makes them more likely to be supportive, to be prepared to respond to further calls for help, or to recommend the organisation as one of authority.

People are more likely to assume a campaign with an air of efficiency is right in its demands than they are of a campaign that is obviously incompetently run. Efficiency doesn't cost money. It doesn't require special talents. It requires a determination to do things properly and to put in the necessary hours.

FUND-RAISING

F FUND-RAISING is the most difficult and dislikeable part of pressure group activity, but also one of the most necessary. No pressure group can operate without spending money, and, unless you have considerable personal reserves, and this is rarely the case, it has to be raised from others.

Any guide to fund-raising is bound to make it sound easier than it is. It requires a book in itself, and I do not, therefore, intend to offer a detailed account of how to raise money (even if I knew).

However, I would like to offer some broad principles that you should apply:

● *Determine exactly what you need*. If you are to formulate an adequate and realistic fund-raising plan, you have to have as precise a target as possible.

- *Try to make it fun.* I always urged my colleagues in Shelter to 'take the D out of fund-raising and make it fun raising money'. No-one likes to beg for money, and the organisation of imaginative 'fun' events that also raise money makes begging unnecessary and can actually contribute to the morale of the organisation.
- Once you have your target, make a list of the most likely contributors. For instance, if you are a pressure group seeking better facilities for disabled children, your first priority will be to obtain a mailing list of parents of disabled children, who are most likely to understand and sympathise with the cause. They will be your priority target. Likewise, if the pressure group is to obtain a couple of pedestrian crossings near a school, the parents of the children attending that school are most likely to contribute to a fund to pay the cost of a campaign.

Priority fund-raising targets will always include:

(1) Those directly affected by the problem;

(2) Those known to be sympathetic to the cause.

- *It makes sense to break the target down into more manageable sums.* If your target is £100,000, then just to look at that figure written on a piece of paper will induce a deep sense of depression and pessimism. But if you break it down into manageable sums and say 'We can raise 30 per cent of that in big donations from wealthy people who are sympathetic, 20 per cent by a couple of "fun" events, 20 per cent from industrial sponsors, 20 per cent from a house-to-house collection, and 10 per cent from other donations and activities', and if you then give responsibility for each of these sections to one individual who has to create his or her sub-committee, then you have spread the fund-raising responsibility across a number of people with more manageable targets.
- *Don't be afraid to use some of the money you have raised to raise more money.* I proposed to colleagues in CLEAR a full-page ad in *The Observer* at a negotiated price of £10,000. 'TEN THOUSAND POUNDS – You must be mad. Think what we can do with that money', I was told. I had to point out that the ten thousand pounds would not disappear. First, the ad would bring back a considerable sum of money as a direct appeal. Second, it would provide through donors and members a mailing list we could appeal to a second and a third time. Third, it would attract massive attention, which would in turn reinforce our other fund-raising activities. Fourth, the unusual nature of such an ad would attract the attention of other media and thus increase coverage generally. All of this happened, and the ad more than paid for itself. Thus we had the same £10,000 to spend at the end that we had at the beginning.

It is the principle I recommend, not the specific idea. I do not suggest that everyone should take a full-page ad in *The Observer*. But for a fund-raising programme to be a success, you have to spend some money to make money.

● *Beware of the fund-raising professionals.* I am not saying ignore them – I am saying 'take care'. Their first priority is to win your business and obtain their fee. Never forget that. That is the profession they are in. That is their objective. You are merely a passing client and a temporary concern. Of course it is their business to make you feel you are much more than that. But why should you be? They weren't involved with you before you turned up on their doorstep to seek their advice.

Second, as they may well emphasise themselves, it will probably be you that will have to do the work. The most some firms can offer are ideas and advice. This can in fact be valuable, but if you have a hope that they will raise the money for you, explain that clearly to them, and make sure that this is the deal you make.

If you wish to approach professional fund-raisers, ask them to spell out on paper *exactly* what they can and cannot do for you, and only if you are really satisfied that their help is both necessary and will achieve the desired results, consider them. Then ask if there are any similar pressure groups they have helped, and consult those pressure groups.

● *It takes people to raise money.* There is no fund-raising machinery. It takes people. The more people you have raising money the more you will raise, and if you can give them specific tasks, and make the whole exercise agreeable, they will raise even more. If you have to raise money – and you most definitely do – then set out to do it with as many people as possible.

● *Don't overlook tried-and-tested methods.* You may groan at the idea of jumble sales, Christmas bazaars, summer fêtes and the like, but the reason that there are so many of them is because they work.

● *You don't have to have all the money raised before you launch the campaign.* If you have formulated a first-class pressure group campaign that will last 18 months or two years, and you estimate that you will need £100,000, you don't need it all on day one. Try to raise sufficient money to cover the first three to six months. If the campaign is effective, it will attract further money.

● *In all that you do, don't forget that you need money.* If you are having a public meeting to spread your message, try to raise money at it as well. If you are writing to local authorities all over the country seeking their support for a national policy why not, if they are likely to pass a resolution, ask them also to make a donation to the cause? (As you will see in my chapter about CLEAR, we not only obtained the support of well over 100 local authorities, but obtained money from them as well.) If someone who you know to be wealthy writes to you in support of your campaign, or by some other act indicates sympathy, don't be afraid to write and thank them and point out in a courteous and friendly way that the campaign costs money and any help they could offer would be much appreciated.

● *Try to create ways whereby the giving of money to your campaign can benefit the donor.* For instance, many companies have a public relations budget, and seek to achieve public goodwill by being seen to be attached to worthwhile activities. Industrial sponsorship can be applied to voluntary activity and pressure groups just as it can be applied to sport, or the arts. The CLEAR Charitable Trust persuaded an industrial company to contribute £15,000 to its international symposium on lead and health. Also, many companies may not donate money but will give practical help that has the same effect. For instance, British Leyland loaned a van to CLEAR for six weeks for its lead-testing unit free of charge. Another company gave Friends of the Earth all its old desks and filing cabinets – sufficient to furnish the whole office. Before you think of buying a thing, ask whether it is possible someone will donate it.

GROUPS

G IF YOU plan a pressure group on a national issue, and you expect the battle to be prolonged and requiring support throughout the country, then you need to think in terms of local groups.

Before you decide whether to set up your own groups, consider whether there is a national organisation of local groups that would be likely to support you and whose groups would take the issue up.

I have had experience of both approaches: Shelter set up its own groups, and at one point had over 350. CLEAR, on the other hand, became associated with Friends of the Earth, and FoE offered to encourage its local groups, over 200 in all, to make lead in petrol a major issue in 1982. (In fact, a number of people where there were no FoE groups decided to set up CLEAR groups, and we ended up with 12 or so. But, on the whole, the FoE groups did all that was necessary.)

So, *you may not need you own groups' network – you may be able to plug into someone else's.* But if that is not possible, then you should consider the following:

● *Be clear what you want from your local groups.* Are they to be fund-raising groups? Local pressure groups? Both? And what are their precise objectives? If they are fund-raising groups, do you intend to give them specific targets? If they are local pressure groups, what do you want them to do? It is vital you answer these questions properly, because the answers will determine the kind of people you are looking for to start groups and the kind of groups you want.

- *Choose the right group leader.* The right personality is one who not only is committed to your cause but has the ability to get on with other people and encourage them to act. Such people are difficult to find. You will often find someone who is completely committed to your cause but alienates everybody around them, wanting to boss the group about, and unable to get co-operation or sympathy. On the other hand you can have someone who is a terrific personality and a lot of fun, but completely hopeless at grasping the message and communicating it effectively. The ideal local group leader will (1) be committed, (2) be able to bring the best out of people, (3) have ideas and energy. The right organiser of a local group can achieve miracles at local level. You can tell within minutes of arriving at a meeting in a town whether the local group is organised by such a person, or by a no-hoper. You can see it in the layout of the hall, and the number of helpers there, and in the size of the audience. So the choice of person is important. If a number of people emerge in an area, it is worth going there to meet them, and if you can recognise such a potential group leader, encourage the others to elect him or her rather than necessarily responding to the first person who offers to do it.
- *Keep your groups well-informed.* Group leaders should receive a special regular briefing giving them (1) up-to-date facts on the cause, (2) up-to-date news on the organisation's progress nationally, (3) up-to-date requests for help and support. It is vital that they feel they are cared about by you and that they feel well-informed. If you are having a big national press conference to launch a new aspect of the campaign, advise the local group in advance – it is upsetting for an active and committed group leader to read in the newspapers at the same time as everyone else what your campaign is doing.
- *Don't be afraid to spend money supporting your groups* and keeping your groups well-informed. That money should come back in terms of even more vigorous activity at local level.
- *Don't give groups more to do than they are capable of.* On the contrary try to give them a set of objectives that develop in size as the group develops. If they begin with a number of simple tasks which they can easily achieve, this is enormously encouraging for them, and they then feel able to take on more difficult responsibilities. If you land them with too much to begin with, they can end up frustrated and disenchanted.
- *It is vital that they believe themselves to be important to you.* The more they feel you depend on them and need them and are enthusiastic about their work, the more they will do. If they begin to feel taken

for granted, they will quickly dissolve, and who could blame them?

● If you appoint one or more organisers to go round the country encouraging and stimulating groups, then you are looking for a remarkable personality. For a start, they have to act as a link between groups and headquarters, and this inevitably puts them in a position where their sympathies are divided. They have to convey the feelings and needs of each to the other without implying a bias one way or the other and alienating either the group or the headquarters staff. Second, they have to be able to go to an area and not only absorb any complaints, and defuse them, and leave the group happy with headquarters, but also leave it full of enthusiasm and rejuvenated. This takes energy and confidence and considerable personality. (If anyone knows such a person, send me their name. I have spent most of my life looking for them.)

● *Try to give your groups as much information and a sense of direction as possible, but leave plenty of room for them to take decisions and to employ their own ideas.* They know their area better than you do. They know their membership better than you do. They know what they can achieve better then you. They should receive plenty of ideas and suggestions from you, and requests from you, but still have the freedom to pick and choose what they do according to their own circumstances, and also to introduce their own ideas.

If they send you ideas for the central campaign, consider them carefully, and even if you can't use them, respond to them positively and gratefully.

● *Try to see your groups as both a whole series of mini-pressure groups and also as a national force.* Wherever possible, they should be doing their own thing at local level when it suits them. But every now and again, if they all come together as a national force, they can be a tremendous source of strength. For instance, if every MP in the House of Commons receives two or three letters from their own locality in the same week, it can cause quite a ripple at Westminster. You can only organise such a concerted campaign about once a year. Likewise, if you plan a series of national events that are going to attract a lot of national publicity, and you know this well in advance, you might encourage all your local groups to have some fund-raising activity in that particular week. That way, they will benefit from the stimulus of the national campaign. This requires a lot of advance planning and advance warning. Often you can produce more cheaply national posters and leaflets which can be distributed on a nation-wide basis to enhance that national effort.

So far I have talked about the organisation of local groups from a national point of view. But what if you have become committed to the work of a pressure group and have decided to form a group in your own locality? How do you go about it? *Organise an event to educate local people about the cause.* This could well be a combined film–meeting–social event. It is vital that this event be well-organised, well-attended, and make a considerable impact, for the nucleus of your group will probably emerge from it. When I was at Shelter a common practice was to organise a showing of the famous television play 'Cathy Come Home', followed by a brief 15 or 20 minute speech by myself or another Shelter speaker, and then have a social event. During the evening everyone would be approached and invited to become a member of a local Shelter group. Their full name and address and phone number would be taken on the spot and a date given for the first meeting of the group. This procedure helped form a considerable number of Shelter groups. However, they required considerable organisation (see P for Public Meetings). If there is to be a film, make it a good one. Otherwise don't bother. If there is to be a speaker, for heaven's sake have a good speaker – someone who will really excite and interest the audience. Try to get a local celebrity to chair it. This will help attract people; also a few words from them at the end can encourage people both to join and to donate money. Finally, you yourself should speak briefly saying why you personally care, why you would like them to support you and work for this cause at local level, and what your plans are.

Never ever let them leave the hall until you have made them answer the question: will they help? If you don't get their names, addresses and phone numbers that evening they may well be lost to you, no matter how interested they are. So, try to get them to commit themselves while you have their attention.

At the first meeting of the group, have informative material to give each group member to take away. The national headquarters should send you ample supplies of its newspaper, leaflets, etc. Be in a position to give a more detailed briefing about the cause. Have your own list of objectives for the local group. Get each person to indicate what their profession is – remember, you are looking for an accountant to be treasurer; someone in the communications business to be press officer; etc. Try to get each person to volunteer for one specific function and give them a title. If someone agrees to be organiser of a couple of local fund-raising events, call them events organiser and encourage them to form a sub-committee consisting of at least one other person already in the group, and others they must recruit themselves. Make sure they all have specific things to do before the next meeting and fix the next meeting while they are all there and have their diaries out. If one or two can't come, find another date when they can. The second meeting is actually more important than the first. Those who turn up for the second meeting have become reasonably committed, will almost certainly have done what they said they would do and thus you are on your way.

- *Try to visit the national headquarters* of the pressure group as soon as you can, meet everyone there, see what literature and material they have, and establish your personality with them and also get to know who the best people are to ring up for specific things.
- *Plan your events with the group over a year in such a way that you are not making your lives impossible.* Your group will dissolve if people are asked to do more than they can cope with. Begin in the first year with a realistic plan of activity that will not overwork everyone, but will maintain the level of commitment and make them feel they have really achieved something at the end of the year.
- *Try to balance fund-raising and other activity* in such a way that they are not always having to raise money, but are also able to do things that they feel are more relevant to the cause.
- *Try to inject as much fun into your activities as possible.* Two or three parties a year are a good idea, but if you are going to have one, why not have a big one and turn it into a fund-raising event as well? That way you all have a good time together, but at the same time you are furthering the cause.
- *Don't constantly be moaning at headquarters.* Even headquarters can be alienated. If you have a complaint, make it firmly, but also good humouredly and tell them exactly how you want them to compensate. ('I know how terribly busy you are, and I don't like to bother you with this, but I have to point out that my request for additional leaflets has been ignored on two occasions. This is making it difficult for me to carry out my plans at local level. So headquarters, what about it? Any chance of posting them today?') This approach is more of a reprimand to headquarters and more of a stimulus to action than an abusive letter ('What the hell are you up to down there?'). If, however, your good humoured approach gets no response, ring up the Chairman, Director, or whoever runs the pressure group, and ask them what is going on. If you don't get a satisfactory answer, then you have to begin genuinely wondering what condition the pressure group is in.
- *Remember that at local level you are the public image of the pressure group.* If you alienate people at local level, or organise things badly, you are not only making your own life difficult – you are also perhaps undermining the national campaign's chances of success. Don't take on a local group unless you really care, are prepared to work hard, and are prepared to make friends for the organisation as enthusiastically as you would like to make friends for yourself.

GIMMICKS

GIMMICKS HAVE their place.

But they should be kept in their place.

Remember, your cause is either of substance or it is not. If it is of substance, it must be argued in a substantial way. Too many gimmicks can create the impression that you don't have a substantial case. Thus, your gimmicks should be few, beautifully timed, imaginative and if possible humorous.

Joe Weston, a Friend of the Earth living in Oxfordshire, had a brilliant idea to draw attention to the potential destruction of some historic fields at Otmoor by the proposed M40. With the co-operation of a farmer on the site, he divided it into thousands of small plots, and sold them to environmentalists all round the world, from Dr David Bellamy in Britain, to John Denver in Colorado, and even to people as far away as Papua, New Guinea. The 'sale' of these plots of land achieved enormous publicity and at the same time created a bureaucratic nightmare because the road could not be built until negotiations had taken place with each of the owners. At the time of writing we do not know how the bureaucracy will find a way round the problem FoE has created, although they no doubt will, but there is no question that he has both put a considerable spanner in the works, and drawn attention to the threat to Otmoor by a simple yet highly imaginative gimmick.

HUMOUR

H THERE ISN'T enough humour in pressure group activity in Britain and that's a pity.

I highly recommend it.

First, it keep you from going round the bend!

Second, it can be the most effective way to make a point.

Third, signs of a sense of humour can be surprisingly reassuring to others. It suggests to them that you have a sense of perspective, that you are not a fanatic, that while you may care passionately, and work hard for the cause, 'you haven't lost your sense of humour'.

You can show humour with one or two cartoons in your newspaper, with the slogans on placards at demonstrations, or with the nature of the demonstrations themselves, with a few jokes or witticisms in speeches, or with light-hearted irony in articles you write or letters to the editor.

Too much humour and everyone will think you're mad. A well-judged sprinkling of humour and they will be convinced you're sane.

Fund-raising with humour – students raise money for Shelter in the City of London

HOLIDAY

HAVE ONE. Whenever anyone tells me 'I have been so busy with the campaign I haven't had a holiday for three years' my heart sinks. If they won't take a break from it, they have probably lost their sense of perspective, and if they have lost their sense of perspective, heaven help the pressure group.

I   IMPOSSIBLE

DON'T BELIEVE IT.

J   JUSTICE

NEVER SETTLE FOR LESS.

K   KILL

DON'T DO IT. There has to be another way.

LAUNCH

L THE LAUNCH of your campaign will be a big factor in your success or failure. The way you launch the campaign will determine your credibility with the media, and indicate to everybody involved whether you are likely to be a campaign of substance, or not. It is necessary at the launch to:

- Be able to demonstrate substantial pre-launch support;
- Have first-class print material, both in presentation and content, and a well-assembled case;
- Stage a press conference that is professional and gives the appearance of assurance and competence.

You will need to plan to spend a fairly high proportion of your resources on an effective launch, but, if it works, it will be money well spent.

The following are *musts*:

- The invitation should go out from as many sponsoring and supporting organisations as possible, in order to indicate that this is a press conference to launch a campaign of some substance.
- If possible the press conference should be chaired by a public personality of some note.
- Choose an impressive place in the centre of London – try to arrange to have it at the House of Commons or House of Lords, or in some other such place.
- Arrange for a small 'leak' to appear in a daily or Sunday newspaper within the previous seven days along the lines of 'A major campaign is to be launched next week . . .', etc. to alert the remainder of the media in addition to the invitation you will have sent.
- Don't just rest on the press conference; do as much prior briefing of journalists as possible. Furthermore, arrange for parliamentary questions or some activity in the House of Commons within the following 24 hours, and hold back a good story for release within a week in order to give the campaign momentum. The launch of your campaign, its objectives, and plans, are sufficient to guarantee you initial publicity; if you have a good story up your sleeve, there is no need to use it at the launch press conference. Spread your ammunition over a longer period.
- Invite representatives of all the supporting organisations and other interested parties to the launch. This makes sure you have a good crowd there and a good atmosphere of anticipation and excitement. (If your press conference is at 11.00 am, you may even think of having a reception for interested parties at 12.30 in order to encourage and enthuse them and make the most of the occasion.

To this you could invite sympathetic MPs.) (See details of the launch of CLEAR in Chapter 6.)

LETTER–WRITING

PRESSURE GROUPS write a lot of letters. *There is no point whatsoever in writing these letters unless you do it well.* A bad letter will have the opposite effect to that intended. A good letter should:

- be brief;
- be clear;
- grab the reader's attention in its opening paragraph and encourage them to read on;
- be precise about what it wants from the reader;
- be neat and clean and without error.

A letter that rambles, is appallingly typed, and is difficult to answer is likely to be put on one side or rejected.

The ideal letter should be written in such a way that it is easy to answer: it should virtually make the decision for the reader.

Letters in response to donations or offers of help are important. I have always given considerable attention to these. When it comes to donations, it is clearly not always possible to respond to every one personally. To begin with, by the time you take into account the cost of the typing, the letter-heading, the envelope, and the stamp, you could end up spending more to say thank you than the value of the donation itself. Thus, standard letters need to be used. If these are well designed, they can be both a standard letter and a receipt. But because this is a standard response, the letter should be written with the utmost care. Those who donate larger amounts should receive a personal letter, not only expressing gratitude, but also indicating to them what their donation would achieve.

Just what this can mean to an organisation is best described by an experience we had at Shelter. At that time we found that if we raised £325 cash, this would be sufficient by the time it was added to local authority loans and improvement grants, for us to buy and rehabilitate a flat for an ordinary-sized family. We received a donation of £1,000 from a generous woman. We wrote her a lengthy letter thanking her, and explaining that we should be able to rehouse three families with the money, and what this would mean to them. By return of post we received a cheque from the woman for £10,000. We wrote once more, deeply grateful, and explaining that over 30 families could be helped with this money. In addition, we enclosed as much material about Shelter as we could in order to make her feel that her money would be well spent. By the time the correspondence ended, her total donation was £22,000 – or 66 families helped. All of this happened because letters showed that her contribution was recognised and invaluable. Clearly this kind of response is unusual, because not many people have this kind of money, but if ever there was a reward for care in letter-writing, this was it. And don't forget – it all began with the reply to the first donation. If we had taken that £1,000 for granted, as can easily begin to happen with a big organisation, the other £21,000 would never have come.

If you are writing an individual letter, make it *individual*. Five of the six paragraphs in the letter may be standard, but at least the sixth should indicate that this letter has been written for this specific individual.

The cynic may feel that this is *too* professional an approach. I would respond with two points: first, I cannot say often enough that if the cause is worthwhile no other approach is satisfactory. Second, I strongly believe that the individual who takes the personal decision in their home to donate money, or offer help to your cause, should be treated with the utmost seriousness. This is someone who cares. This is someone who is a supporter – someone who is with you in what you are doing. Your campaign should reach out to them with the enthusiasm with which they have responded to your campaign. You owe it to the donor – as well as to yourselves. One of the most exciting things about being involved in voluntary activity is to see donations and letters of help and support arrive in the post. They come often from people that can little afford them. They come from people who have listened to what you have to say, who believe in you and have put their trust in you, and believe you will spend their money, or use their help well. It is a great compliment to you and a great credit to them. An enthusiastic and warm and grateful response should be a natural response.

As for all other forms of letter-writing – to those in authority, to contacts, or to others who you can believe can help – remember that letter writing

- takes time;
- costs money;
- engages your energy;
- can be counter-productive if the letter isn't good.

For these reasons you *must* do it properly. The letter should be typed. This makes it easier to read. It should, if at all possible, be restricted to one page. And it should be neat. If you achieve this, you can guarantee that it will be read. If it is hand-written, lengthy and untidy, it could be passed on to a secretary, or put aside or only half read.

It is crucial that the first paragraph engages their interest or sympathy. It should if at all possible begin with a reference to them, linking them with your cause.

Dear . . .
I know that for many years you have been concerned about freedom of information, and I was most impressed by your article in. . . . I believe, therefore, you will be supportive of our campaign to achieve greater rights of access to information.

The campaign is organised by . . . and its organisers include. . . . Its objectives are. . . .

We would be particularly grateful if you could help. We need . . . and believe that if you . . . we would achieve this objective.

If this is possible, perhaps your secretary could telephone me to arrange ten or fifteen minutes of your time, when we could discuss it more fully.
Yours sincerely. . . .

The above letter draws the recipient in by reminding him or her that they have committed themselves in the past. It quickly conveys that this is a campaign of substance, and what its objectives are. It has sought initially a contribution that will not be difficult for the recipient . . . that does not require him or her to act at all; it merely asks that his or her secretary arrange a meeting. It would be difficult for the recipient to refuse.

Finally, I also believe it of importance to answer abusive letters as well. When I was at Shelter, I received some appalling letters, usually attacking the families because they had too many children, or accusing us of only helping blacks. These vicious and racist letters were often upsetting, and it was very tempting to reply 'Listen you racist bastard, we need your help like a hole in the head . . .'. The trouble with such a letter is that it would confirm the hatred and the prejudice in the mind of the writer.

My approach was to always write back as follows:

Dear . . .
Many thanks for your letter. I read it with care. It does indeed illustrate the size of the task we have to create greater harmony and understanding in the community and to help all of our fellow citizens to the ideal of a decent home. I can assure you we will do all in our power to achieve that worthwhile end.
With all best wishes.
Yours sincerely. . . .

MEDIA

MCONSIDERING THE central place the media has in our everyday lives, it is extraordinary how it maintains an undeserved mystique. The media – newspapers, radio and television – is a business just like any other business. On the whole, the media will help you if there's something in it for them. That 'something' is 'a good story', whether it be a news item or feature, and, of course, the best story is a good story that is also exclusive.

Pressure groups and the media need each other. Pressure groups are the source of well-researched, controversial stories to the media and the media is necessary for the pressure group to make an impact. The best way to deal with the media, therefore, is to be businesslike and professional and try to achieve a feeling of partnership. There is no need to be subservient; on the other hand, there is every reason not to be unfriendly or hostile. Whatever you do, avoid 'the problem with this country is the media' attitude. There is, of course, some truth in it, but as a basis for partnership with the media, it is disastrous. You can't change the media. You have to work with it as it is. This is possible and can be fruitful.

Perhaps the best way to avoid becoming anti-media is not to think of the media as one entity, but break it down into constituent parts. First, break it down into newspapers, radio and television, then break it down into national and local, then break it down to the sections of the media that are sympathetic to you and those that have proved a waste of time, and then break it down to the individuals who you find are most responsive to your cause and develop a special friendship and partnership with them.

Over the years I have increasingly dealt with the media in terms of a relatively small number of individual journalists who I have come to respect and trust and with whom it is possible to 'do business'. By this I mean it is possible to sit down with them and discuss a potential story, and make an arrangement on the timing of it and how it will be handled. This way, they obtain what they want – an exclusive in their own field. You obtain what you want – the best possible story at the best possible time in the most appropriate place.

At the same time as developing this partnership with individual journalists, I also maintain an overall media service for the pressure group, and it is possible to achieve colossal publicity for your cause if you follow a number of basic principles:

- First, as always, *it requires hard work and a highly professional approach*. Many of those who condemn the media for indifference or inadequacy have in fact been responsible for the poor coverage themselves. They haven't worked hard enough. They have communicated with the media in an inefficient and unimpressive way. And they have often lost the confidence of the media by over-stating their case, by being over-aggressive, or by presentation that raises serious questions over their credibility.
- *Get to understand the media and how it works*, its needs and eccentricities.
- *Master the few fundamentals* – how to write a good press release, how to evolve and sell ideas for future articles, how to interview

well on radio and television, how to organise a press conference, and how to manage personal relationships with journalists.

Obviously I have been helped by the fact that I was trained as a journalist. In fact, I wanted to be a journalist from the age of ten and still call myself 'journalist' on my passport. I have the instincts of a journalist, and this, unfortunately, not every pressure group organiser can hope to have. But thought, and experience, can enable any able individual to work with the media to the advantage of their cause.

Recently it has been a practice of pressure groups not to have a press officer, but to encourage each campaigner to develop his or her own contacts with the media. This has some advantages, apart from saving the cost of a salary, and the main one is that you present a number of different faces to the media and the public, and this is healthy. Furthermore it is always best if the central figure, whether it be the director of the pressure group, the chairman, or a specific campaigner on his own subject, talks directly to the media, because these people tend to be the most knowledgeable and practised in talking on the subject and come across with a greater sense of authority and experience. However, the top-class press officer meets this point by fielding the top personalities or the relevant campaigners to do the actual interviews, while he or she does the media planning. I believe that if a national pressure group can afford it, it should have a press officer, and even voluntary local pressure groups should appoint one of their number as press officer. This person should maintain surveillance of the media, maintain press clippings files (essential), be constantly looking for opportunities for new stories and features, be dealing with day-by-day enquiries quickly and efficiently, be developing a photograph file, and generally providing an efficient and professional service that will make the campaign spokesman's life easier and more effective.

Often the specific campaigners do not have as much time as they would like to maintain links with journalists; the press officer to some extent can maintain the partnership for them. Just the same, as both chairman and director of pressure groups, I have always given the maintenance of close relations with key journalists *the* top priority. Pressure groups, particularly in the public domain, need frequent and positive coverage, and the chairman or director who won't set the time aside to do it, has almost definitely got his or her priorities wrong, and when they complain about the media, often fail to realise that the poor coverage is their own fault.

Returning to the press officer, however: this should be a full-time job quite simply because there is no end to the opportunities that can be created by someone with imagination and energy. If your cause is urgent and just, then there are a thousand stories to be written about it. And out there somewhere, on the features pages or women's pages of local and national newspapers, on the hundreds of radio and television programmes broadcast every week, there are thousands of journalists looking for those stories. The press officer's job is to bring the two together.

There is so much to be done that I simply cannot conceive of a situation where the press officer of a pressure group could ever be under-employed. One could write a whole book about the mechanics of dealing with the media, and in fact a number exist, but by far the best is Denis MacShane's book *Using the Media*. Although it is written primarily for trade unionists and workers' organisations, the advice can be adapted to all kinds of pressure groups. I will concentrate myself, therefore, on the broad principles.

Before looking at each sector of the media in turn, let's look at some of the facets of media relations that are common to all:

Press releases

The desks of news editors are piled high with press releases. Some of them contain news of real importance. Some of them are appalling public relations garbage. Don't add to the pile unless you really believe your story is likely to survive the early morning shake-up that diverts most of these press releases into the wastepaper basket. *Your media performance should not be judged on the quantity of the material you send out, but the quantity that is published.* Far better to send out six press releases a year containing the basis for good stories, and thus win the respect of the news desk and the reporters, who can operate on the principle that 'if it comes from that pressure group it is likely to be good' than win a reputation for besieging their office with paper, most of it of no value.

- *Keep it as brief as possible* (say all that you have to say but no more).
- *Present it cleanly*. It should be typed, and be easily handled by the journalist who has to adapt it or rewrite it for publication.
- *Tell them what they need to know in the first paragraph*. This is essential. If you don't grab their attention with the headline and the first paragraph you have probably lost them.

Denis MacShane explains this particularly well:

Every press release should begin with the Four W's, and should start off by stating:

What is happening;
Who is doing it;
Where it is happening;
When it is happening.

The fifth W is Why something is happening.[9]

Thus, the first paragraph could read as follows:

Friends of the Earth	Who
will dump 10,000 empty bottles	What
on the doorstep of Schweppes Ltd	Where
tomorrow morning (Saturday).	When
The Friends say Schweppes should use returnable bottles	
to save the waste of a million tons of glass a year.	Why

The remainder of the press release will give the details, and a suitable quote from the campaign, but the opening paragraph will have caught the news editor's attention.

- *Use the maximum of fact and the minimum of opinion.* The opinion should be in a specific quote from a spokesman of the campaign to isolate it from the facts making up the remainder of the story.
- *Don't be pompous* or pretentious. Say what you have to say clearly, authoritatively, and let the story speak for itself.
- *If you wish to send a story in advance, you can embargo it.* If this is your intention, make it clear on the press release ('Strictly embargoed until 12 midnight, Saturday April 3'). Only employ an embargo if it is really necessary; otherwise date the story for the day after you post it, i.e. if you post on April 1, it should be dated April 2 so that it is seen to be operative and up-to-date when it arrives on the newsdesk.
- *Learn the basics:* that you should type the story double-spaced, on one side of the paper only, with wide margins, etc.
- *Don't forget to include the name and telephone number of a contact.* If it is a good story, the newspaper will wish to develop it in their own way, and will inevitably wish to follow-up your press release with its own questions. Alternatively, your opponents may seek to contradict or undermine your press release, and you have to be reachable to answer this.
- If the press release is about a lengthy speech, or a report or publication of your pressure group, the press release should summarise it briefly, pin-pointing the most newsworthy aspects. The full speech or report can then be attached if the newspaper or programme wishes to develop it further.
- *Don't send photographs to radio stations.* I know it sounds absurd, but any news editor of a radio station will tell you that he still receives plenty of press releases accompanied by photographs. Apart from the fact that this looks sloppy, it is also an appalling waste of money. Make sure that what you mail is appropriate.
- *Ensure that your media list is comprehensive and up-to-date.* Compile a list of all appropriate media, broken down under different headings – daily newspapers, weekly newspapers, magazines, radio, television,

etc. Make sure the list is comprehensive and in tune with your objectives and the audience you wish to reach, and make sure it is up-to-date. Any newspaper would tell you that it still receives press releases addressed to editors or news editors who have moved on, retired, or possibly are even dead. Don't automatically send every item to the whole list – the more you can break the list down into segments, the more you can target your press releases to where they have some chance of publication. The principle should be to never send a press release to a publicâtion you know won't use it; not only are you wasting your valuable resources, but you alienate the publication concerned, and thus miss out when you do have a suitable item.

Press conferences

The press conference has the advantage of being an event. It implies that what you have to say will have added significance, and a newspaper or programme that decides not to attend, takes the risk that it may miss a good story.

This will only apply if your pressure group has a reputation for a sense of perspective. If you organise press conferences willy-nilly, irrespective of the importance or newsworthy nature of what you have to say, you will quickly find that they are badly attended and possibly not attended at all.

● *Only have a press conference on special occasions* when you can justify it on the highest news criteria.

Although CLEAR received almost unprecedented media coverage during 1982–83 we only held four press conferences in those two years: the first was to launch the campaign in January 1982; the second was to launch our autumn campaign and a CLEAR report on local authority lead monitoring in September 1982; the third was to launch our report on lead in city vegetables in March 1983; the fourth was to launch our report on lead in paint in September 1983. Sorry, there was a fifth – the press conference to mark our success in achieving a decision to phase lead out of petrol. That took place two and a half hours after the press conference of the Royal Commission on Environmental Pollution, and one hour after the press conference by the Secretary of State, and the journalists simply moved on from one press conference to another.

Usually the best time for a press conference is the morning, about 11.00 am, and keep it brief. If you have more than one speaker, then the speakers should be fully briefed on the subject-matter they should cover, and should be kept to time. The chairman of the press conference should, if they are talking too much, slip a note in front of them with a one-minute warning.

- The journalists should be given the press releases and copies of any other documents when they arrive as some have early deadlines and may not be able to stay for the whole press conference.
- If there are likely to be radio or television interviews, you should try to have a separate room available, so that these can be done quietly. Often the radio and television people will wish to do their interview before the press conference, because of deadlines, and you should allow for this possibility. Clearly it makes sense to do the interviews in another room, otherwise the whole press conference hears what you have to say and it can create a feeling of anti-climax for the press conference.

Press enquiries

An active pressure group will receive many telephoned press enquiries. They should always be dealt with courteously and comprehensively, and the image created should be of an efficient, concerned pressure group with all the time that a journalist needs. No matter how ignorant the journalist, how lazy, or even how stupid (there are such individuals), be patient, and help them achieve their objective – the information they need for their story.

If you are impatient, rude, aggressive, or intolerant it will quite likely be reflected in the story that is published. Whatever you do, don't divert press enquiries to a junior. Remember, if whatever is said is published it will be magnified by the number of copies that newspaper produces. If you say 500 when you should have said 50 to a reporter, that error can be read by millions of people if it appears in a newspaper like the *Daily Mirror*. Perhaps it won't matter. On the other hand, it could be disastrous.

Feature ideas

The media is a creature with an insatiable appetite. Every day it eats up every idea it can get, and the next day it needs more. It never stops devouring ideas. It operates 365 days a year, 24 hours a day. Any creature with an appetite like that needs help. You can be that help. You are the experts on your own area. You know all the facts, all the victims, all the injustices and needs. The media is a people business and you are concerned with people issues. There are, as I have said, a thousand stories to be unleashed by your campaign. The media will not dig those stories out itself. You have to do it for them.

Always be looking for possible feature ideas for radio, television, and newspapers. But remember, you don't exist just to serve the media, but to work with it. Therefore, the story you will wish to sell should have two ingredients: it should be newsworthy or fascinating in its own right, but it should also serve your cause. Thus, at Shelter, we would look for feature articles that might:

● Feature the plight of a homeless family (good human interest story for the newspapers) but also convey with a few statistics the size of the housing problem and the way that families can innocently become its victims.

● Feature an unfair eviction, thus producing a good confrontation story for the media (landlord versus tenant) but, with one or two good quotes from the pressure group, also dramatise weaknesses in the Rent Act or security of tenure provisions that enable it to happen.

● Expose conditions in hostels for the homeless (a scandal – just what the media likes) but containing a number of points furthering your call for firm rules on the treatment of homeless families by the authorities.

● Feature the achievements of a local housing association, a good positive people story, especially if it can contain a family reunited because it now has a decent home. At the same time, it communicates the positive side of your work.

And so on.

In the selling of the story, it is of importance to convey to the journalist why they should do it. You must picture the feature article in your mind and describe it to them as they might write it. A professional journalist will recognise a good feature as you describe it although, of course, they may do it differently.

When you meet the journalist to brief them in full before they do the feature, this is the appropriate time to negotiate the references to the pressure group that you would like. Most journalists are reasonable. If you give them a sheet of paper with facts and figures on the national problem, so that they can put the specific story in context, and if you give them one powerful quote, they will normally do all in their power to use it.

Reaction to events

Unfortunately, you don't entirely control the media coverage you receive. Often, you have to react to what your opponents have said. Or to announcements or events. Often you have to react to attempts to smear you. Keep calm. Remain businesslike. Deal with the matter factually.

It is no good, when a journalist telephones you to say that a Minister has described your organisation as 'emotional' and issued some alleged statistics that whitewash the problem, shouting down the phone to the journalist 'The man's a bastard – how dare he?' Far better to say:

The Minister may like to create the impression that our campaign is emotional, but unlike his statistics, ours are reliable. He says there are only twenty thousand homeless people in Britain, but of course this statistic is based on the number of homeless actually in hostels. A vast number of other families are split up, living with inlaws, overcrowded, or living in slums. We would argue the number of *genuinely* homeless is more like a million. It is deeply regrettable that the Minister should attempt to play down the problem instead of face up to the policies that are necessary to tackle it – the provision of more houses at rents that poorer families can afford.

This calm but factual answer succeeds in demolishing what the Minister has tried to do without being abusive. Remember, if you respond emotionally, you prove his point.

If the government has announced a major change in policy, and it is the opposite of that your campaign seeks, you may be interviewed on a radio or television news programme. At the most, they are likely to have a 15 to 30 second extract from what you say. Do not appear excessively angry or emotional. Speak firmly and clearly and make a simple point.

Anyone who has studied the evidence of the health risk to children will be bitterly disappointed that the Minister has decided to perpetuate the use of lead in petrol instead of banning it altogether. I am afraid, because the medical evidence accumulates steadily, that he will be forced to reverse this decision. Our campaign will continue with even greater vigour until that is done.

National newspapers

As I have said earlier, I have become convinced that the best way to achieve consistent and reasonable coverage in national newspapers is to develop a small list of key contacts. It is wise to try and have at least two on each newspaper, because of holidays, sickness, or the possibility of one journalist being away on assignment at a key time.

● Read the newspaper carefully, for some weeks, noting the subjects covered by different reporters. You will quickly be able to work out which writers are most likely to understand your cause and be sympathetic to it. Arrange to meet them for a drink or inexpensive lunch, and seek their advice. Tell them about your organisation, the cause, what you hope to achieve, and what your plans are. Discuss possible stories. Ask them if you could maintain contact. Usually, provided they respect you, they will be only too pleased to establish a relationship, for you are a likely source of stories, and a reporter is only as good as his or her contacts.

● *Don't bother them or hound them.* If they write a story and it isn't published, it's not their fault. They have been beaten by the subeditors or a busy news day. They feel as bad about it as you do. There is no point in being accusing; just sympathetic. When you speak to them next, ask if there is any way the story can be revived, indicating that you realise there was little they could do about the earlier failure.

● If stories emerge in your particular field which do not justify a press release or press conference, but if given exclusively to one journalist, become stronger, offer them to one of your contacts. This is a point worth noting: some stories are only stories because they are exclusive. A document that would not be considered news-worthy if it were sent to every newspaper, becomes one if the reporter can say '. . . this is revealed in a document obtained exclusively by the *Daily* . . .'.

● Your contacts can often help you by signalling a forthcoming story to the remainder of the media. For instance, before the launch of a major campaign I usually leak a small-half story to a contact, who is happy to do a piece on the lines of 'a major campaign to eliminate the use of lead in petrol is to be launched in Britain next week . . .'. The deal has to be that they have the minimum of facts, so as not to break the embargo or undermine the press conference, but at the same time have just enough to whet the appetites of the remainder of the media.

● When it comes to a major story, you have to take the decision whether to release to all the press, or just to one contact. If you believe the story will achieve widespread coverage, it is probably best to publish it in a press release at a press conference. Explain to your contacts that you are doing this. They will understand. The advantage of a friendly and honest relationship with a journalist is that you can discuss these things. If you find you can't, abandon the relationship. On the other hand, if they think you are being devious or manipulative with them, they will abandon the relationship.

● Naturally, the national newspapers vary dramatically. The thinking behind news selection for the *Sun* can be very different from *The Guardian*. There is a tendency in pressure groups to obtain publicity in *The Times* and *The Guardian* and feel a sense of achievement. This coverage is, of course, of considerable importance, because these are the newspapers read by decision-makers and they have an influence out of all proportion to their readerships. At the same time, the importance of the popular newspapers is their effect on a considerable number of voters. With the popular papers, it is particularly important to try to develop useful contacts, ideally with columnists, or editors of specific pages, who have some extra influence.

● *Don't forget letters to the editor.* These columns offer many opportunities to communicate ideas, comments, and responses to what the opposition is doing. Keep them brief, be witty if you can, and make sure that they make their point emphatically. The mistake most people make is to try and cover too much ground in a letter and at the end the reader is not really clear what it is you are saying or why. Thus, if there are six points you wish to make in a letter, reduce them to just one or two – the ones you can make most clearly and that are most relevant to the news item that has sparked off the letter in the first place.

Local newspapers

To a local pressure group, the local newspaper is vital. Fortunately, you are equally important to it. It often has to fill a considerable number of news pages with the activities and personalities of a relatively small area, and is extremely grateful for all the material it can get, particularly if it is well-presented and useable without the deployment of scarce manpower to follow it up. Often your press releases will be published as written.

Study your local newspaper, define the different opportunities that exist within its covers – on the news pages, in its 'diary', in its letter page, on the woman's page, on the feature pages, etc. – and then spread your stories and input to the newspaper over these different sections.

That way you can appear frequently in the newspaper without appearing to overdo it as far as any one section is concerned.

Pictures

I don't know whether a picture really is worth 'a thousand words', but it can often be the best chance of getting an item published, or alternatively it can draw what would usually be an inside page story on to the front page.

The decisions on the deployment of photographers and the publication of photographs is usually in the hands of a picture editor. It often pays to send press releases and separate letters to him or her. They too need ideas, and often get forgotten. Often a photographer will turn up where a reporter doesn't, and in that way you still make the newspaper.

If the photograph you intend to circulate involves other people, ask them to sign a permission form on the lines of 'I hereby authorise the Campaign for . . . to distribute for publication the photograph involving myself taken on . . .'. This is an essential safeguard.

A good photograph for local media – FoE members present a book on bicycle planning to a council official: it combines parents and children, smiling faces, and bicycles, and is bound to achieve a positive response from the reader.

Television

Essential to working with television people is to understand that they do not care about you. This is probably the most self-centred, manipulative, and ruthless profession there is. I have been dealing with television people for pressure groups for nearly 20 years and I have learnt to live with them, but never to believe them.

The world of charities, pressure groups, and voluntary organisations, is littered with people who have been let down and become disenchanted by television programmes.

I do not intend to waste space with anecdotes, or to sit in judgement on their behaviour. Suffice to say that we have to live with television as it is, and television news and current affairs programmes have a morality all of their own. (They also have an extraordinary ability to justify all that they do. I doubt if they will recognise themselves in what I say, or accept a word of it. The fact is that by their own values their behaviour is legitimate.) There is only one way to deal with television and that is accept it as it is and try to achieve the best you can in the circumstances.

Usually you will first be approached by a researcher. That researcher is often the most idealistic and genuine person on the programme, but

Before you do a television interview, reflect for a moment or two on the main message you wish to convey in the interview. No matter what question you are asked, find a way of conveying that message.

he or she has no standing whatsoever. Once the director, producer and reporter become involved, the researcher is swept aside. The researcher will no doubt paint a picture to you of a worthwhile programme, sympathetic to your cause and your organisation, and you will visualise an item on the news programme, or the documentary slot, presenting your case fully and fairly and enabling your representative to make the key points, if not at length, at least adequately. That is what you would like – it is not what you will get. What television seeks to do is to hold viewers. Television assumes that most people have little intelligence or patience and thus seeks to present the argument in black and white terms, with eye-catching picture, and as much drama as possible.

They will drain the pressure group of every bit of information it can provide. They will try to bend you to their will, making you go to all sorts of inconvenient places in order that they can have a suitable background. (Not that it will matter, because they will still show only your face or head and shoulders so that you could be anywhere. For instance, on the lead in petrol issue, I was constantly being dragged out to the sides of motorways. All you saw in the picture was my head but you couldn't hear a word. Ministers, on the other hand, insist on being interviewed in the studio or at their desks in their office. The result is that you look windswept, untidy, and are shouting above the traffic, while they look authoritative and calm and important sitting in their office.) Every director sees himself as a kind of Cecil B DeMille. The whole story can be completely changed to meet television's need for pictures rather than words.

There are some ways in which you can protect yourself with television and improve your coverage:

- If it is a nightly regional news programme *try to appear live* in the studio. That way they can't cut you to pieces in the cutting room.
- Don't let them walk all over you. If you don't like the place where they wish to film you, don't go. There is no need to be aggressive – just say firmly that unfortunately you had not realised they needed this amount of your time, and you have another arrangement, and therefore will have to be filmed in your office or wherever you are.
- *Don't let them put you in an undignified or degrading position.*
- *Don't feel you have to answer their questions.* Use the opportunity to make the points you wish to make. Thus:
  Question: 'It has been suggested that your organisation is more concerned with publicity than results. What do you say to that?'
  Answer: 'Without the publicity we could not communicate the urgency of this issue – and the issue is the risk to hundreds of thousands of children by the widespread dissemination of a known poison – a neurotoxin – in petrol. Our case is that this practice is unnecessary, it has been stopped in other countries and it can be stopped in Britain, and it should be as quickly as possible.'
  In this way, you have calmly brushed aside the accusation in the question and made the point you wished to make.
- If a programme like Newsnight asks you to come to the studio early and record your interview or discussion, ask yourself why? It should be more convenient for them to have you live. There can be only two possible explanations: either, they intend to cut you, or secondly, they intend to have the opposition in the studio to answer you without you yourself being present. Insist on appearing live if you possibly can.

MEMBERSHIP

WHETHER OR not you have a formal membership of your campaign must depend on its likely duration.

If, as in the case of CLEAR, or the 1984 Committee for Freedom of Information, the plan is a short, sharp campaign aimed at a relatively early success, then there is probably little point in a membership scheme and the developing bureaucracy it can cause. In these circumstances it is far better to just call those who wish to support the campaign 'supporters' and have their names on a supporters' list.

The difference between a 'member' and a 'supporter' is that the former implies some influence on the policies and decision-making of the organisation. If it is decided to have a membership, it is essential to develop a democratic structure that enables its voice to be heard. Organisations that don't do this nearly always end up in trouble.

Before you fix your membership or supporters' fees, think carefully about the number you are likely to receive, and what kind of people they will be. Many organisations are afraid to set a realistic membership fee, and spend more to service the membership than is received in return. Members or supporters are those who have indicated their basic sympathy for the cause, and are those most likely to donate generously, so it makes sense to set a realistic figure that makes it possible for you to service them effectively, and makes their support a source of financial strength.

It also makes sense to set the figure in the first year at a sufficient level to hold for two or three years, for all sorts of complications are caused by increased membership fees, particularly in these days of bankers' orders and the like. Alternatively, fix a rising membership fee from the start, making it clear that each year it will increase by a fixed sum.

Remember that your members or supporters are a crucial source of strength and keep them informed about what you are doing and about the progress of the campaign. This is where a campaign newspaper can be helpful (see N for newspaper on pages 94–99).

Watch your membership figures very closely for any trends. The start of a drop in membership should be a warning signal that either you are not maintaining proper contact with members or servicing them properly, or that the cause is losing some appeal. If there is a sudden drop in membership, contact the members and find out why. A series of telephone calls will quickly indicate whether it is a reflection of financial circumstances, a recession or whatever, or whether there is a rising tide of discontent about your policies or approach.

Finally, as in all other aspects of your campaign, keep in mind when you plan your membership scheme or build up a list of supporters what your objectives are in doing so. If it is money you want from them, plan the scheme so that you can raise as much from them as possible, as painlessly as possible. If it is action in their localities, build up your membership scheme accordingly, perhaps developing it around local groups.

NAME

N

THE DECISION on the name of your campaign should not be taken lightly. Ideally it should be:

- brief;
- positive (i.e. *for* rather than *against*);
- convey an image of what you want to achieve.

All of these criteria were met by Shelter – The National Campaign for the Homeless, and by CLEAR – The Campaign for Lead-free Air.

We were unable to come up with such a straightforward solution for our campaign on freedom of information, launched at the beginning of 1984, and so decided to call it the 1984 Campaign for Freedom of Information, hoping that the link with 1984 would convey the point of the campaign, and deliberately encouraging the Committee to become known as the 1984 Committee (rather than the 1984 Committee for Freedom of Information).

If you have an acronym of your title (i.e. CLEAR – Campaign for Lead-free Air) that's marvellous, but don't strain so much to achieve it that your title actually fails to convey in the one word what the campaign is all about.

Above all, the name should speak for itself.

NEWSPAPER–YOUR OWN

A CAMPAIGN newspaper is in my view an essential – the most versatile and valuable means of communication you can have. The need for a well-designed, well-compiled campaign newspaper is simply not understood by most pressure groups to their disadvantage. When the CLEAR campaign was being planned, and I mentioned that I intended to have a campaign newspaper, one of my most senior and valued colleagues protested vigorously. It was a waste of money, he said. I responded that if we spent money on no other piece of material, we should spend money on a newspaper. Furthermore, I argued we should spend whatever was necessary to produce a newspaper of high quality. The arguments for a newspaper are these:

- The format is flexible and enables the presentation of all the information you have in a variety of different ways.

FoE

FRIENDS OF THE EARTH

AUTUMN '83
50p

PESTICIDE SCANDAL!

Products on Sale in Britain Were Cleared on Basis of Invalid Research

by Maurice Frankel

CONFIDENTIAL

Some pesticides used in the UK have been cleared for use on the basis of safety studies now known to be invalid. The studies were carried out at what used to be the largest independent toxicology laboratory in the US — Industrial Bio-Test Laboratories Inc (IBT) — and have been crucial in obtaining safety clearance for pesticides, pharmaceuticals, food additives and cosmetics throughout the world.

Four senior IBT executives are currently standing trial in Chicago charged with falsifying data. Government prosecutors claim that they deliberately omitted evidence of hazards from some reports, fabricated other data, and then conducted test data when they learnt they were under investigation. Major chemical companies are also implicated — prosecutors say they knew what was happening and the lab to get the results they wanted.

A toxicologist from the giant Monsanto chemical company is one of those on trial. He worked at IBT for 18 months supervising tests on a Monsanto product before returning to Monsanto. The prosecution says he rewrote key sections of the IBT report omitting evidence that the chemical, an anti-bacterial agent used in soaps and deodorants, damaged exposed rats.

IBT provided some 800 vital health studies on 140 pesticides registered in the US. The Environmental Protection Agency (EPA) now says that three-quarters of these

were so badly performed as to be useless. Some of these studies have since been replaced, but this July the EPA announced that 35 pesticides

There is increasing worldwide concern about the inadequately controlled manufacture and marketing of pesticides.

Friends of the Earth is undertaking the research and the groundwork for a major British campaign on the issue to be launched this autumn.

FoE is the UK leader, and Oxfam the international leader, for a British coalition of organisations which will campaign under the banner of the Pesticide Action Network.

Fuller story – page 3.

would be suspended unless IBT data on them was replaced by new valid studies. Sweden banned 7 IBT tested products in 1978, and several have been banned or restricted in Canada, where 24 other products must carry special warning labels until IBT data has been replaced.

Some pesticides used in the UK were originally cleared at least in part on IBT safety studies. But anyone trying to find out what has been done about them faces an overwhelming obstacle — official secrecy. The Advisory Committee on Pesticides (ACP) recommends which products should be cleared under the UK Pesticides Safety Precautions Scheme — but it publishes no annual report on its work. All the information provided to it by industry is treated as confidential: officials will not even say what kinds of safety studies have been carried out on a particular product, let alone disclose the findings. ACP officials say they have identified the cases where IBT data was submitted, and wherever it played an important role have obtained new studies from the manufacturers. As a result, they say, it has not been necessary to ban or restrict any IBT tested product in the UK. But the Advisory Committee will not identify the products involved, will not say how important IBT data was, and will not reveal what the new studies have found.

Much of the information we have comes from America, demonstrating the value of the US Freedom of Information Act which gives citizens a legal right to much government information. The first list of IBT cleared pesticides was obtained using the FOI Act. A Washington group using the FOI Act discovered that the government was considering giving expensive new contracts to

This story illustrates the importance of the need for greater freedom of information in Britain and an end to abuse of secrecy.

See 'Thinkpiece' on page 24 and Maurice Frankel's article on page 5 explaining why environmentalists should be concerned about secrecy.

IBT even after the fraud had been suspected — the disclosure put a quick end to that.

The US list of IBT-cleared products contains the names of at least 18 pesticides also sold in the UK by the some manufacturers. In some cases the faulty data may only have played a minor role — but in others it appears to have been essential. For example, Ciba-Geigy sell chlorbromuron ('Maloran') in the UK. The product's US registration was based in part on four important IBT studies — all now known to be invalid — which Ciba has so far not agreed to replace. Chlorbromuron has already been banned in Canada and is under threat of a US ban. It is still cleared for use in the UK as a weedkiller on crops of carrots, parsnips and potatoes.

Another product used in both countries is Monsanto's 'Ramrod' (propachlor) registered in the US on a set of data which included 17 IBT studies, only one of which is valid. Monsanto has so far not agreed to replace crucial cancer and reproduc-

tive studies, and is now under threat of a US ban. The product remains cleared for use in the UK as a weedkiller on onions, leeks, cabbage and other crops.

The problem with some pesticides is not that the data was invalid — but that so little was ever required. The herbicide dichlobenil was permitted in the US without a single cancer, birth defect, mutation, infertility or nervous system study. Because the information is confidential we have no way of knowing whether the British manufacturers of this chemical were ever required to do better than this. ■

Sizewell

FoE forces admission that the Sizewell Inquiry will side-step safety . . . CEGB cornered on economic facts . . . FoE identifies British purchase of PWR as a factor in nuclear proliferation . . . Full details on these and other energy stories pages 6 & 7.

8
Page
DEBATE WITH THE PRIME MINISTER...
Margaret Thatcher answers FoE's environmental questionnaire . . . And FoE answers Margaret Thatcher's answers.

11
Page
LEAD BATTLE GOES ON...
CLEAR stresses that the battle on lead in petrol continues until there is "an early and firm date"... Campaign on lead in paint begins.

16
Page
THE FIGHT FOR THE COUNTRYSIDE
FoE's Countryside Campaign begins — Full reports.

One of the most valuable weapons for a pressure group is its newspaper: on the following pages the newspapers produced by the author for CLEAR, Friends of the Earth, and the 1984 Campaign for Freedom of Information

Govt. disarray over lead in petrol as CLEAR wins overwhelming support

Reliable sources at Westminster report considerable concern at high levels within the Conservative party at Ministerial disarray on the lead-in-petrol issue as public support for CLEAR has proved to be overwhelming.

It is said there is particular concern at the way Ministers and civil servants have contradicted each other, and also at the way Ministers have frequently been humiliated by CLEAR's exposure of their ignorance of the key scientific issues, of their inaccuracies and their distortions of the facts.

There is also widespread parliamentary indignation that the House of Commons was, at the time of the 1981 decision, kept completely in the dark on two crucial issues: first, that the nation's chief medical adviser, Sir Henry Yellowlees, had warned Ministers in unmistakable terms that the evidence of a serious health hazard was accumulating steadily; second, that the petroleum industry had actually recommended a direct move to lead-free petrol but their offer to produce it had been rejected.

As they review the position after a few months of the CLEAR campaign, Ministers have to acknowledge the following unpalatable facts:

(1) The report of the Lawther Committee, the main basis for their policy, is now discredited, and has been abandoned on a number of key points by several of its members. The most scientifically respected committee member, Professor Michael Rutter, has publicly stated that the report under-estimated the contribution to body lead levels of petrol lead.

> **"The reduction of lead in petrol to an intermediate level is an unacceptable compromise without clear advantages and with definite disadvantages."**
>
> *Professor Michael Rutter, MD, FRCP, FRCPsych, DPM*
> *Professor of Child Psychiatry, Institute of Psychiatry, London*

On Lawther's support for a safety threshold of 35 μg/dl, Rutter admits "it never was justified to assume that levels below 35 μg/dl were safe." He has further called the decision to reduce lead levels to 0.15 grams per litre "an unacceptable compromise".

(2) While they were publicly stating that there was no evidence for a reduction in the safety threshold below 35 μg/dl, their civil servants let it be known that they wanted a safety threshold of 25 μg/dl. This has led to a complete lack of confidence in

official policies on a safety threshold.
(3) It is now publicly known that they took the decision not to ban lead in petrol after their chief medical officer, Sir Henry Yellowlees, had warned them of accumulating evidence of health dangers in a letter that remained confidential until it was leaked to CLEAR and published on the front page of The Times earlier this year *(see page 4).* Since then, the Yellowlees claim that "new evidence is accumulating all the time —and it always points in the same direction as the existing evidence, so that the health case becomes steadily stronger and stronger", has been proved correct by eight major new pieces of evidence confirming the trend. As Professor Rutter says "Since 1980 there have been several studies that have examined the effects in the range below 35 μg/dl. All of them have demonstrated ill effects and none has produced evidence that there is a threshold below which there is safety.

(4) They have been completely unable to answer an article published in The Guardian *(and republished on page 7 of this newspaper)* by CLEAR's Chairman, Des Wilson, demonstrating that on at least 12 occasions Ministers have deliberately distorted the facts or the arguments.

(5) The leak of an internal BP document to CLEAR revealed that the petroleum industry in 1980/81 offered lead-free petrol to Ministers and actually recommended it as preferable to a reduction to 0.15 grams per litre. Ministers rejected the offer but the vast majority of MP's had no idea that it had been made.

(6) Overseas findings have shattered their position that lead from petrol is a relatively small factor in lead pollution. The US has announced that after four years of beginning to phase lead out of petrol, blood lead levels fell by 36.7%.

(7) They have completely under-estimated public concern on the issue

and were reported to be stunned by an opinion poll that showed 90% of British people supported the CLEAR position rather than their own. Over 200 Members of Parliament, including 35 members of their own Conservative Party, have signed CLEAR's objectives. Major institutions, such as the BMA, the Institution of Environmental Health Officers, and the National Society for Clear Air, have all accepted in their evidence to the Royal Commission on Environmental Pollution that the position is more serious than they previously believed, and most have called for the phasing out of lead in petrol. Over 85% of local authorities surveyed say they want a ban. And every other political party, with the exception of the Conservatives, has now committed itself to a ban on lead in petrol.

The Guardian has described the position of Ministers as "untenable".

Opposition party leaders are considering a supply day debate in the autumn to further embarrass Ministers.

Des Wilson told a press conference that "CLEAR has achieved every one of its campaign objectives so far—first, we have united all of the opposition parties behind our case, so that if the Conservatives remain obstinate, we at least know that lead-free petrol is to come one day. Second, we have demonstrated overwhelming public concern and that people are prepared to pay a few more pence a gallon for petrol to protect their children. Third, we have shown that we can win the debate in the medical and scientific arena and that our campaign has a sound scientific basis. Fourth, we have proved conclusively that lead-free petrol is possible within a relatively short time.

"The behaviour of Ministers has been so dishonest and so self-serving in the way it puts political convenience before the safety of our children that it shatters one's faith in the capacity of the established authorities to protect public health".

They said our concern about the health hazard caused by lead in petrol was "emotive". They said there was no serious scientific and medical evidence to justify our campaign. They said our children were safe.

So in May CLEAR invited respected researchers on lead pollution from all over the world to come to London and present their studies. CLEAR invited everyone concerned with lead pollution including every Ministry, and everyone known to be critical of CLEAR's position. Finally, CLEAR invited the world's most respected child psychiatrist, Professor Michael Rutter, who had been a member of the Lawther Committee, and who is universally admired for his scientific independence and integrity, to chair the symposium.

In other words, CLEAR put the serious medical and scientific evidence on the line.

The Observer said we had taken an extraordinary gamble. We did

not see it that way. We always knew that the evidence of a serious health risk to our children from lead in petrol existed and was unanswerable—if only others would listen. Our international symposium showed that our faith was justified.

At the conclusion of the symposium Professor Rutter summed it up. While Ministers say there's been no evidence since the Lawther report to justify a reappraisal of their policies, Rutter concluded that there has. Furthermore, he acknowledged that the new evidence was consistent, that it raised a serious question-mark over the safety threshold of 35 μg/dl, and that it contradicted the Lawther/Ministerial view that lead in petrol contributes only between 10 and 20% to body lead burdens.

He also rejected the search for conclusive evidence. "No one study ever finally resolves the scientific questions in these circumstances and it would be scientifically foolish as well as politically irresponsible to

wait for the perfect study to be undertaken".

Professor Rutter was careful to stress that the elimination of lead from petrol would not dramatically alter the world for the better, but concluded that a further reduction of environmental lead "should make some worthwhile difference to some children and that ought to constitute a quite sufficient justification for action now".

He was unequivocal on one point: "In my view, the reduction of lead in petrol to an intermediate level is an unacceptable compromise without clear advantages and with definite disadvantages".

Be in no doubt—the Rutter conclusions represent the complete collapse of official policy on lead in petrol in this country, and he has plenty of heavyweight medical and scientific support. The case for action is made. The obstinate refusal of Ministers to respond to public concern represents a genuine national scandal.

US Battle

Lead in petrol looks like becoming as big an issue in the United States as it is in Britain *(see full story on page 12).*

Since 1975 all petrol stations in the US have been required to have lead-free petrol available and all new cars have had to be manufactured to run on it. That policy of phasing out lead in petrol continues. However, the Reagan administration promised their friends in the petroleum industry to relax the regulations.

The very latest news is that the Environmental Protection Agency has, on the basis of fresh evidence of the health hazard, recommended that rather than weaken the regulations on lead in petrol, it should tighten them further, but the Office of Management and Budget, a branch of the executive offices of the President, is still seeking to block the EPA policy.

UK Cover-up

The petroleum and lead industries have both refused to make available their evidence to the Royal Commission on Environmental Pollution.

CLEAR published its evidence and sent it to other "witnesses" with a request that they return the courtesy. The industries have refused to do so.

In this respect they differ from most other organisations, nearly all of whom have sent their evidence to CLEAR. These include Ministries.

CLEAR's Chairman, Des Wilson, says that "this behaviour reflects their cynicism. What is at stake is not national security but public health. Yet they operate in secrecy and have no wish to share with the public their so-called evidence. CLEAR has sufficient confidence in what it has to say to publish its evidence for all to analyse and comment upon."

SECRETS

Political Leaders back call for freedom of information

'Our right to know'

The most substantial British campaign ever for freedom of information and a statutory "right to know" has been launched with such clear and categorical support from the leaders of all opposition parties that success at least in the longer term appears inevitable.

The Chairman of the 1984 Committee, Des Wilson, read to a press conference to launch the Campaign for Freedom of Information on January 5 supportive letters from Neil Kinnock, David Steel, and David Owen, and named over 150 Members of Parliament and 50 Members of the House of Lords who supported the broad objectives of the campaign.

Neil Kinnock stated that: "A thriving democracy depends on clear, full information, fairly presented, for all our citizens. Information is the lever of power and in a free society free people should have maximum access to and control over that lever.

"I want to emphasise both the importance of the issue itself and the commitment of the Labour Party to new freedom of information legislation which will strengthen Britain's democracy by requiring authorities to justify withholding information."

(The 1983 Labour Party Manifesto promised a Freedom of Information Act.)

David Steel, leader of the Liberal Party, wrote that "freedom of information is vital to the regeneration of our society. Resting on our laurels as the oldest modern democracy, we have become smug and complacent…our government is too centralised, too bureaucratic and too secretive, and is desperately in need of reform.

"It is ironic that the Freedom of Information Bill sponsored by my colleague Clement Freud MP should have fallen due to the intervention of the 1979 General Election. **I welcome this opportunity to renew our commitment to freedom of information.**

"The Campaign for Freedom of Information could be the vehicle for this reform and it has my best wishes for every success in its efforts."

(The Liberal Party-SDP Alliance promised Freedom of Information legislation in its 1983 programme.)

David Owen wrote: "The public has the right to know whether it is being governed lawfully and efficiently. Whoever needs information for any legitimate purpose in our society should be able to get it unless there is some clear, specific and valid reason why it should be withheld. The SDP policy is to introduce a comprehensive Freedom of Information and Expression Act which would include such measures as the establishment of the principle that all government information is freely available unless otherwise stated. The legislation would also include the right of individuals to have access to information on themselves, subject to a code of practice defining exceptions and limitations."

"I welcome and support the 1984 Campaign…I emphasise the importance of the issue itself and the commitment of the Labour Party to freedom of information legislation."

*Rt. Hon. Neil Kinnock
Leader, The Labour Party*

"I pledge the full support of my party…whoever needs information for any legitimate purpose should be able to get it unless there is some clear, specific and valid reason why not."

*Rt. Hon. David Owen
Leader, Social Democrats*

"Government is too centralised, bureaucratic, and secretive, and is desperately in need of reform…the campaign could be the vehicle for this and has my best wishes."

*Rt. Hon. David Steel
Leader, The Liberal Party*

Commenting on the considerable political support for the campaign, Des Wilson said that the organisers still hoped that the Thatcher Administration would respond to the widespread concern about excessive secrecy and would support freedom of information legislation rather than unconvincing voluntary changes.

"In any event, the opposition parties are surely committed to the point where a failure to act, if they come to power, would be seen as a fundamental betrayal of the electors. Not only have they stated in their 1983 manifestos (and will presumably repeat in subsequent manifestos) that they will legislate, but the three leaders most likely to be at the helm when the next election occurs have committed themselves clearly and categorically.

"At least we now know that just as it is inevitable that the present ruling party will one day, rightly or wrongly, be dismissed by the electorate, so it is inevitable that we will have freedom of information legislation."

He pointed to all-party support for the campaign, including support from Conservatives, and named organisations that would be fully involved in the campaign, contributing finance, research, and campaigning staff. In addition, other organisations had indicated their basic concern by becoming observer organisations.

Individual activists in the campaign included Bernard Donoughue, former No. 10 Downing Street advisor; Harold Evans, former editor of The Times and The Sunday Times; Peter Jay, former UK Ambassador to Washington, and Chairman of the National Council for Voluntary Organisations; Michael Shanks, Chairman of the National Consumer Council; Dame Elizabeth Ackroyd, former Director of the Consumers' Association, and now Chairman of the Patients' Association; and television campaigner Esther Rantzen.

The campaign's broad objectives are headed by a drive to secure a statutory right of access to all information held by government and other public sector bodies, other than that for which specific statutory protection is provided, and to place on these bodies an obligation to disclose such information.

Thus the campaign is concerned with both national and local government and also with other public organisations and utilities.

However, the campaign extends its objectives to organisations in the private sector, requiring a statutory obligation to give access to and disclose such information "as may be required by the public interest".

It seeks to promote a Freedom of Information Act and to repeal the Official Secrets Acts and replace them by one Act giving such protection to official information as may be necessary for national security.

In addition to pressing for this major legislation, the campaign hopes to monitor all Bills introduced into Parliament and to add provisions for public access and disclosure where relevant.

It hopes to identify and seeks to repeal all unnecessary secrecy provisions in existing legislation.

However, the campaign emphasises also what it will *not* seek — it acknowledges that an element of confidentiality remains necessary and will not seek the disclosure of information that would endanger national security, impair relations between governments and others, adversely affect sterling or the reserves, adversely affect law enforcement, breach genuine commercial confidentiality, or invade individual privacy.

A subject of considerable debate by the Council for Freedom of Information, the campaign's policy-making body, was whether advice, opinions, or recommendations intended by civil servants and others to assist with Ministerial policy-making should remain confidential. It was finally concluded that an element of confidentiality was necessary for free and frank policy-making discussion, and that the campaign would not seek legislative controls over confidentiality of such advice, provided it was broad advice, and not specific scientific and technical advice based on fact and expertise. This should be widely available.

Mrs. Thatcher 'to be convinced'

The political battlelines on freedom of information are likely to be drawn over whether or not it requires legislation. All the main opposition parties share the view of the 1984 Campaign that it does. The Prime Minister, however, is to be convinced.

In a lukewarm letter to the campaign the Rt. Hon. Margaret Thatcher "welcomes any move to help ensure that public demands for information are heard and as far as possible satisfied", but she adds "we already have a clear policy to make more information available and the necessary machinery to do so".

Mrs. Thatcher once introduced a Private Members Bill to open local authority meetings to the public but she has since been criticised as a defender of secrecy. The Times in a leading article in 1979 said: "Mrs. Thatcher has passionately criticised the closed shop in many areas of British life. She should not now countenance a closed shop for information." More recently — in 1983 — it warned her "government is public business — not a private firm — it should comport itself accordingly".

The Prime Minister, however, argues that Ministers are accountable to Parliament and "a statutory right of public access would remove this enormously important area of decision-making from Ministers and Parliament and transfer ultimate decisions to the courts. No matter how carefully the right were defined and circumscribed, that would be the essential constitutional result. The issues requiring interpretation would tend to be political rather than judicial, and the relationship between the judiciary and the legislature could be greatly damaged. But above all, Ministers' accountability to Parliament would be reduced and Parliament itself diminished."

- A newspaper has enormous versatility – it can be used for propaganda; it can also be used for the presentation of relatively dull but essential facts of information, and can be used for humour; it can be used for every kind of communications technique.
- People are accustomed to reading newspapers, and normally can assimilate more information from a newspaper more quickly than they can from any other source.
- A newspaper enables the campaign to talk about itself in the third person. This is a particularly valuable aspect of this medium. Whereupon to be constantly saying 'We did this and that' sounds self-centred and sometimes boastful, a newspaper can report about the activities of 'the campaign . . .' as if it is objective, third-person reporting and it has an entirely different note.
- A newspaper can constantly be updated. It can be linked to specific campaigns and have specific themes whilst retaining the central information from issue to issue.
- The newspaper can also be the basis for the campaign's appeal to its supporters and thus a fund-raising weapon.
- The newspaper can be sent to a wide variety of organisations, and inserted in a wide variety of other organisation's mailings. Whereas another organisation would think twice to agreeing to a fund-raising appeal being included in a mailing to their supporters, they are more likely to find a newspaper acceptable, on the grounds that they are conveying to their members information, albeit with a fund-raising appeal included.

The four major campaigns I have been mainly involved with – Shelter, CLEAR, FoE, and the 1984 Committee – have produced newspapers, each of them different, but each of them essential.

The Shelter newspaper was published to coincide with major appeals – at around Easter time, at the time of the publication of Shelter's autumn housing reports, at the time of its autumn political campaign, and for its Christmas appeal. Its combination of stories about the homeless, coverage of the work of Shelter, and fund-raising appeal, meant that it raised considerable sums of money from the campaign's mailing list as well as being the ideal piece of information to hand out to interested individuals and groups.

The Friends of the Earth newspaper is given as a service to all supporters and this substantial newspaper, together with all the news it contains of FoE's works, makes supporters feel that their support is worthwhile. Once more, it is the ideal publication to hand out to people who are interested in knowing what FoE is all about.

If you plan a newspaper, there are a number of factors you should take into account:

- *It should be of the highest possible standard* in design, writing, and editing, otherwise it will be completely counter-productive. Try to recruit the help of a designer, and if you cannot obtain voluntary help, pay for it. The design of the newspaper should achieve two objectives at once: first, it should reflect the image of the organisation; second, it should *look* like a *newspaper* – and thus achieve the image of objectivity and urgency that a newspaper conveys. Likewise, it should be well and sharply written. The size of the newspaper should be defined by the information and propaganda you wish to convey. Don't fill it with waffle. The reader should wish to turn from page to page and be impressed by the variety and extent of the information, as well as its authority. This requires imaginative editing.

● In addition to professionalism, *the newspaper requires careful tactical thought*. Unlike the design of an ordinary newspaper, where the aim of the exercise is impact and readability, this newspaper is designed also to achieve objectives. Every item in the newspaper should be there for a good reason – either to create greater concern about the problem, or to convey the breadth and quality of the organisation's work, or to stimulate help and support. The reader should put down the newspaper more knowledgeable about the cause, impressed by your organisation, and wanting to help.

Do not give the newspaper a specific date or imply regularity, but rather *time your newspaper for when it can be most valuable*. I personally believe three or four issues a year is more than adequate, one about February to launch your early-year activities, one about May to carry the campaign across the summer, one in September to launch your autumn campaign, and one just before Christmas to raise money and tie up the year's activities. But this can be varied according to your particular cause, and the most appropriate occasions for publication.

My own view is that a few substantial newspapers is better than a lot of small ones, remembering the cost of postage, and also the ability of the variety of people you want to read it to cope with too much information.

OPINION POLLS

O PROFESSIONAL OPINION polls are expensive. Few organisations can afford them and even fewer can afford them very often. But *a well-timed opinion poll is a ploy that you should at least consider*.

In the case of CLEAR, an opinion poll proved to be a critical factor in our success. We spoke to the MORI organisation, and found that for

£1,000 they would include four questions in a multi-question sample of nearly 2,000 people they did on a regular basis. We discussed at length what the questions would be, and their advice was helpful. What we wanted to discover, in a nutshell, was whether the public supported a ban on lead in petrol. The first question was calculated to find out whether they knew that lead was in petrol and that it was a poison. The second and third were calculated to find out whether they supported a ban. And the final one was intended to discover whether they were prepared to pay more for unleaded fuel. It revealed overwhelming support for CLEAR.

The question now was what to do with the poll. Operating on the basis that we could achieve the maximum exposure by offering a newspaper an exclusive (see M for media on pages 79–92), I discussed the matter with *The Observer*. 'If I allow you to publish this poll exclusively on Sunday,' I asked, 'Will you run it as a front page story?' They said they would have to see it. This was fair enough, and once they did they quickly confirmed acceptance of the terms. Their reasoning was simple enough: it was a good story. In fact, I didn't realise how good a story it was, until *The Observer* arrived that Sunday, and I found it was the front page lead. The BBC picked it up on the Saturday evening and ran it as the first item on the radio news. The other daily newspapers all published the results on Monday.

The opinion poll was worth thousands of pounds to CLEAR, far more than the thousand pounds it cost. First, we could not have bought that media exposure for ten thousand pounds. Second, it shook the politicians and the opposition by showing the strength of our support. Both *The Observer* and *The Guardian* published leading articles drawing on the opinion poll and condemning the authorities for obstinacy. We were able to quote the opinion poll time after time to demonstrate that we spoke 'for the British people'. MPs, with an election due within a year, were not slow to get the message, and it was fascinating to see our Westminster support grow.

Incidentally, I did find some money for a follow-up opinion poll nine months later. There was a minor downwards shift, reflecting that we had had a quiet two or three months, but the support was still sufficiently solid to indicate that the remarkable result of the first poll was not a reflection of a high public profile at that time.

It should be said about opinion polls that they do not necessarily need to be professionally undertaken. Local groups can organise their own opinion polls in their own area and these will often achieve considerable local media publicity and be effective in shaking the complacency of local officialdom.

9 in 10 say 'Ban lead in petrol'

by GEOFFREY LEAN

NINE out of 10 people in Britain want lead banned from petrol, according to a public opinion poll published today.

The near-unanimity of the poll, conducted by the MORI organisation for the Campaign for Lead-free Air (CLEAR), is likely to prove an embarrassment to the Government, which has privately believed that pressure to ban the toxic metal had little support. Only 6 per cent of those questioned supported the Government's view that a ban is unnecessary.

It will also increase the likelihood that the three main opposition parties, whose leaders have supported CLEAR, will adopt lead-free petrol as an electoral commitment.

Mr Des Wilson, the campaign's chairman, said last night that MORI had told him that the findings provided some of the most decisive figures they had seen.

Ninety-one per cent of those questioned said that they believed lead was a potential health hazard and only 4 per cent said it was not. A detailed breakdown shows that 46 per cent rated it a 'very serious hazard,' 33 per cent 'a fairly serious hazard' and only 12 per cent 'a slight hazard.'

Eighty-nine per cent said lead should be banned, 55 per cent adding this was 'urgent.'

Three-quarters of those questioned said they would be prepared to pay more for lead-free petrol.

Asked 'Do you think the Government should introduce a law to ensure that all petrol sold in Britain is lead-free, even if this would put up petrol prices by a few pence per gallon?' 77 per cent said 'yes,' 15 per cent 'no,' and 8 per cent didn't know.

Mr Wilson said: 'This poll should confirm the determination of the opposition parties to commit themselves to lead-free petrol and, unless this Government is prepared to act, it will become isolated on an issue that rates high priority.'

Mr Gerald Kaufman, Labour spokesman on the environment, said last night that the results of the poll were 'very important indeed.' He said that Labour would continue to press for lead-free petrol as soon as possible.

In a speech on health policy due to be given at an SPD members' conference yesterday, Dr David Owen, the party's parliamentary leader and a former Health Minister, said it was 'crucial' to 'enact a timetable for the phasing out of petrol containing any lead.'

MORI interviewed a representative quota sample of 1,911 adults, 18 years of age and older, in 159 constituencies throughout Great Britain between 18 and 22 February.

The front page lead story in **The Observer** *based on the exclusive leak of CLEAR's opinion poll and the accompanying leader*

If you plan to undertake a local opinion poll, however, it is essential that:

- *You design the opinion poll so that it has credibility.* Positive answers to loaded questions will impress no-one. The opinion poll must be carried out with the appearance of independence and objectivity. Remember that you don't have to publish the results if you don't like them.
- *It should be a substantial sample* – sufficient for your opponents not to be able to decry it as unrepresentative.
- Like all else you do, *it should be done efficiently and professionally* and the results should be well-presented.

PETITIONS

P
ANOTHER FORM of opinion poll is the petition. Unlike the opinion poll, however, this does not pretend to be an objective test of public opinion but rather a demonstration of support.

Personally, I think that petitions have been rather over-done, and as a result the authorities tend to be less and less impressed by them. *If you plan a petition, therefore, you should try to design the operation in such a way that it cannot be easily brushed off.*

Let's say it is a local problem – the need for a pedestrian crossing near a school. An impressive petition would be one that contained the signature of *every* parent, or *every* household in the surrounding streets. Thus you are not only handing over to the authorities a huge collection of names, but a summary sheet that states that the community is 100 per cent behind your objectives. This is extremely difficult to ignore. A huge collection of names on sheets of paper does not necessarily represent a force that has to be answered; but a list of names within a given area or constituency, that has the capacity to organise itself and that will still be there tomorrow and the day after is a different matter.

Once you have taken the trouble to organise a petition, maximise its publicity potential. Arrange to hand the petition over to a local MP or celebrity with the media present. It is often possible to obtain local television and newspaper publicity as well as to impress those to whom you are handing the petition.

My own view is that petitions are best used on local issues, and rarely.

POLITICAL PARTIES IN OPPOSITION

IF YOU plan a national campaign, then it is a mistake to aim to influence the Government only. There are three reasons why you should seek to win over the major opposition parties:

First, *you isolate the Government politically* on the issue and, particularly on a non-major issue, this makes them *feel* isolated, look obstinant, and behave as if they are on the defensive. It also undermines their confidence on the issue.

Second, *you can obtain publicity in the process* of winning over the other major parties, and they can become enormously helpful in furthering your case at Westminster, and with the public at large.

Third, if you fail in your immediate objective of persuading the government to act, *you have sewn up the other parties so that when eventually one or other of them is returned to power, it is committed to your objective* and thus, belatedly, you will win the day in that way.

I will describe in detail in Chapter 6 how we did this with the CLEAR campaign. Suffice for the moment to say that we did, and it achieved all these objectives: first, by winning over all of the other parties, we completely isolated the Government and put them very much on the defensive. Second, we achieved considerable publicity and advantage by the conversions of the other parties, one by one. Finally, they were all so committed in their manifestos, that had any of them been elected to office, it would have been extremely difficult for them to do other than ban lead in petrol.

I would like to be able to say that winning the opposition parties over requires the same level of argument that is necessary to win with Government, but unfortunately this is not true (not, perhaps, 'unfortunately' for the pressure group, but unfortunately for the quality of political decision-making). The opposition is motivated by its desire for power and to achieve that it has to embarrass the Government. It is thus more open to pressure groups able to demonstrate that the Government is vulnerable on a particular issue. I have to say that none of the three major opposition parties – Labour, Liberal, or Social Democrat – in my view carefully studied the lead in petrol issue before committing themselves. They responded to the politics of the issue rather than the issue itself. Whether or not this is desirable, the pressure group has to be aware that this is possible. Sometimes the urgency of the cause is such that the pressure group must simply play that political game. *There is a case, however, for seeking to argue the issue in as much depth within the opposition parties as possible, so that when they come to government they are genuinely committed and not superficially committed on the issue.* For instance, on the lead issue, we felt so confident of our case that we would have happily argued it at every level within the Labour Party, or within the other parties. In fact, we were never called upon to do so.

The Labour Party

It is difficult for the Labour Party in opposition not to be sympathetic to most community/cause pressure groups, because it is committed to its image of compassion and concern, equality and justice. To be fair, the vast majority of its members are genuinely committed. Therefore, pressure groups can expect sympathy and support within the Labour Party. However, this is not enough. That sympathy and support has to be turned into action, either in terms of pressure on Government, or in terms of a commitment to act when in Government itself. (I am speaking now of Labour in opposition.)

It is notable, for instance, that although the Labour Conference had voted for a ban on lead in petrol, although the NEC had approved a statement to that effect, although the Shadow Minister for the Environment, Gerald Kaufman, achieved considerable publicity by committing himself to lead-free petrol, although the Party Leader, Michael Foot, put his name to the campaign from the start, although a number of trade unions signed a letter to members of the Shadow Cabinet requesting that Labour give half a supply-day to the issue, in fact the Shadow Cabinet at no point set up a debate in the House of Commons on the issue. Thus, although the party's sympathy and support was stated in every conceivable way, it was not reflected in the one form that the pressure group requested – a supply-day debate. (A supply-day debate – see W for Westminster on pages 124–129 – is a debate chosen by the Labour Party on one of the days supplied to it to raise issues of its own choice.) It was also noticeable on the lead question that Labour had not acted while in office. Nearly all the reductions in lead levels in petrol had come from the Conservatives.

So you can see that the expressed sympathy and support of the Labour Party did not necessarily mean wholehearted commitment. That is why a campaign within the Labour Party has, in my view, got to go a lot deeper than conference resolutions, or support in principle. It must seek to persuade the Party in depth, and commit it absolutely.

One way to do this is to get a full-scale debate and decision at the Labour Party Conference. These days these tend to be far more influential than they were in the past. To do this, it is necessary to get considerable support from within the Party, both at constituency level, and from the trade unions. It is not enough to get one constituency party to submit a resolution. There has to be such an inflow of resolutions on the issue, from such a broad front within the party, that the resolution survives all the opposition from other resolutions, plus from those who have their own reasons to try to stop the resolution getting on to the final agenda.

The Liberal Party

There are two ways of making an issue Liberal Party policy: one is by having a resolution passed at the quarterly meeting of the Party Council; the second is to have a resolution passed at the Liberal Assembly. The value of the second is that you have a bigger audience, and the possibility of considerable television and media coverage. For instance, as a Liberal, I was able to move a resolution on lead-free petrol at the Liberal Party Assembly and in addition to winning Liberal Party support and getting considerable newspaper coverage the next day, appeared on both television channels at the same time. Whilst there may not be a huge audience watching party conferences, it is still substantial exposure.

Liberals call for ban on lead in petrol

By ALAN TRAVIS

Mr. Des Wilson has swung the Liberal Party behind the campaign to ban lead in petrol within five years.

Lead in petrol was "Britain's No. 1 public health problem" which threatened the mental health of hundreds of thousands of children, he said.

Mr. Wilson, a Kidderminster Liberal and chairman of the Campaign for Lead Free Air, said the only answer was a total ban.

With the Alliance behind the campaign "Conservative ministers would be isolated with their friends in the multi-nationals as the only people left in Britain still refusing to accept the medical and scientific evidence of the health hazards." He told the Liberal Assembly in Bournemouth that the evidence of risk to children was well established.

Even low levels of lead exposure can lead to mentally retarded or hyper-active children, he warned.

The Liberal Assembly backed his call to phase out lead in petrol within five years. This

would enable new cars to be produced for lead-free petrol while older cars were phased out. Petrol stations would be required to supply lead-free petrol by law. Earlier in the afternoon's

debates a fierce attack on President Reagan's foreign trade policy was launched by Mr. Richard Holme, prospective Liberal candidate for Cheltenham.

Mr. Holme, policy adviser to Mr. David Steel, the Liberal leader, said President Reagan had done more "damage to the fabric of international relations in the past two years than anyone would have thought possible.

He said the dispute over the Siberian gas pipeline had shown that the US had put the cold war above commonsense.

"We sometimes feel in Europe that the Reagan administration thinks of Paris and London at best as backdrops for a B movie. But we are the lucky ones. They can't even place Bonn or Brussels on the map."

The Liberal Assembly also voted yesterday to bring down the age of consent for homosexuals from 21 to 16.

It came as part of a resolution calling for a uniform age of majority to entitle young people to become fully independent at 16.

Recruitment of support of opposition parties and the TUC has many benefits, one being additional publicity

Lead-free petrol pledge by Labour

By Philip Webster
Political Reporter

The next Labour Government will move swiftly to ban lead in petrol, the party's national executive committee promises today.

In a statement agreed at its meeting last Wednesday, the NEC pledges that it will press for the introduction of lead-free petrol to be included as a top priority in the next election manifesto.

Under the commitment the next Labour government would require by law that all new cars sold in Britain be manufactured to run on lead-free petrol; all petrol stations would have to have lead-free petrol available for sale to the general public; and the use of leaded petrol in existing cars would be phased out "over a generation of cars", fuel duties would be changed to make lead-free petrol cheaper

The likelihood of the commitment appearing in the next Labour manifesto is high. Labour's environment spokesman have spoken in favour of a ban and last year's party conference passed a resolution calling for a complete ban on the use of lead in petrol"

The NEC says that is making the party's position clear now so that oil companies planning to make changes to comply with the Government's decision last year to reduce the lead content in petrol from 0.4 to 0.15 grams a litre from 1985 can go the whole way. "The oil companies may choose the zero option today if they realize that the costs they would incur for the Tory transition will have to be repeated under Labour".

The NEC says that lead poses a sinister and serious health risk. It points to evidence that the mental health of children can be adversely affected at relatively low levels of lead exoosure; lead in petrol is not only the major source but it is also the course which is easiest to control.

Other countries have gone much further than Britain, the NEC says. In the United States every post-1975 car has been required by law to take lead-free petrol, Japan is almost lead-free and Australia is phasing lead.

"The costs to the oil companies of going lead-free have always been exaggerated...", it states. "The Tories have made a gesture to poison our children a little less quickly but the poison will be still there"

T.U.C. move on lead in petrol

A demand that all new cars sold in Britain after January 1, 1985, should be made to run on lead-free petrol was approved by T.U.C. delegates today.

A motion by the Iron and Steel Trades Confederation at the Brighton conference said the use of lead additives in petrol constituted a far more insidious threat than lead used in paint or water supplies, particularly to the mental health of children and the mental and physical well-being of unborn children.

Mr. Bill Sirs, the union's general secretary, said lead damaged the central nervous system, the heart and kidneys, caused anaemia and high blood pressure, and was likely to cause still-births.

Frank Chapple, Right-wing leader of the electricians union, was elected president of the T.U.C. General Council.

In order to get the resolution on the agenda, it was circulated to every constituency association together with a letter signed by myself, Stephen Ross, the party's environmental spokesman, John Bates, the chairman of the Liberal Ecology Group, and Lady Banks, President of the Liberal Women's Federation, all urging the association to forward it to the Assembly Committee. As a result of this procedure it was submitted by more associations than any other resolution and this made it almost impossible for the Assembly Committee to reject.

The Liberal Party in the House of Commons is, of course, much smaller than the others, and thus their MPs are extremely busy. On the other hand, they have a better understanding than many other politicians of the importance of campaigning politics, and will do their best to assist by tabling questions if you can brief them well.

The Conservative Party

It is much more difficult to achieve any kind of policy influence on the Conservative Party, partly because their conferences are not really intended to establish party policy. The best chance of achieving success within the Conservative Party is by finding leading Conservatives who will take up the issue within the party on your behalf.

Whereas the Labour Party and the Liberal Party often have community/cause pressure group activists in their ranks, and there is considerable dialogue between party and pressure group it is less likely that community/cause pressure group members will also be in the Conservative Party.

However, one should never write off the Tories. I should mention that the Chairman of CLEAR's Advisory Committee in the House of Commons was a Conservative MP, Martin Stevens from Fulham, because his constituency was one of the worst-affected by heavy traffic and lead pollution, and there is no question that in dealing with a Conservative administration there were advantages to having a Conservative helping in the House.

An instance of how invaluable the recruitment of support from opposition parties can be is that of the launch of the 1984 Campaign for Freedom of Information. We were able to obtain forceful letters of support from the leaders of the three opposition parties, Neil Kinnock, David Steel, and David Owen, and the publication of these with the launch of the campaign, together with a substantial list of political supporters, guaranteed more widespread publicity, as well as helping to overcome the common assumption that freedom of information was not achievable given the vested interest of all politicians in the status quo.

So firm were the commitments of the three party leaders, that the existence of the campaign became even more essential in order to continue to create situations for these promises and pledges to be repeated so that the parties were fully committed should any of them come to power within the next few years. And that is tadvantage of committing the opposition parties – that there is at least a chance you are committing a future government.

PUBLIC MEETINGS

THE DIFFERENCE between public meetings in the television age of today and pre-television is that they now have to be much better organised and require much harder work for the 'opposition at the fireside' is formidable. As always the first question is: what is the object of the exercise? There is no point in having a public meeting unless there are specific things you can achieve. Usually they are held to publicise the issue in a given locality, thus embarrassing the local MP, local authority, or some other target, by the publicity they will achieve, or they are used to recruit helpers for a longer-term campaign.

The easiest public meetings are those that arise out of local uproar about some problem. For instance, the word gets out that a local power station is being demolished, and that the contractors are not being careful about the release of asbestos into the local community. The local newspaper runs stories, an action group is formed, and often a considerable number of people will turn out to register their objections, to hear what is going on, and to support the group.

More difficult is a public meeting to support an on-going campaign, like for instance CLEAR's campaign on lead in petrol. However, it can be done, and the following are a few useful hints:

- *Define the objective of the meeting carefully, and then organise it to reflect that objective.* If it is to recruit help, decide what kind of helpers you want, and then aim for an audience comprising such people. Make sure the meeting is organised so that you achieve the objective at the actual meeting itself (I will return to that later).
- *Fix a target audience in your mind.* (I am a firm believer in targets, whether it be for fund-raising, attendance at meetings, or any other activity. Unless you know exactly what you want to achieve, it is extremely difficult to organise to achieve it.)

  Make your target audience realistic. It is amazing how many people organise meetings in halls for 4–500 people when the most they could possibly hope to attract would be 40 or 50. Even if the total possible audience, 40 or 50 arrive, the meeting looks a failure because the wrong-sized hall has been booked. Always book a hall slightly smaller than the audience you expect, for it's far better to have people standing, or to have to pull in more chairs, than to have a relatively small number of people in a huge hall. A half-empty hall kills the sense of occasion, discourages the organisers, and suggests to the audience that this is a loser.

● *Choose your hall with care.* Try to get one that is not only the right size, but also has some sense of atmosphere. It is amazing what a difference a good hall, comfortable seating, and sensitive lighting can make. A big, bare, draughty hall with huge lights on the ceiling hardly has a sense of atmosphere, and makes it all the more difficult to create a sense of community in the room. A smaller hall, intimate, with softer lighting can make the meeting more pleasant for speakers, and more exciting for the audience.

● *Try to offer your audience an attractive package.* Don't just call it a public meeting but have a well-known personality as chairman, a good speaker, some kind of visual aids and perhaps a social event afterwards, and then sell the evening as a really worthwhile *event.*

For instance:

> Lead in petrol – is it really a threat to our children? Dr David Bellamy (or whoever) hosts an evening for you to meet CLEAR, The Campaign for Lead-free Air, at the . . . Hall on Thursday, April 1. Speakers: Des Wilson, CLEAR's Chairman, and Dr Robin Russell Jones, CLEAR's medical adviser. Film. Wine and cheese party to follow. The full story on a major public health controversy and a pleasant evening as well. Not to be missed.

● Make sure there is *print material on the chairs* for people to read while they wait, and also that there are plenty of stalls selling all of your material.

● *Make sure your chairman is well briefed* (with a typed outline script) and that your speakers are placed behind a substantial table, with a lectern for the speaker, and glasses of water. It never ceases to amaze me how organisers of meetings never think of these details. Yet in my view speakers are twice as effective if they have a table lectern in front of them to rest notes and lean on. It gives them confidence and also enables a speaker to handle his notes more comfortably. Also, many times at key meetings I have found my throat dry and have croaked on because the organisers did not think of the speaker's need for water.

● *Try to avoid having your speakers on a platform.* It is best to create a circular seating arrangement with the speakers at a table half-surrounded by the audience. This creates greater intimacy. What is really bad is to have your speakers on a stage about 4 ft high and a big gap between them and the front row of the audience. Obviously in a big hall with a big audience you do need to have them on a stage, but the closer you can get your speakers to the audience the better for speakers and audience, and for the atmosphere of shared concern you wish to generate.

● If you have chosen the correct hall, you probably won't need amplification. Microphones do create a distance between speakers and audience. But, if it is a fairly big hall, and you do need amplification, have it checked thoroughly and ideally have a professional to look after it. I have seen many a promising meeting ruined by all sorts of disasters with the microphones. Likewise with the projector and screen. If you intend having visual aids, or if your speaker says he or she intends to bring slides or a film, it is vital – repeat *vital* – that you have the correct equipment and someone who knows how to work it. I have seen meetings completely disrupted by cock-ups with slide projectors and with movie projectors. It can have the effect of disrupting and holding up the meeting, making the speaker feel a fool, irritating the audience, and above all making the organiser look completely incompetent.

- *Don't let the audience go until you have got every bit of commitment you can.* At the end of the meeting the chairman should ask everybody who wishes to become involved to fill in a very brief form with their name, address and telephone number. Helpers should stand at the end of the rows, as if for a financial collection, and take the pieces of paper. In this way people have to make a decision about whether to help while they are there and hopefully feeling enthusiastic.

  If you say to them 'If you want to join the group, then telephone so-and-so', you let people off the hook. Even if they think they will do so, the probability is that they won't. It must be a case of 'We'll ring you . . .' and you have to get their telephone number in order to chase them up. Don't feel this is exploiting them. They don't *have* to fill in the form, they don't *have* to come to the next meeting, but at least you are making it easy for them if they want to.

- *Don't invite a busy person to come and address a meeting unless you are able to organise it properly.* There is no more dispiriting experience for someone who is already working long hours because they believe in a cause than to waste a few hours by travelling all the way to a meeting in another town only to find half a dozen people there because the organiser has not really cared enough to make the event a success. Organising a public meeting these days requires a tremendous amount of work . . . don't organise it unless you are prepared to do that work.

- A key to the success of the meeting is publicity, both before and after. Try to get a profile of the speaker in the local newspaper. Try to get the issue more topical locally, by getting a number of different people to write letters into the local paper, and by getting news stories in the local paper about the meeting. Advertise in the 'forthcoming events' columns of the local paper, and also arrange leaflet deliveries house-to-house, particularly in the areas affected by the cause (if they exist in your town), and also in the areas nearest to the hall. Put up lots of posters. Organise the meeting in sufficient time to write letters to all local organisations, and see that the subject is raised at their own meetings. Try to get other bodies involved in the organisation of the meeting and this will increase the numbers there considerably. Even better, make it a joint meeting with other organisations. For instance, if it is a CLEAR group, it should try to unite with a local Friends of the Earth group, and any other conservation groups plus parent–teacher associations.

Also do your best to get the local media at the meeting in order that a full report appears in the newspaper the following week. If they don't come, write up an account *that evening* and hand it in the following day, preferably with a photograph of the speaker. This is important. If those attending the meeting see a story in their newspapers they get a feeling of being involved in something of importance.

Yes, public meetings can still be organised, and are still very useful. But, like all other aspects of campaigning, their success or failure depends entirely on the work you put into them.

PUBLICATIONS

AS ALWAYS, begin by asking yourself: 'What is the object of the exercise?'

Given the cost of print these days, no pressure group can afford a lot of material, and it is therefore vital that the material you produce is genuinely *useful*. I stress the word 'useful' because a lot of pressure group material looks attractive, but in fact it is of very little *use*.

I have often heard people say 'Well, first of all we need a leaflet'. My reply is always 'What for?'. Perhaps a leaflet is needed, but at least one needs to be clear why it is needed, who it is for, when it is going to be used, and in what numbers.

I have already suggested that most pressure groups should have a campaign newspaper. Obviously the size and quality of this newspaper will depend on resources available, and on whether it is a national or local campaign. A local newspaper may, in fact, be more in the form of a duplicated newsletter, or maybe just four pages of tabloid. A national newspaper, like the CLEAR newspaper or Friends of the Earth newspaper, may be up to 24 pages and properly printed.

CLEAR's print material consisted of:

(a) The newspaper, three or four times a year;
(b) A fairly expensive handbook. We justified this because of the need to develop the authority of the campaign in an area that required medical and scientific evidence. We knew we had to convince many

people in local authorities, national organisations, medical and scientific institutions, and in political office, of the seriousness of the issue, and therefore felt that it was necessary to have a more expensive handbook than would otherwise be the case.

(c) The back page of the newspaper was maintained in every edition, with a summary of the case against lead in petrol, the need for CLEAR, the role and objectives of CLEAR, and the help that we needed. This was then run on as a special *one-page leaflet* for putting on chairs at public meetings, for having on literature stands at public meetings, for fund-raising events, for house-to-house distribution by local FoE or CLEAR groups, and other such activities where a relatively brief but comprehensive item is required.

(d) *Posters.* Our poster was designed so that there was space on it for local organisers to put in details of local meetings or whatever. It was, therefore, an all-purpose poster, being capable of being used in itself to propagate the message, but also being used to publicise local events. This is the most efficient expenditure on posters. Be careful with posters – many organisations spend a lot of money on them, and end up with most of them in boxes in the basement. There is not as much use for posters as is commonly assumed. We printed a relatively small number, and used them in the main to help local groups publicise local activities or to decorate meeting halls, etc.

(e) *Car stickers.* Imaginative car stickers can be a good idea. You can sell these, and therefore they should cost the campaign little, provided you don't order too many.

The other CLEAR material tended to be special reports and publications based on our research.

As you will see, we did not have a wide variety of print material, nor in my view is it needed. The quality of the presentation and the clarity of your message is of greater value than the quantity of material you produce.

Remember: sloppy print material suggests sloppy organisation and that suggests a sloppy campaign. Why should anyone support it?

POWER

THROUGHOUT THE book I have referred to the 'target' of your campaign. The target, in this context, is the individual or oganisation responsible for the decision you seek. I don't employ the word for dramatic effect, but rather to emphasise that all your activites need to be targeted to apply the necessary pressure on the decision-maker or decision-makers. Activities that achieve publicity, or arouse attention, but do not reach the target area, or will not lead to pressure on the target area, may well be a waste of time.

In order to identify the target of your campaign, however, you have to identify where power lies in any given situation. There is, of course, no one answer to the question: a lot of factors influence it. If the decision is a governmental one, then there are different power centres. During the early 1980s, for instance, it has been generally recognised that considerable power is exercised at Prime Ministerial level. In some administrations, however, the centre of power can be the Treasury, and the most powerful politician the Chancellor of the Exchequer. The extent of the authority of individual Secretaries of State or Ministers is defined by the extent that the Prime Minister genuinely delegates. Where it is the case that the power definitely lies with individual Ministries, it does not necessarily follow that the powerful figure is the Minister him or herself. Once more, this differs from Minister to Minister, some having a firm grasp of departmental affairs and exercising considerable personal authority, and others being little better than public relations 'fronts' for their civil servants.

The campaigner, therefore, has to undertake the necessary enquiries to establish exactly who is likely to take the actual decision in any given situation (in contrast to who may announce it or have to defend it). If power lies with the Minister, then you need to decide how to apply the necessary pressure on this particular Minister. This also depends on a number of factors – the Minister's political vulnerability, the proximity of an election, the political potency of the subject, the position of his civil servants on the issue, the influence and determination of the pressure groups opposed to you, etc.

In the case of lead in petrol, the decision lay with the Secretary of State for the Environment, who delegated day-by-day handling of the matter to a junior Minister. They were implacably opposed to the CLEAR campaign to begin with, not least because they had announced an alternative policy less than a year earlier, and did not wish to abandon it or admit error. The proximity of an election, and the huge public support for CLEAR, made the Minister vulnerable, but the lukewarm support for the Ministerial position by the Prime Minister herself made him even more vulnerable than usual. Therefore our strategy was to emphasise governmental indifference to the threat to children in a period leading up to a critical election, and thus force a decision for political reasons (it having become clear that they would not be swayed by the argument itself). Sceptics argued that the issue was not sufficiently politically sensitive to worry the Thatcher Administration, particularly as the Administration was shown to be way ahead of its opponents in the opinion polls. However, politicians, even the Prime Minister, experience considerable insecurity prior to an election and if they can deal with potentially embarrassing problems at little cost (as was the case with the lead in petrol issue) they are tempted to do so. Throughout the campaign we judged that the junior Minister, Mr Giles Shaw, would have no ultimate influence on the question and was merely being exploited by his Secretary of State, Tom King, as a front man to take all the flack. Thus it was that a week before Tom King reversed the policy, Giles Shaw was still defending it on a television programme and offering little hope of change. We deliberately concentrated our fire-power on Shaw in order to 'save the face' of Tom King, while at the same time demonstrating our potential strength.

When it comes to local authorities some research into where power lies is particularly important, because it varies from council to council. On some local authorities, the leader of the council has so much power that he or she is effectively a city boss, and is the only realistic target. On others, the leader of the council has less influence, and the chairman of the particular committee is the key figure. On some local authorities, the councillors do not carry a lot of weight compared with their officials and it could be a key official you wish to influence. A chat with the reporter on the local newspaper who covers the local council and some consultation with one or two members of local political parties, and perhaps a local councillor, will produce the answer. Incidentally, don't believe the first person you speak to. It's best to talk around a bit and gradually a consensus view will emerge. If you have talked to, say, six different people, and four of them have said that the leader of the council is the person, or a particular committee chairman, the probability is that this is where the power does indeed lie.

If your target is a big company, a nationalised industry, or some other kind of major organisation, it is necessary to establish whether the chairman or the chief executive is the most powerful of the leading characters. Sometimes the chief executive can be conservative, whereas his or her chairman can be more bold. In these circumstances it is best to win the chairman's support before you approach the chief executive. In other organisations, the chairman tends to be a highly conservative figure, while the chief executive is thrusting, and in these circumstances your approach will be reversed.

In defining your target you should distinguish between who is responsible for the problem, and who has the power of decision to solve it. The aim of the exercise is to achieve change and it's the decision-makers you have to influence. Time spent establishing exactly who the decision-makers are can be time saved.

QUOTES

Q

ALL PRESSURE groups should have a 'quotes' file. Everyone involved in the campaign should be on the look-out for relevant remarks made by 'targets' or by other public figures, for suitable paragraphs from official reports, books, or other publications on the subject, and for any other quotes that can be deployed in articles, speeches, and, above all, in print material, to lend authority to the case.

One well-chosen sentence or paragraph can, if quoted at the appropriate moment or in the appropriate place, have considerable impact. I am always on the look-out for entries for the 'quotes' file and draw on it on almost a daily basis.

RESEARCH

R SO YOU are concerned about a problem. You are angered by an injustice. You are committed to a cause. You decide to launch a pressure group. Now . . . before you go any further, *become an expert*.

No matter how committed you are, or how much you think you know, before you launch any campaign, research the subject thoroughly from A to Z. You cannot lose by this but you can gain in four ways. First, if there is any possibility that you are wrong, your research may save you a lot of energy and heartache. Second, if you are right, it will nevertheless throw up a considerable amount of additional information and strengthen your case. Third, the research will help you to define the possible solutions and to define your objectives and priorities. Fourth, the research will make you impregnable when you launch the campaign, and the opposition opens fire. You have to be able to answer every question, be right on every detail, have anticipated every thrust of the other side – the research will help you do all this.

Before the Shelter campaign was launched, no-one involved questioned either the need for the campaign or the justice of the cause. Just the same, I spent three months travelling the country from one end to another researching the problem of housing in different cities, and putting together a briefing book on housing and the homeless. From that emerged the case we were able to argue for the whole five years I was involved. From that also emerged all the themes and key phrases of the campaign. I describe this exercise in Chapter 5.

Before the launch of CLEAR, we undertook massive research to accumulate all of the medical evidence from all over the world and details of all the actions of different countries, in order that we could present an unanswerable case. Throughout the campaign we continued the research, spending a lot of our resources on it, for we recognised that the lead-in-petrol campaign would only be won if we could convince the authorities and the nation of the seriousness of the problem and of the strength of the scientific case.

Detailed research has been a feature that has distinguished Friends of the Earth from some other environmental pressure groups. On nuclear energy, pesticides, transport policy, facilities for cyclists, energy conservation, recycling of resources, and many other issues, FoE has commissioned and carried out extensive research in order to add authority and greater relevance to its campaigns. Typical is the pesticides campaign currently under way; although the campaign manual produced by Friends of the Earth for the Pesticides Action Network consisted of around 10,000 words, the research document that backed it up contained over 120,000 and is probably the most comprehensive document in existence on pesticide use.

In my view, the research is so important to the nature of the campaign itself, to its message and themes, that you should not even consider your objectives, targets, or campaign plan, let alone the design of your material or the way you intend to put it across, until the research is complete, and you are able to study it and its implications in depth. Research is not just about the information to support your case – it is also about the choice of arguments and the presentation of the case itself.

With research comes knowledge and with knowledge comes authority and with authority comes conviction and with conviction comes a greater chance of success. Whatever you do, don't economise on research.

SPEECHES

S I AM afraid I have to say it once more: *I never cease to be amazed* how people who care so much and know so much about a cause will devote so little attention to their presentation. This is particularly noticeable in public speaking.

Public speaking is a necessary part of campaigning, and *it is essential that you field a team of effective speakers*. This does not require talent (although to be a brilliant public speaker may do). You can perform adequately with no more than confidence and careful preparation.

As always, we begin with the question: what is the object of the exercise? Is it to inform people who have little knowledge of the problem? Is it to inspire the knowledgeable to become involved? Is it to argue the case as an advocate? Be clear what the purpose of the speech is. I have spent many, many hours sitting on platforms listening to other speakers, and in an extraordinary number of cases they clearly have not bothered to be briefed, or have been badly briefed, on the nature of the occasion. Their speech is entirely inappropriate, either in subject, or in style. Many make the same speech, irrespective of the audience or the occasion, because they feel safe with it, or are too lazy to adapt their performance. All these bad performances have their inevitable result: a bored or disenchanted audience. Don't bother to make a speech unless you are determined to do it properly, and if you do, you will be surprised how much it will achieve.

Points to note:

- *Get a clear understanding of the nature of the occasion*, the audience, the other speakers and what they intend to do, your own place in the function, and the time at your disposal.

- First, *prepare an outline of what you intend to say*. The *structure* of the speech is all-important. Each point should lead naturally to the next, so that you appear to be answering each question in the audience's mind just as it arises. For instance, a basic Shelter speech for me would have consisted of:

  (a) Attention-grabbing introduction on how many homeless families there are in Britain and what conditions they are living in;
  (b) Explanation of how and why people become homeless;
  (c) Explanation of what the authorities are doing, and where they have failed;
  (d) Explanation of why Shelter has been set up and what it can do;
  (e) Explanation of what the audience can do;
  (f) Inspirational call to action.

  Thus I have taken the questions that any sensible individual would ask – what's the problem?, how has it occurred?, what are the authorities doing about it?, what can you do about it?, and what can I do about it? – and answered them.

- *Make sure you have a lectern and a glass of water* (check when you arrive at the meeting whether the organisers have supplied it. They probably have not. Insist on it. You must feel comfortable, and that comes from being able to refresh yourself as you speak, and having a lectern to stand behind, lean on, and rest notes on.)

- When deciding whether to use notes, ignore all advice from public speaking books and do what you feel you can do best. If you can speak with only a few headings, use only a few headings. If you need full notes, don't be afraid to use them, but practise using them. After many years of public speaking I still write major speeches in full, although I have practised the art of speaking from them so that few in the audience realise this is so. Don't read speeches badly or mumble them, desperately trying to follow your own unintelligible writing. This is a disaster. If you intend to read a speech, have it well and clearly typed out so that you can follow it quickly. And practise reading it interestingly.

- *Don't go on and on and on.* Although nearly every speaker begins with a joke about it being their intention not to strain their audience's patience, nearly every speaker does. Of all the speakers

I have heard, and there have been hundreds and hundreds, only about five per cent could judge the correct length for a speech. The other 95 per cent spoke for too long. I have been listening to speeches as a journalist, as a campaigner or politician, for approaching 30 years, and I have never heard a speech that was too short!

● *Don't be over-emotional.* It is possible to speak with feeling and with power without the use of excessive emotion. Excessive emotion in a speech embarrasses the audience, makes everybody feel uncomfortable, and tends to undermine the authority of the rest of your speech.

● *Prepare a list of the 20 most awkward questions you could expect, and jot down one paragraph answers.* You may not have time to refer to them on the platform, but the exercise in itself will have helped. It is no sign of weakness to be prepared for awkward questions; there are inconsistencies and weaknesses in everyone's case. That's life. There is no harm in taking care to prepare the most effective answers. Incidentally, don't be afraid to acknowledge a good point, even if it is not helpful to your case. You can gain credence with the audience with the way you handle the difficult moments. ('That's a fair question, and indeed it does appear to be an inconsistency in our case. However, what you have to take into account is. . . .')

● *Be friendly. Be good-humoured. And acknowledge your audience.* These people could be at home watching television, could be at the movies, could be at the pub, could be almost anywhere else except in this hall listening to you. Acknowledge that. Draw them in. They are your potential helpers.

● *Adapt your speech to the circumstances on every occasion.* No speech is quite the same because no occasion is quite the same. Think about it and adapt. For instance, if you are invited by an all-party committee of MPs to speak to them, remember they are extremely busy and also extremely bad at listening. The 30-minute speech you give to a public meeting will be hopeless. At the most take ten to 12 minutes and put the emphasis on information. Likewise, the speech you will make to a Labour Party meeting will be entirely different from the one you make to a Conservative Party meeting. The speech you make to youngsters will be different to that you make to adults. Adapt it, vary it, and make it relevant to your audience.

Your audience will respect the fact that you have taken care, put together the best speech you can, and have considered the occasion and them. They won't mind if you are not a world-class orator. That attention to detail, and your sincerity, will be more than enough. Audiences only ask that you try your best . . . but *do* do that.

TELEVISION

T IT IS advisable to maintain close surveillance of advance television schedules, for a major documentary, play or film related to your cause offers a remarkable opportunity to rally support.

Shelter was launched on a wave of concern about the homeless caused by the Jeremy Sandford drama-documentary 'Cathy Come Home'. It was shown on television on three occasions and I would put a cash-donation value on it of over £100,000, quite apart from its contribution to understanding about the problem and its help in recruiting support. The film 'Cambodia – Year Zero' made by ATV led to over £1,000,000 in donations from viewers. Granada's 'Life for Christine' helped MIND in its campaign to convey the plight of the mentally ill. The BBC's 'Edna: The Inebriated Woman' by Jeremy Sandford increased understanding of the single, elderly homeless. 'Alice – A Fight For Life', Yorkshire Television's film on a victim of asbestosis, did much to boost campaigners on the health hazard caused by asbestos, and Yorkshire Television's film on the possible link between the nuclear power plant at Windscale and instances of cancer and leukaemia led to a governmental inquiry. And one can go on.

Pressure groups or voluntary organisations can benefit enormously from these television programmes, but it takes planning and it is necessary sometimes to invest some money to achieve the desired result.

For instance, if you plan a direct mail appeal for funds, clearly it makes sense for that direct mail appeal to arrive in mail boxes the day after a television programme on the subject. As I have said, at Shelter we placed advertising in the national papers and church newspapers for the days immediately after the screenings of 'Cathy Come Home'. If you have sufficient advance warning of a suitable programme, you can arrange for local groups to hold wine and cheese evenings on the evening of the programme so they can watch it together, and discuss it. At the very least you should let all your supporters know about the programme, for it will have the effect of rejuvenating their concern.

If the programme is on a campaigning subject, it can make sense to advise sympathetic MPs, and even to arrange for questions to be put in the House.

TIMING

YOU ARE sitting in your office and someone comes in and hands you a piece of information. It is dynamite. It will strengthen your campaign. You reach for the phone to telephone a friendly journalist who can probably have it on the front page of *The Guardian* the following day. Now . . . STOP!

I repeat – STOP!

Is this the right time?

Timing is crucial in any campaign, whether it be a military one, a political one, or a pressure group one.

The best time for any action is the time when it is likely to have the greatest effect. One of the secrets of success in pressure group activity is a sense of timing – knowing just when any particular action is likely to achieve its full potential. (For an account of how a piece of leaked information can be deployed at the best possible time see Y for Yellowlees on pages 131–135.)

A number of factors need to be calculated: If it is a politically sensitive piece of information, you have to use it at a time when it is likely to be most politically effective. If there is no particular time when it is likely to be more effective than another, then it should be used either just prior to, or at the same time as, you plan a fund-raising (or other) activity, to reinforce the impact of the organisation overall at that time. Alternatively it can be used between already-planned activity to maintain the momentum of your campaign.

If it is likely to damage your 'target', you may decide to hold it until your damaged 'target' is already virtually on the floor and then employ it as the final blow. If you know your 'target' is about to score a point on his or her side, you may decide to employ it the day before, on the day itself, or on the day after to defuse the effect of the target's' own campaign.

Timing comes into every consideration: the structure of your campaign, the launching of it, the holding of different activities and events – almost the second question you ask yourself after 'What are we going to do' is 'When?'. So don't *only think ideas and activities, think TIMING.*

TRUTH

YOUR PRESSURE group must always tell the truth. If you don't you will be caught out, lose your credibility, and fail. In any event, you will deserve to fail, for there will be no moral difference between you and the other side. Build a reputation for being truthful – build it with your supporters, build it with the media, build it with your opponents. After all, is your message valid or not? Is your cause just or isn't it? If it is, you don't need to tell lies. Honesty is what you want of the world at large; it will only be achieved if it starts with you.

UNIONS

U THE TRADE union movement in the Thatcherite days of the 1980s may not be the power in the land that it once was, but it is still an ally that pressure groups should seek. These days trade unions are increasingly concerned with the quality of their members' lives, health and safety, working conditions, housing, etc. Many of them have dedicated and skilled researchers and campaigners. You should, at an early stage, therefore, identify the trade unions likely to be sympathetic to your campaign.

Try if possible to avoid writing directly to the General Secretary in the first instance. It is better to establish who the official is whose responsibilities are likely to cover your area, and make contact with him or her. They can best advise how to seek union support, including possible financial support.

● Try to have an influential trade unionist on your committee or council.
● Submit articles to trade union magazines – these have big circulations, and are read by the union leaders as well as the members.
● Seek to demonstrate how your reforms can be beneficial to the unions' members.
● Try to avoid a request for money at your first approach; best to achieve the union's support for the principle and then return for money at a later date if you have to.
● In approaching the union, try to get the support of someone they will respond to – i.e. a letter to the union on your behalf signed by another leading trade unionist, a leading member of the union itself, or even a leading member of the Labour Party sympathetic to the union as well as to your cause, could be helpful.

It may be helpful if I describe how CLEAR won widespread trade union support for its campaign on lead-free petrol.

First, we knew that Clive Jenkins of ASTMS had a first class record of concern on pollution issues and a good team in his union working on these matters. We therefore approached Clive and asked if he would be a trustee of the CLEAR Charitable Trust and he accepted the invitation. (This was a particularly courageous act as many of the employees of Associated Octel, the main manufacturer of lead additives to petrol, belonged to Clive Jenkins' union and he courted some unpopularity by his support.)

Second, we arranged that Bill Sirs, General Secretary of the Iron and Steel Trades Confederation, would submit a resolution calling for lead-free petrol to the annual Trades Union Congress. As the main resolutions on economic and political matters tend to be drawn from the big unions, the smaller unions will often be open to the idea of a resolution that is less likely to come from the big ones, and thus more likely to create an opportunity for their General Secretary to make a speech at the Congress.

We discovered that the TUC General Council met at the conference venue, Brighton, a week before the Congress itself, and arranged a reception for the General Council at the conclusion of its afternoon session on the Thursday before Congress. It was hosted by Clive Jenkins. On this occasion I was able to talk directly with union leaders who wished to be reassured that there would be no economic or employment effects on their particular members by the introduction of lead-free petrol.

The following week the resolution was passed unanimously at the Trades Union Congress and this achieved widespread publicity in newspapers.

Did it matter?

Yes, for three reasons:

First, because of the publicity and attention it received.

Second, because it made it more difficult for the commercial companies involved to use economic and employment arguments when trade unionists had indicated that they cared enough about the problem to support action.

Third, once it became trade union policy, it was possible for CLEAR to return to trade union leaders for further support. This we did in two ways: first, by a financial appeal. Second, by asking them to sign letters, either to newspapers, or in one case, to the Labour Party Shadow Cabinet asking them to keep a supply day free for the issue. Many of the trade union leaders were co-operative and this was extremely helpful.

For the 1984 Campaign for Freedom of Information we went to the National Union of Journalists before any other union to seek their full involvement and support. We argued that our aims and those of journalism were the same – the provision to the public of all the information they were entitled to have. We won their support and this was a tremendous boost to the campaign before it was even launched.

Another pressure group, Transport 2000, dedicated to the preservation of a decent public transport system, naturally went to the rail unions for support and received it.

Unions can be helpful in other ways. For instance, their leaders are influential within their industries, and can often help create opportunities for meeting people, or make personal submissions where the pressure group leaders cannot themselves achieve access to the senior industrialist concerned.

Clive Jenkins, for instance, is a man to be reckoned with in most industries and when he, during an informal chat with Sir Michael Edwards, then Chairman of British Leyland, suggested that it would be helpful if British Leyland loaned a van to CLEAR for a month for its lead-testing unit, Sir Michael indicated he would be happy to do this. A letter followed and as a result of this CLEAR was loaned a brand new van.

Trade unions can be extraordinarily bureaucratic, slow in their decision-making, and even those involved in the trade union movement will acknowledge that the unions still have many faults. They also come under many pressures and tend to be extremely busy. However, I have always found trade union leaders to be warm and sympathetic and a group who genuinely care about their members. If they can be persuaded that what you want will be helpful, they can be generous in their support.

VISUAL AIDS

V ONE OF the effects of the television age is that people are used to being communicated to in pictures. One way to hold your audience, whether it is at a press conference, a public meeting, or in any other circumstances, is to use visual aids.

In the presentation of the CLEAR case, I found that I had to use a number of quotations from organisations and medical experts, and in order that the audience would grasp their importance, and take them in, I had slides made of the quotations and showed them on a screen as I read them during my speech. When this was added to slides of charts and diagrams, it became an effective slide-show illustrating rather than replacing my talk, and enabling me to keep the audience's attention longer and make a greater impact.

This idea of showing the actual words on a screen was adapted from the television news programmes where, when they are quoting from a speech of a politician or whatever, they often show a still picture and beside the picture the actual words. It is still, I think, a rather unusual approach, but one that I find invaluable.

We had one particular diagram that we showed often during the CLEAR campaign: it showed how over a number of years the lead in blood streams of children in New York ran almost parallel to the sales of lead in petrol. You could make that remark with as much emphasis as you wished on a public platform, and not really communicate the point. The chart, however, was dramatic and made a considerable impression. It was worth having a projector and screen for that one slide alone.

A good set of visual aids don't cost that much, and can be used frequently. It is worth sending your key group organisers a set of slides and an accompanying script. They can then take them round local meetings and it helps them enormously to communicate the case. You can even hire them out if you wish to recoup the money.

Of course these days we live in a video age, and the possibility exists now, and will increasingly exist, for pressure groups to make relatively inexpensively powerful video cassettes conveying their argument with illustration. This, too, you should consider.

WESTMINSTER

W AT THE end of the day it is most likely that you will succeed or fail in the Palace of Westminster – either with the introduction of a regulatory change, or a piece of legislation, or by refusal to introduce it. In Britain today the vast majority of the decisions that pressure groups seek will be taken by Government, and the Palace of Westminster is the place where these measures can be advocated, the place where they have to be debated, and in the final analysis, the place where they have to receive endorsement.

The bigger pressure groups these days employ parliamentary lobbyists whose sole responsibility is to represent the cause at Westminster. They spend their whole day talking to Members of Parliament, attending and observing parliamentary committees, circulating briefing documents, reporting back to their campaign, and generally trying to ensure the smooth progress of the campaign's activities in the Houses of Commons and Lords.

(Let me at this point distinguish between this section and the following section on Whitehall. The basic difference is that this section is concerned with influence on Members of Parliament, or influence by Members of Parliament on Ministers; the section on Whitehall is concerned with the Ministers themselves, and the civil servants. On the whole, you don't make your approach to Ministers via the Palace of Westminster, although this could be the place where you apply pressure upon them. Thus, this section is really concerned with influencing, or employing on your behalf, the backbench Members of Parliament.)

In setting out to achieve the maximum support in Westminster there are a numbers of steps that you can take:

● Look at the history of the issue and identify those Members of Parliament who have asked questions related to it, spoken on the subject, or have some record of concern. Choose from them those who you believe would be the most helpful or influential and invite them to form a parliamentary advisory committee. Begin by finding a good chairman who will sign a joint letter with you inviting the other members to serve. Make sure it is all-party, and try to have at least some members on it who you know will spend a little time actually doing things on your behalf. This parliamentary all-party advisory committee also looks good on your campaign material.

- Circulate a list of your objectives to all Members of Parliament with a letter inviting their support. Send a form for them to fill in so that their support is on record. This will often enable you to launch your campaign by indicating the extent of parliamentary support. CLEAR, for instance, was able to announce on its opening day that it had over 130 MPs behind it; the number later well-exceeded 200.

- Parliamentary Question Time offers a wide variety of opportunities to maintain pressure on Ministers. Arrange with two or three of your friendly MPs that they should table a series of questions at a time that links in with other campaign activities in order to keep the Minister on his toes.

For instance, after lead-free petrol had been announced in 1983 William Waldegrave, a junior Minister at the DoE took over responsibilities for seeing the measure introduced. By the autumn it was clear that he needed to be closely watched and continually pressed. Thus, as soon as Parliament reassembled, we arranged for a whole series of questions to be put down, and for them to reappear in different forms over the following weeks. He knew very well where they were emanating from, but the point was that we were reminding him of our existence, of our ability to raise the matter in the House if we wished to, and that he would not get away with indolence on the issue.

Parliamentary questions can also be useful for obtaining all sorts of facts. Sometimes they can be used to force the Prime Minister or Chancellor of the Exchequer to confront an issue they have until then avoided. For instance, on the lead-free petrol issue, once the famous Yellowlees letter was published (see Y for Yellowlees) the Prime Minister found herself personally embarrassed by questions from the leaders of both the Labour Party and the Liberal Party in the House the following day and the issue finally arrived on the doorstep of Downing Street itself. It is worth learning the rules for questions in the House, and learning how they have to be drafted, for they are a crucial weapon in your armoury.

- If your aim is legislation, and it is clear that you are unlikely to achieve governmental priority, you might consider a Private Member's Bill. When the ballots take place for these, only the first 6–10 MPs in the ballot are likely to actually achieve any parliamentary time for their Bill. Thus it is necessary to have a proposal and a Bill ready, and to circulate the idea to all MPs before the ballot takes place in order to plant the idea in their minds. It is of equal importance to know on the day who the top ten are, and to immediately circulate them with the draft Bill and a further reminder, or even try to get them on the telephone.

Some great pressure group achievements have been by Private Member's Bill: one thinks of Alf Morris's Private Member's Bill on behalf of the disabled, or the Bill introduced by Stephen Ross to create greater protection for homeless persons. Abortion and divorce reform came about by Private Member's Bill. In all of these cases, the Member of Parliament concerned was enormously helped with briefings and research and other support by pressure groups.

● There are two particularly useful parliamentary devices for drawing attention and indicating support for your cause:

A member may introduce a Bill under a 'Ten Minute Rule'. If he or she succeeds in doing this, he or she is able to introduce it immediately after Question Time and make a short speech in support of the Bill – usually around ten minutes. This may be followed by a speech from a member who opposes the Bill and after that the speaker will put the question that leave be given to introduce the Bill. If it is carried the Bill is presented and has its first reading. It may die there but there is an outside chance it can go further. Whatever happens, it presents a first class opportunity to publicise an issue. Alf Dubs, a London MP, introduced a Ten Minute Rule Bill for lead-free petrol and both obtained publicity for the cause and put on record in Hansard the case for it. It was a useful exercise.

Another useful device is the Early Day Motion. This is usually put down by a member, with support from other members, and it appears as an order paper to be debated on an 'early day'. In fact they are very rarely debated, but often form a way whereby the parliamentary support for a measure can be demonstrated. If it is possible to get 200–300 MPs to sign it, then the government is warned that this is an issue that it cannot take lightly.

● If there is to be a major debate on your subject, it is crucial to brief MPs well, both on the main arguments for the action you require, but also with answers to whatever defence or case that Ministers may put before the House.

● The Houses of Parliament are not only a place of influence but also a useful facility. With the help of a Member of Parliament it is possible to arrange meetings, press conferences, receptions, and even dinners in the House. It is a useful and impressive venue and you should always consider this.

(opposite) MPs seek publicity in their local newspapers for their support for lead-free petrol

Campaigning MP urges total ban on lead in petrol

A CAMPAIGN to stop children being poisoned by petrol fumes was stepped up this week.

MP Graham Bright (Con, Luton East) wants the Government to ban lead in petrol in Britain, because of the harm it can do to the health of youngsters.

Mr Bright was one of the first MPs to demand a ban on lead. He started his campaign at a time when many scientists believed lead was reasonably safe.

Then scientific tests were carried out and they showed Mr Bright was right to be worried.

Said Mr Bright: "There is growing evidence that lead in petrol is more serious

By RON LOFT

Norman Fowler about the danger of lead. Mr Bright has

MPs work or lead- e petrol

WORTH and IP, Alf Dubs, is

Cut out lead—MP

KENSINGTON'S MP Sir Brandon Rhys Williams is to intensify pressure on the Government "to give a strong stimulus to the lead - free - fuel campaign".

A recent poll in a Sunday newspaper showed that nine out of 10 people want all lead out of petrol — and the majority would be prepared to pay more for it.

"I believe the residents of Kensington — and particularly young children — are at risk in view of the heavy traffic which passes through Inner London," said Sir Brandon.

He wants to see a speedier development of a new engine design to run on a fuel that doesn't create severe health hazards. This could compensate for the "expensive exercise" of eliminating lead from petrol altogether.

The newly-formed Campaign for Lead-free Air (CLEAR) is demanding that the Government speeds up its plans to cut lead content to 0.15 grams per litre — and that should be for existing cars only.

From 1985, CLEAR wants all new cars on the UK market to be forced to run on lead - free petrol. And to encourage motorists to buy it, the Government should put higher taxes on ordinary petrol, the campaigners believe.

In the first issue of CLEAR's newspaper, the chairman, Mr. Des Wilson, talks of the "legacy we owe our children" the air they breathe should be safe and clean.

In an anniversary lecture to Shelter, the London Housing Action Centre, last year, Mr. Wilson asked what history's verdict of this generation will be.

"Will history record that we capitalised on all the sacrifices of those who went before and we took all the benefits of the present, but could not care less for the fate of our children and their children?"

Mr. Wilson believes this will be so if we go on squandering the world's resources and polluting the air and water — leaving our children to reap the destructive harvest.

● Try to give Members of Parliament who help you some support in return. For instance, press releases to their local newspapers saying that they are involved on your parliamentary advisory committee and welcoming their support. Help in achieving publicity in their constituency for the good they are doing will be gratefully received and is no less than they are entitled to.

● MPs are entitled to give limited access to the House of Commons for research assistants, and many pressure groups find it worthwhile to offer a Member of Parliament who particularly cares about their cause some research assistance in return for this accreditation. This an be extremely useful.

However, you should not forget that the House of Commons is the final destination for your campaign and your cause. It is a mistake to arrive on the floor of the House before you have created the necessary publicity and support outside. The attention you will receive from MPs, and the likelihood of success in the House of Commons, will owe a lot to their perception of its political priority.

There are three ways of impressing Members of Parliament with the importance of the issue:

First, widespread national publicity and signs that there is genuine support.

Second, pressure from their constituencies, in terms of publicity in their local newspapers, questions at local meetings, and above all, letters from constituents. One cannot over-state the importance of arranging for Members of Parliament to receive letters urging their support, or their presence on a particular day when an issue is to be raised.

Third, Members of Parliament have to survive, i.e. they have to be re-elected. If you can show that they themselves can achieve some favourable publicity, or reward for their support, this will be helpful.

Use the House of Commons for what it is:

First, a national forum where there is opportunity for drawing attention to your cause.

Second, a forum that is entitled to call for information that can be helpful to you or embarrassing to the opposition.

Third, a forum where it is possible to directly confront Ministers, even the Prime Minister, with your cause.

Fourth, ultimately the place where Members of Parliament will one day have to vote for or against your measure.

It is worth becoming an expert about the ways of the House of Commons, its rules, its opportunities, and its weaknesses. There can be no greater folly than to build up a huge and effective campaign only for it to founder because you have given inadequate attention to its projection at Westminster.

(I have given little space to the House of Lords, but many of the opportunities provided by the Commons are also provided by the House of Lords, and often there are even greater opportunities for lengthy question-and-answer sessions, or debates in the Lords. Many of the techniques described above should also be applied to the Lords.)

WHITEHALL

I OFTEN feel that Whitehall is like a sponge. If you hit it, your fist appears to make an impact. The sponge gives under the pressure. But when you withdraw your fist the sponge re-shapes and looks exactly as it did before.

It is extremely dispiriting to keep hitting a sponge.

It can sometimes be equally dispiriting to make what appears to be an impact on Whitehall.

To begin with, your cause may actually be affected by more than one Ministry. For instance, on the lead-in-petrol issue, there were a whole series of Ministries involved: the Department of the Environment, because of environmental protection; the DHSS because of the health risk; the Department of Education because the main threat appeared to be an adverse effect on the ability of children to learn; the Department of Transport, because of the effect on the motor industry; the Department of Industry, largely influenced by the petroleum industry; and the Treasury.

Second, government departments have ways of de-fusing, delaying, or deflecting issues – which can be infuriating.

What you have to remember is that government departments are enormous great bureaucracies but that high up at the top of them sits a Secretary of State or a senior Minister. Depending on the nature of your cause, and its likely political importance, often the best way to force that bureaucracy to respond with any speed is to embarrass the Minister. Ministers don't like to be embarrassed. Senior civil servants don't like the Ministers to be embarrassed. It's bad news. Ministers are concerned about votes. They are concerned about their standing in the eyes of the Prime Minister. They are concerned about their image with their colleagues. Civil servants are concerned about their department's image in Whitehall – above all, with their peers and other departments. Embarrassment or humiliation for a Ministry is unwelcome.

My approach has always been to approach Whitehall in the orthodox way, seeking information and a response, and if possible, a sensible dialogue. But once it becomes clear that the departmental response, no matter how nicely wrapped-up in platitudes, is a negative one, and likely to remain so, I have tended to re-direct the attack straight to the top. One way to disconcert Ministers is to prove to them that the advice or information they have been given by their civil servants is wrong. This not only makes them wonder if perhaps you don't have a point, but undermines their faith in their own case – a case which very often they don't really understand and which has been foisted upon them by civil servants whom they trust to be right about these matters. The lead in petrol battle was a classic case of abandoning a debate with Whitehall entirely, and concentrating on politicising the issue and embarrassing Ministers. (See Chapter 6 for the full story.)

A few thoughts about dealing with Whitehall:

● Where a number of Ministries are involved, write with the same questions, etc., to each of them. Sometimes the difference in answers will be very interesting; sometimes one civil servant in one Ministry will be more forthcoming than the others.

● Where possible get ordinary supporters to write the questions to Ministers. The civil servants are particularly careful in replying to pressure groups who they know are capable of exploiting the weakness in their arguments. Sometimes they will give away in a letter to an individual constituent a little bit more than the Minister.

● If you are not having any luck getting answers from Whitehall, persuade your MP either to table a parliamentary question or to write to the Minister. Ministers do feel a responsibility to answer MPs in more detail, particularly if they are MPs of their own party. In fact, it is worth noting that at all times you can be more effective in pushing a Minister if you can do it with the help of one of his own side rather than the opposition.

● Find out where the Minister is speaking, particularly in a situation where he may be taking questions, and try to have two or three people in the audience with sharp and pointed questions who will test his grasp of the subject and perhaps embarrass him sufficiently to make further investigations when he gets back to the office.

Most of the above assumes resistance by Whitehall to what you want. However, I must stress that I believe that one should begin by trying to explore all the possibilities of a more positive approach. Be courteous in your early enquiries and seek if possible to achieve a meeting with civil servants. If your pressure group begins to make its mark, it could well be that the civil servants will encourage submissions and evidence and may even seek to meet some of your points. If you can manage to maintain a reasonable working relationship, this is a very good thing. It could possibly also lead to a meeting or meetings with Ministers. You could also try inviting the Minister to address a conference. There are obvious reasons why you have to begin in this way: Firstly, no-one has the right to be aggressive or critical without first giving the other side the opportunity to respond positively and explain their case. You need to have demonstrated that you are constructive if you are to have any hope of a constructive response. Second, sometimes in the earlier frank encounters you can separate the positive from the negative and it helps if you know who within Whitehall is a possible friend and who the opposition is. Third, meetings and encounters give you the opportunity to demonstrate your expertise. It is more difficult for a Minister to discount you as 'a crank' if he has met you and your colleagues and found that you really know your stuff. Finally, you have to be able to demonstrate to MPs and others that an aggressive public campaign has been justified by private indifference by Whitehall.

However, one warning: Whitehall is clever at drawing you in, making you feel you are being consulted, patronising you, and thus weakening you as an effective fighting force.

XMAS

X IT HARDLY needs saying that Christmas is a crucial time for charity appeals. It can, also, be an appropriate time to raise money for pressure groups less traditionally associated with compassion at Christmas.

Christmas parties or Christmas fairs can combine fund-raising opportunities with exhibitions and other propaganda activity.

Or, if your cause has a particular poignancy at Christmas, you can hammer home the message in posters or advertising (for instance, the 'Christmas – you can stuff it' ads placed by Shelter in the Sixties and referred to in Chapter 5).

Every pressure group should give some thought to how it can benefit from the heightened 'peace and good will' at Christmastime. If businesses can begin in January to consider how they will exploit the Christmas tradition the following December, charities and pressure groups, with more right to do so, should have no compunction in following suit.

YELLOWLEES
(OR HOW TO HANDLE A LEAK)

Y PRESSURE GROUPS seek to establish contacts within 'the system' and the ability to do this can be the difference between success and failure. You can't beat for sheer value the equivalent on your particular subject of John Le Carre's 'mole'. However, as I pointed out under T for Timing, to obtain the leak is one thing, to achieve its full potential another. Even the best leak can be of only minimal help if the pressure group bungles the exploitation of the information.

If you obtain a leak, a number of questions immediately arise:

- What can we achieve with this?
- How shall we handle it?
- Who should we entrust with it?
- When should we use it?

To rush out to the first journalist is not the answer. You have to guarantee that you will get the maximum impact, at the crucial time, to the maximum effect.

To illustrate how a leak can be exploited to such effect I intend to tell you at some length the story of the now famous Yellowlees letter.

In the planning of the CLEAR campaign in late 1981 one of our main concerns was to establish medical and scientific credibility. We knew that the industries and Whitehall would seek to destroy our credibility by implying that our campaign was over-emotive and not based on any medical evidence. We therefore accumulated as much supportive evidence and opinion as we could, but nevertheless we knew this would remain a problem. Imagine, therefore, what it meant to CLEAR when a few weeks before the campaign was launched someone walked into my office and handed over a photocopy of a letter. It was written by the Chief Medical Officer of Health at the DHSS, Sir Henry Yellowlees, to senior Whitehall colleagues, and it was, in political terms, dynamite. It completely vindicated our concern about the risk to health of lead in petrol. He had written:

> I am taking the unusual step of writing to you about this matter. . . . A year ago . . . there was a degree of uncertainty, but since then further evidence has accrued which although not in itself wholly conclusive, nevertheless strongly supports the view that:
> (a) even at low blood levels there is a negative correlation between blood lead levels and IQ of which the simplest explanation is that lead produces these effects.
> (b) lead in petrol is a major contributor to blood lead acting through the food chain as well as by inhalation.
> . . . it is doubtful whether there is anything to be gained by deferring a decision until the results of further research should become available. . . .
> . . . There is a strong likelihood that lead in petrol is permanently reducing the IQ of many of our children. Although the reduction amounts to only a few percentage points, some hundreds of thousands of children are affected . . . I regard this as a very serious issue.

And so on.

This, we knew, added the medical weight to our campaign that we had needed. Once we saw it we knew that if we handled this correctly, we could not lose. Naturally, the temptation was to employ it at the launch of the campaign on January 25th, 1982. There is no question that by dramatically producing this letter and showing it on a screen at that press conference, we could achieve considerable effect, and launch the campaign with a bang. In fact, we did not. We entered that press conference with the Yellowlees letter in our pockets and never referred to it.

At the risk of sounding immodest, I would suggest to the reader that this required considerable discipline, judgement, and the sense of timing I referred to earlier. The holding back of this letter at this point was to prove vital for exactly the reasons we thought it would.

First, we knew that the launch of our campaign, because of the number of organisations involved, and the strength of what we would say at the launch press conference, plus some additional medical evidence at hand, would guarantee fairly substantial publicity. We intended to follow the launch press conference in London with a series of provincial launches, and because of the nature of the topic, knew we would achieve widespread radio and television publicity at local level around the country. We did not need the Yellowlees letter for the initial impact. We *would* need it, however, to answer the main charge that would be levelled – that we did not have a convincing scientific case. We decided, therefore, to hold our big gun back, open the attack with the remainder of our artillery, and let the opposition fire back. When their initial ammunition was wasted, we would hit them with the big gun.

There was one other reason for holding the Yellowlees letter back. As a leak, it was an extremely good story. As an 'exclusive' to one newspaper, it clearly was a real scoop. If we held it back to after the launch, we could choose the most appropriate newspaper – perhaps one that up to now had not adequately covered the story – and negotiate the best possible terms for its publication on an exclusive basis.

The campaign was launched and the launch went according to plan. We had considerable opening publicity, and the petroleum industry and the politicians hit back with just the charges we expected: that they were already doing enough, that the health evidence did not justify our campaign, that everyone should remain calm and not be impressed by campaigners operating on the basis of 'emotion'.

We were not particularly happy with the coverage in *The Times* and decided that there were two reasons why we should offer the leak exclusively to that newspaper. First, because, of course, it is a highly influential newspaper. Second, because the editor at the time, Harold Evans, was known and rightly respected for his campaigning journalism, and we felt that he would not be able to resist the combination of a scoop plus the campaigning nature of it.

There were one or two problems, however. First, because the letter had identified the mole, all we now had was a typed-out version of it. Would this typewritten sheet of paper be sufficient to convince Evans, let alone excite him? We decided that if we could not show him the actual letter, the next best thing was to show him the newspaper headlines. Therefore, we had a special newspaper front-page printed. The idea was to run off two thousand copies of it, and on the day *The Times* appeared, to have it on every MP's desk, and to circulate it to other opinion-formers.

We were in Liverpool some ten days later, while the newspaper page was being printed in London, when we decided the time had come to play the Yellowlees card. I telephoned Tony Holden, the Deputy Editor of *The Times*, who I knew, and told him that I had a vital document I believed to be 'dynamite'. I said I was prepared to offer it to *The Times* exclusively, but wished to come and see Harold Evans personally. Holden knew that I was a professional journalist, and not likely to make a dramatic gesture without reason. He fixed for me to meet Evans at 3.00 pm the following day.

Because of the timing of our provincial launches, I had to fly down from Manchester. I met Evans and Holden in the Editor's office. They accepted without reservation that it was a major newspaper story.

What were my terms?

I said simply that I would like it on the front page, that I would like it clear that it came from our campaign, and that I would like the opportunity to write a back-up feature article putting it in its perspective within the lead controversy. These were not unreasonable terms. It clearly was a front page story. It was only fair that the source, CLEAR, should be referred to. And a campaigning article on the subject on the same day was reasonable journalism. I did, however, have one other request. Although this was Wednesday, I wished it to be published the following Monday. The reason for this was that I needed time to have that newspaper on every MP's desk by the time they arrived back from the weekend.

The following Monday the story appeared as a front page exclusive in *The Times*, with the full letter published on page 2, and my article opposite the leader page. The following day *The Times* published a leader calling for a ban on lead in petrol. At the same time, all the other national newspapers, radio and television, took up the theme of the Yellowlees letter. Michael Foot, the leader of the opposition, and David Steel, leader of the Liberal Party, challenged the Prime Minister in the House of Commons on Tuesday. The publication of the Yellowlees letter hit the lead-in-petrol issue like a time-bomb, spread-eagling the opposition and convincing almost everybody that CLEAR's case was vindicated and action had to be taken. It was a classic case of a leaked document causing the maximum possible embarrassment. I would suggest to the reader that its impact had as much to do with the use of the letter as the letter itself.

I quote this case at length in the hope that it will encourage all pressure groups to think carefully how to use such information to maximum advantage, remembering what impact they wish to make, how to do it, and, above all, *when*.

Z   ZERO HOUR

THIS IS what we all face if we don't listen to the pressure groups for peace.

PRESSURE IN PRACTICE

5 SHELTER – CASE HISTORY OF A CHARITY – PRESSURE GROUP*

THERE WAS NO greater political scandal in the 1960s than the Profumo Affair, but for all the drama it caused at the time, its longterm effect had little to do with spies or sex. One of the cast of characters in the affair was Mandy Rice-Davies, the mistress of a slum landlord called Peter Rachman. The newspapers, anxious to maintain the momentum of the Profumo scandal while it sold millions of additional copies, looked into Rachman's background and activities and uncovered a fresh scandal, that of appalling treatment of the desperate families who were tenants of his properties. There were stories of ruthless evictions, and brutal bullying by rent collectors with alsatians. Such was the impact of the disclosures that the word 'Rachmanism' assumed a permanent place in the English language. It is now to be found in my Chambers Family Dictionary:

> Rachmanism, n. Conduct of a landlord who charges extortionate rents for properties in which very bad slum conditions prevail. (from the name of landlord exposed in 1963)

As the full details of the number of slums in London and other major cities, and the treatment of tenants, emerged, the 'never had it so good' image of the Conservative administration of Harold Macmillan was

---

* To write this chapter, I have drawn heavily on my own contributions to two publications of the Sixties – *The Shelter Story* and '*I Know it was the Place's Fault*'.

severely dented. The Milner Holland Committee on London's housing, set up in the wake of the scandal, produced an unequivocal condemnation of housing policies. Harold Wilson, leader of the Labour opposition, promised half a million new houses a year if Labour were elected, plus a Rent Act to create security of tenure for tenants of unfurnished accommodation. Labour was elected in 1964 and *did* introduce that Rent Act, and also increased house-building until for the first time ever it exceeded 400,000 houses a year. Thus, what began as a politics-and-sex scandal emerged as a contributor to social policy.

The legacy of bad housing, overcrowding and insecurity was colossal. The voluntary sector's input was in the form of charitable housing trusts. In cities like London and Birmingham these trusts would purchase big, older houses, improve them, convert them into flats, and let them at cost-rents to families that otherwise would live in one room or in an unhealthy slum or break up altogether. Because the housing trusts could obtain mortgages from the local council, together with improvement grants, they found that it would cost about £325 per flat for an ordinary-sized family. The problem was to raise the £325.

As a result of an initiative by the Notting Hill Housing Trust and its Chairman, Bruce Kenrick, discussions began on plans for a national charity to raise money for existing housing associations or trusts, and to encourage the formation of new ones. The first step was to try to achieve the maximum co-operation of everybody already in the field. There were at that time four main national charities – the National Federation of Housing Societies (in the form of its Housing Society's Charitable Trust), the Catholic Housing Aid Society, Christian Aid, and the British Churches' Housing Trust. These, together with the Notting Hill Housing Trust, were persuaded to merge their appeals into one, and all to back Shelter. Each had a representative on Shelter's Board of Trustees. This merger of activity was vital because it meant that the public would not be confronted with conflicting appeals and messages on behalf of the homeless, and it meant that existing goodwill towards the cause could be mobilised behind our campaign.

(The creation of coalitions, or at least the maximum level of co-operation between like-minded organisations, is in my view an essential first step in the launch of any appeal or pressure group . . . see C for Coalitions on pages 56–57.)

I became involved in the planning in early 1966 and in June became the first full-time worker, opening a small office in James Street, W1. My first responsibility was to research the problem. I studied all the existing material, talked to housing academics, went to the Ministry of Housing, visited local authorities, studied closely the work of housing trusts, and produced a substantial report.

My research confirms that thousands of families are fighting for their very existence in appalling housing conditions and that many are falling through the net of the welfare state. Many of these families are urgently in need of help and without that help may disintegrate.

I believe that my research shows, too, that the role of Shelter is clearly defined by the circumstances and its arrival on the housing scene is timely. Therefore it is not difficult to be excited by the challenge of the problem rather than depressed by its size and ugliness.

The report identified the worst hit areas under a number of headings: overcrowding, unfit housing, people in hostels for the homeless, the spread of multiple occupation, council waiting lists, the record of the local authorities in housing, and the view of authorities such as officials at the Ministry of Housing. It concluded that the outstanding blackspots at that time were Glasgow, Liverpool, Birmingham, and London.

The report reflected a sense of shock at what I discovered. For instance, it described one house in Church Road, Birmingham, where 27 people shared one toilet and one cold water tap and there was a family in every room. Gas and electricity bills had not been paid by the landlord for months and those services were about to be cut off. The floors were unsafe and there was a fire risk. I wrote that 'It is doubtful whether this house would survive one of the criteria under the Housing Act Unfitness Standard'. One family with four children lived in a room ten feet by eight feet, and the mother slept upright in her chair with a child on each arm.

Of Liverpool, I wrote:

> The state of disrepair in multi-occupied buildings in Liverpool appeared to be worse than anything I had seen in London or Birmingham. For instance, one house in Prince Avenue is in an appalling state of repair; broken windows, garbage all over the front yard, and no security – anybody can get in. There are holes in the floor and there is access through almost every window. A couple with their five children are all living in one room, the eldest being five and the youngest a few days old. They pay £2 10s. They all sleep in one big bed behind a partition, making a bedroom four feet wide. Seven people sleeping in one bed in a room four feet wide! No hot water, the toilet is broken, and the piping to the toilet and bathroom have been stolen. They have to take a bucket of water on every visit to the toilet which is in an appalling state.

I reported that the housing problem was so bad in Glasgow that, had I not seen it with my own eyes, I would not have believed it.

The research confirmed the knowledge of the Steering Committee, chaired by Lewis Waddilove of the National Federation of Housing Societies, that there was desperate need and that a campaign like Shelter was needed to act as a spearhead for the voluntary housing movement, both in terms of money and to raise money. It also defined the role of Shelter:

First, it emphasised the emergency nature of the problem:

Shelter does not need to create an emergency situation. It is there. All that is necessary is that it should be imaginatively, responsibly and dramatically publicised.

Second, it suggested that if Shelter was to be seen to get results, it should concentrate its money on the blackspots – the four major cities.

Third, it discussed what Shelter's definition of homeless should be. According to the authorities, 'truly homeless people' were 'those who have come to welfare departments for shelter and temporary accommodation'. At the time this represented about 12,500 a year. Shelter, on the other hand, was to base its campaign on the principle that the home was the basis of family life, and that any family was actually homeless if it was split up because its home was too small, or if it was living in housing conditions so unfit or overcrowded that it could not lead a civilised family life.

> The home should meet two criteria: firstly, it should be a place where individuals and families can be themselves for better or worse, and can obtain peace and security. Second, it should be an effective base for daily life, providing rest and relaxation and the mental and physical strength for participation in our pressurised and competitive society.
>
> Thus, Shelter believes any family is homeless if it is nagged by insecurity, or overcrowded so that it lives with constant strain and tension, or lacking any kind of privacy, or surrounded by dampness and infestation that spread disease, or living in physical danger because of the unfitness of the property, or cheated of the essential facilities that others take for granted.

The national statistics were appalling. They showed, according to an official White Paper, that 'Three million families in Britain still live in slums, near slums and in grossly overcrowded conditions'. They showed that 1.8 million houses in Britain were 'unfit for human habitation', that 1,641,270 people were statutorily overcrowded, and at least 390,610 people were extremely overcrowded. Some 4,364 children were 'in care' for no other reason than their families lived in unsatisfactory housing conditions. And all of the above figures, with the exception of that for overcrowding, were for England and Wales only.

Thus, my report suggested a number of themes for the campaign:

(1) We should convince people that the housing situation was out of control and only an all-out effort from everybody could save hundreds of thousands of families from disaster. We decided to emphasise that Shelter was a 'rescue operation' in a national emergency. 'This is a national emergency, and in an emergency we all unite', our literature said.

(2) We should emphasise the statistics of the housing problem to show that people were not homeless because of their own inadequacy but because of the scarcity of housing – 'In an emergency situation like this there have to be innocent victims.'

(3) We should emphasise the Shelter definition of a homeless family, and constantly refer to 'the hidden homeless'.

(4) Recognising that the particular spirit of the Sixties was a desire by people to become involved, we should emphasise involvement in all our publicity. 'Shelter involves you' became a campaign theme, and the slogan on T-shirts and badges.

The weeks of research, and the research document, were a key to the success of the launch of Shelter. Not only did we produce material that was accurate, detailed, and comprehensive, and enabled us to present ourselves as an organisation that really understood the nature of the housing problem, but also the research had helped to identify the campaign themes.

Between the sponsoring organisations and a bank loan based on guarantees from one or two generous individuals, we were able to put together a small budget to launch the campaign. We were, however, confident that our initial advertising would achieve a positive response, and committed ourselves to considerably more expenditure than our resources justified.

Now the lengthy preparation for the campaign began. First, we had to fix targets. We decided on an objective of £1 million a year by 1970, with a 1967–68 target of £200,000, a 1968–69 target of £½ million, and a 1969–70 target of £750,000. We devised a fund-raising strategy and budgets. These decisions made, we set out putting together the print material, booking and designing the advertising, and laying the ground for the launch of the campaign.

The name Shelter was chosen. This did not emerge overnight. Lists of possible names were circulated, some favouring a respectable-sounding name like 'The National Housing Trust' and others more jazzy names. The word SHELTER appeared on a number of lists. Some reacted unfavourably, saying that it would be confused with air-raid shelters, or refuges of tramps (one person helped collect £26 in the north of England in the belief that he was raising money for a new bus shelter) but, once the campaign was launched, everyone seemed to think the word Shelter was a 'natural'.

There were to be three main elements to the launch:

- National newspaper advertising;
- Editorial coverage;
- Direct mail to churches and other bodies most likely to be supportive.

An advertising agency was appointed and briefed, and advertising booked for the launch of the campaign on December 1. A leaflet was produced for mailing to churches, etc. The hardest work was the preparation of the editorial coverage. I listed every single relevant national, local and specialist newspaper and magazine together with the journalists we hoped would write the story, and the angle that would be most suitable. Each was telephoned or visited in advance of the press conference. This person-to-person campaign included television and radio programmes and lasted nearly ten weeks. We decided to launch Shelter in the Crypt of St Martin-in-the-Fields. It was central, free, and offered a suitable atmosphere. We persuaded a photographic company to enlarge photographs of the homeless free of charge. These surrounded journalists at the press conference and were taken for the provincial launches in Birmingham, Liverpool and Glasgow. These were planned for the week following the launch, and were to involve not just the media, but local dignitaries. All was set for what we felt confident would be an effective launch.

There was, however, one unexpected factor. Every campaign needs a bit of luck. With the CLEAR campaign it was the Yellowlees letter (see Y for Yellowlees and also Chapter 6). With Shelter, it was the screening on television a few nights before of the launch of Jeremy Sandford's now famous documentary-drama about a homeless family, 'Cathy Come Home'. It is often presumed that the launch of Shelter resulted from Cathy, or was planned to follow the screening of Cathy. This is not so. We had no idea the play was planned. In fact, I did not see it. I was busy in my office that night putting the finishing touches to the print material for the campaign and had no idea that at the same time half the nation was being shocked by a play that would guarantee our success.

In the days after Cathy was screened there was an uproar about its revelations of the nature of the housing problem and the way the homeless were dealt with. It had created the ideal atmosphere for the launching of Shelter, for when our press conference took place on December 1, everyone knew exactly what we were talking about. The impact was immediate. The months of pressure and persuasion had worked and the media coverage was enormous.

The result from newspaper advertising was staggering. For instance, an ad in *The Guardian* which cost £300 raised £7,000, and an ad in *The Times* which cost £1,800 raised £12,000. An ad in the *Church Times* costing £105 raised £1,000, and an ad in a British weekly costing £57 raised £700. Within a month over £50,000 had flooded in and Shelter was well off the ground. Subsequently I was invited by a magazine for the advertising and public relations industry to write about the launch of Shelter:

Firstly we clearly set out our launch objectives back in June – to launch Shelter as 'a rescue operation in a national emergency' – and remained faithful. to those objectives despite temptations to change during the months up to December. This steady focus on one theme, assisted by the screening of 'Cathy Come Home', helped us to hit the nail on the head.

Secondly we chose a number of catch phrases – 'Hidden homeless', 'rescue operation', etc. – and a few basic facts – 'three million families in Britain today live either in slums, near slums, or grossly overcrowded conditions', etc. – and hammered away at them with every single item of advertising, direct mail and public relations. We had the satisfaction of hearing them independently repeated on radio and television a score of times.

Thirdly, we planned and planned. The relentless person-to-person contact with the press was most effective.

Finally, I believe that the enthusiasm and the pace we worked at in those final weeks created its own sense of urgency which got under the skin of journalists who came into contact with us, and nothing thrilled us more than the crusading zeal that many eventually carried into their features and reports.

The BBC decided to repeat 'Cathy Come Home' early in 1967 and this, together with a follow-up advertising campaign, helped Shelter past its first £100,000. By now, a number of things were becoming clear:

First, the churches were highly sympathetic to the appeal, and we therefore concentrated a lot of our energy on communication with them.

Second, there was a huge desire by ordinary people all over the country to become involved, and so we appointed a groups organiser, to help these people form themselves into local groups to raise money for Shelter.

Third, the appeal had made a particular impact within the young, and therefore we appointed a Youth Campaigner to explore ways of realising the potential for Shelter of this concern.

Three young women, all aged 22, came to work at the James Street Headquarters. They were Eileen Ware, who was to become Youth Director, Liz Wills, who was to become Groups Director and later Public Relations Director, and Cindy Barlow, who became Administrator and secretary of Shelter. These three were to serve throughout my time as Director of Shelter and their contribution was beyond measure.

One of our main activities throughout 1967 was travelling round the country speaking at public meetings. We persuaded the BBC to give Shelter exclusive rights to 'Cathy Come Home' for at least a year and the play's author, Jeremy Sandford, offered to forgo his author's royalties, and the cast, with the co-operation of Equity, also co-operated. These meetings were extremely well-attended and formed the basis for the setting up of Shelter groups.

We took a stand at the Ideal Home Exhibition. It did *not* feature an ideal home – just the opposite. The centre piece was a one-room home of a family of six in Notting Hill. (Incidentally, organising a stand at such an exhibition can turn into a nightmare. It is expensive, and there are all sorts of organisational problems, but it made a considerable impact.) As all the television programmes tend to visit the Ideal Home Exhibition, it made an unusual feature for them, and we attracted additional publicity by arranging for Carol White, the actress who played Cathy, and Jeremy Sandford to visit the stand, and also the then Liberal Leader, Jeremy Thorpe.

One Shelter approach was to take a fund-raising idea that had been proved to work at local level and 'nationalise' it. For instance, Shelter raised a lot of money from sponsored walks, and to encourage all sorts of groups to organise a walk, we created Shelter's own 'Walk Week'. In 1967 there were 160 walks in Walk Week, and more than 6,000 took part. We also organised a 'Jumble Sale of the Year'. This mainly consisted of lots and lots of local jumble sales, but all taking place on the same day, and having the advantage of the one lot of 'Jumble Sale of the Year' posters and publicity material.

In the autumn we introduced what was to become a regular feature of Shelter campaigning and still is today: the 'shock report' on housing.

The first was on the theme of 'Back to school from a holiday in the slums' and it demonstrated that hundreds of thousands of children went to school each day from housing conditions so oppressive that their capacity for education was restricted. The report was made up almost entirely of comments from school teachers and social workers. It was published on the eve of the new school term, and also on the eve of the party conferences. It achieved massive publicity. The idea for the campaign came from Eileen Ware, and the secret of the report was its simplicity – one idea that everybody could grasp.

We developed this formula in the years to come. Each shock report was itself the basis of a total campaign, including newspaper advertising, a mailing of our newspaper to our supporters, appeals to schools and churches, public meetings and rallies, and fringe meetings at the party conferences. We also briefed journalists in advance so that feature articles and television programmes could appear on the day of publication.

In 1968 we followed it with a shock report on eviction and harrass-ment by landlords. The report 'Notice to Quit' was launched at a crowded press conference and once more achieved considerable publicity.

Perhaps the major success was the 1969 report, however, called 'Face the Facts'. The theme of this report was that the nature of the housing problem was covered up by the official definition of a homeless family. This enabled ministers to claim there were only 18,000 homeless people in Britain, whereas Shelter claimed there were over a million. 'Face the Facts' outlined the slum conditions, overcrowding, and insecurity that still existed, using case histories from throughout the country. Its theme was that we could not solve the problem until the authorities 'faced the facts'. We backed it up with a hard-hitting advertising campaign, almost unique at the time, a rally in Trafalgar Square, and meetings with standing room only at Labour and Liberal party conferences. The impact of the campaign was such that two of three party leaders – Jeremy Thorpe, and Harold Wilson, the Prime Minister – referred to it in their closing speeches at the party conference, and in one day four different Ministers made speeches in different parts of Britain attacking Shelter for its report.

Even today Shelter publishes a hard-hitting report on housing in the autumn and the technique, even down to the design and the way they are written has been followed by countless charities and pressure groups since.

What made these campaigns particularly effective was the way whereby a variety of activities took place at the same time, each designed to reinforce the other. Thus the report provided the editorial publicity, the advertising campaign was based on the same theme, the supporters received a newspaper at the same time to revive their concern, and direct mail shots were planned to coincide. The effect was that each activity reinforced the other. It could be possible for a Shelter supporter to see an item on television one evening, a feature article on the report and a news story the following morning, an ad in their national newspaper appealing for funds, and to receive in the post the Shelter newspaper on the same day. The result was that we managed to create the impression of colossal activity.

For Christmas of 1967 we launched our 'House a family for Christmas campaign', challenging churches and schools to raise £365 at Christmas time to house a family. This proved a huge success. It definitely helps when approaching groups, like schools, churches, or other organisations, to create a project that will capture their imagination. It should have a manageable financial target and you should be able to indicate what the fund-raising campaign will achieve. While churches, schools, and other organisations will respond to an appeal to organise a fund-raising event, they will respond much more enthusiastically and usually are far more effective if they know they are raising an exact sum of money to achieve a particular objective.

About this time we changed our advertising agency and had the good fortune to strike upon a brilliant team of copy-writer and designer who came up with an entirely different approach to charity advertising. They recommended that instead of the usual, sentimental Christmas advertising appeal, we should reflect the bitter feelings of families spending Christmas in the slums. The headline of the main ad said:

Christmas – you can stuff it for all I care.

It continued:

Christmas – the bright lights, the big send-up, the family get togethers, the sentimentality – it's an insult to a family like this.

You are looking at the hopeless, helpless anger of Britain's three million slum dwellers. People who have been rejected so often that they reject everything.

Yet surely, the Christmas message was meant to bring hope to people like these.

Get them out of their dreadful overcrowded rooms.

Give them a decent home. Let them start living again.

This is what Shelter wants to do.

All of this below a picture of a family standing in a doorway of a damp Glasgow tenement.

The ad caused a sensation. Many people were horrified. Public figures complained in the media. As a result, the advertising achieved a considerable amount of editorial publicity, notably an article in *The Observer*:

> The photograph and the advertising is raw: poverty without pathos. The headline is blunter still: 'Christmas? You can stuff it for all we care'. Shelter, the National Campaign for the Homeless is one year old now and this week takes possibly its biggest gamble: debunking Christmas with a brutally direct advertising campaign that is a world and a half away from conventional tinselly images of the fund-raisers' best season.
>
> Shelter is gambling that the public is ready to accept that for the old, the lonely and the homeless, Christmas is the cruellest month – the time that rubs in the contrast between the 'haves' and 'havenots'. One ad is a photograph of a squalid lavatory system: 'Christmas is a time for sharing. Twenty-three people share this'.

The advertising was so controversial that I was asked to comment on it to a Working Party on Charities set up by the National Council of Social Services. I wrote to them:

> This ad was not attacking the festive season. Nor was it using strong language to shock just for the sake of shock. What it was doing was questioning the way in which we celebrate Christmas. We believe we can only express the bitterness of the poor by using the words of the people themselves. This was truthful. This was uncompromising. Certainly there was a risk that we might alienate some of our supporters. But we were truly representing the feelings of the people that we were formed as an organisation to represent. The response was that more money came in from that ad than from any other. And I believe it proved that people respond to truth. They respond to urgent need when it is presented to them in an urgent way.
>
> We are asked whether the public is likely to react against more hard-hitting advertising. There may be a risk in this, but are they likely to respond to a return to a more conservative approach? Do we want charity to be neatly fitted into our society and not to become so conspicuous that people become uncomfortable, or do we want charities and voluntary organisations to express their concern and the isolation of their beneficiaries in such a way that it cannot be ignored?

"Christmas? You can stuff it for all we care."

Christmas – the bright lights, the big spending, the family get-togethers, the sentimentality – it's an insult to a family like this.

You are looking at the hopeless, helpless anger of Britain's 3 million slum dwellers. People who have been rejected so often that they reject everything.

Yet, surely, the Christmas message was meant to bring hope to people like these?

Get them out of their dreadful, overcrowded rooms. Give them a decent home. Let them start living again.

This is what SHELTER wants to do. The voluntary housing groups that SHELTER helps are doing just this. But we need money.

This Christmas you are going to spend money. So spend some of it to help people live like human beings.

SHELTER
Help SHELTER to house a family

The famous 'Christmas – you can stuff it' advert for Shelter

There is little doubt that this advertising campaign changed the face of British charity advertising.

Also at Christmas, 1967, BBC Television's 'Blue Peter' children's programme had an appeal for stamps for a Shelter housing project. The response was phenomenal. More than 120 million stamps were collected. These were sold to pay for the conversion of a house.

On December 1, 1967, we were able to report that in our first year we had raised £200,000, got homes well under way for 1,000 people, had undertaken a persistent programme of publicity for the homeless, sent speakers to about 350 meetings, screened the film 'Cathy Come Home' more than 400 times, launched over 100 Shelter groups, and involved many thousands of younger people so that Shelter was practically a youth movement.

We marked the occasion by going back to St Martin-in-the-Fields, this time to have an exhibition in a big marquee outside the church. It was visited by the Minister of Housing on Christmas Eve.

Two ideas from 1968.

● It was announced that 960 million half pennies in circulation would be collectors' items after August 1969. Within 48 hours we printed a leaflet and distributed it to children all over the country. As a result of the Blue Peter exercise, we had learned that kids love to collect things, and our faith was not misplaced. By July 30, 1969, they had collected 6½ million half pennies for Shelter – enough to rehouse 45 needy families.

● We launched a 'Tycoon contest'. The basis was that each boy or girl would be given 2s 6d by their mum or dad and have a fortnight to make the money grow. This project came from a group of youngsters in Surrey who had raised £600 in a fortnight in that way. This illustrates that many of the best ideas can come from your supporters. (Only one boy failed – he put his half a crown on a horse and it lost!)

And so I could continue, but as the emphasis of this book is on pressure groups, I do not intend to devote a lot of time to fund-raising. Suffice to say that Shelter exceeded its target in every year and achieved its ambition of a million pounds a year by 1970. The key contributors were:

● National newspaper advertising;
● Fund-raising by Shelter groups;
● Fund-raising by school and youth organisations;
● Fund-raising by churches;
● Twice-a-year donations from supporters in response to the Shelter newspaper;
● Special events.

(below and overleaf) Young people raised a fortune for Shelter and did it with humour and imagination

(below) Eileen Ware was Shelter's brilliant Youth Director. In 1969 she and her small team raised nearly £300,000, mainly from schools

(A lot has changed since those days. Charities do less advertising, because while advertising has become more and more expensive, the sums that people give have remained fairly constant. Thus someone who gave £5 to Shelter in 1966 would probably still donate £5. While the cost of advertising for that £5 will have multiplied five times, the five pounds in the donor's pocket seems in his or her mind to have retained its value. Also, Shelter raises a lot less money from Shelter groups and from schools. The main source of income is direct mail appeals.)

What I wish to stress, however, is the pressure group activity of Shelter. Initially, its objective was quite simply to arouse the public conscience about the problems of the homeless, and create greater political priority for housing. Helped by 'Cathy Come Home', and the huge publicity at the time that Shelter was launched, we were able to do this. In our first couple of years we bothered little about the specific housing policies, concentrating instead on the one main message – that we had to spend a higher proportion of national and individual income on housing. However, as I have argued earlier, experience in dealing with the problem produces knowledge of possible solutions and we felt that we had no alternative but to press for those solutions.

First, we were demonstrating with our money what could be done with older property. Up to that point, housing policy had been to tear down the slums and build new. The problem was that every new house built had to replace one that was knocked down, and therefore the stock was not being genuinely increased at the rate that housebuilding figures would suggest. We therefore put heavy emphasis on the need to devote more national resources to rehabilitation. While I would accept that the authorities had come to much the same conclusion, there is little question that Shelter's activities contributed to a substantial initiative to make improvement grants more widely available, and to encourage rehabilitation instead of automatic destruction of older housing.

At the same time, many of the families we had to deal with came to our attention because they had been unlawfully evicted or forced out of their accommodation. Our major campaign, built round the report 'Notice to Quit' helped to end the complacency that existed after the introduction of the 1968 Rent Act. In addition to meetings at the party conferences, we organised a special Rent Act Conference at a hotel in London. A full transcript of the Conference, together with the recommendations of a study group, were sent to the minister, and also to a governmental committee on the subject.

One of the roles that a pressure group can play is to undermine the effect of cover-up propaganda. Perhaps the classic case was that of the housing surplus. In the late Sixties we achieved a situation where there was a surplus of homes over families in Britain. This did not mean, however, that the housing problem was solved. The housing problem is not about an equal number of homes to families over a country as a whole, but having homes in the right place (where people have to live in order to work), at the right price (at rents and prices people can afford), of the right size (all families in one room were included in those statistics), and of the right condition (all slums were included in those figures). The question of the housing surplus arose in 1967 when the then Minister of Housing, Anthony Greenwood, referred to it in a speech. To be fair to him, he put it in some perspective, saying:

> I have seen it said recently that the demand for housing will fall sharply in the 1970s. I am absolutely convinced that this is wrong. We know that over 100,000 houses a year will be needed simply to keep pace with the growth in households. More, we know now we have between two and three million slums and potentially unfit houses. This indicates our major housing problem in the 1970s.

Unfortunately, abbreviated press reports of this speech concentrated on the potential surplus and Shelter decided to destroy the myth as soon as possible. We wrote to Greenwood at that time saying:

> In order that the misleading publicity be properly balanced with the real facts, we believe that you should in forthcoming publicity shift emphasis from the tremendously encouraging achievement to the huge and heart-rending problem of the homeless and hidden homeless that still remains a major responsibility of the nation as a whole and each individual within it.

Greenwood replied agreeing.

However, in February 1969, under attack from Conservatives in the House of Commons, his junior Minister, Kenneth Robinson, predicted a surplus of one million houses by 1973. Athough he qualified this to some small extent, he used the housing surplus as the main plank in his defence of the Labour administration's record, and the tone of his speech was reflected in a *Guardian* headlines 'Cathy may come home to housing surplus in 1973'.

We decided to reverse the trend of the publicity with a major drive, and issued a press release immediately afterwards condemning Robinson in the highest possible terms. The attack was sufficiently scathing to make the World at One and headlines in the evening newspapers. *The London Evening News* reported:

> Shelter chief slams Commons housing claim.
>
> Mr Kenneth Robinson's claim in the Commons yesterday that there would be surplus of a million houses by 1973 was described by the Director of Shelter today as 'either a cruel joke, an unscrupulous deception, or an indication of Mr Robinson's abysmal ignorance of the realities of the housing problem.'
>
> Commenting on the claim by the Minister of Planning and Land that the seller's market would be finished, Mr Des Wilson said there was 'a colossal difference between ending the theoretical shortage of houses and

ending the real housing problem. It is not enough to have an equal number of units of accommodation to families,' he said, 'they must be in the right place at the right price, of the right standard, and of the right size. There is no chance of us meeting any of these conditions by 1973 or even 1983.

(See M for Media on pages 79–92. This news story shows that a pressure group can demolish official propaganda. In two paragraphs it forces the minister on to the defensive and outlines the full reply to his claims.)

The Guardian published a special article by myself the following day in the form of a letter to Cathy, explaining to her, 'You are the victim of a piece of political deception'. The newspaper itself ran a leader describing 'this kind of calculation as an exercise in inexcusable complacency'. The television programme 'Twenty-Four Hours' invited me to debate the issue with Robinson. That evening just before I left home, I was telephoned to say that Robinson would only appear if he was alone. I could, therefore, not represent our side of the story on the programme. I saw no reason why he should be allowed to escape that easily, and immediately issued to the Press Association the facts about the 'Twenty-Four Hours' programme. The result was that the story made the front pages of every newspaper the next day. Robinson had, by refusing to debate, made certain that the maximum attention would be drawn to my answer to his claims in the House of Commons.

It was significant that little was heard of the housing surplus for some time.

This special role of a pressure group, to maintain surveillance on what the authorities claim, and to correct mis-information and undermine complacency, is a vital one. We put high priority on the creation within Shelter of an efficient 'press comment' operation that was capable of writing, duplicating and distributing press releases around Fleet Street within an hour. In addition, we could write a press release and dictate it to the Press Association in a matter of minutes. Given the dramatic illustration potential of our cause and our campaign activities, we actually employed a full-time photographer with his own darkroom. The research office was responsible for reading the newspapers, distributing all press clippings to do with housing, and drawing the attention of campaigners to news items that Shelter could reply to. The speed of the operation was such that, for instance, when Enoch Powell once made a speech criticising the council house programme, we were able to pick it up in the first edition of the *Evening Standard* and have our own comments extensively reported in the later editions and in radio programmes by the end of the afternoon.

In 1970 I summarised what I believed had been achieved by Shelter's pressure group activities:

Firstly, the involvement of far more people in a voluntary capacity, both in Shelter, and in many other types of housing organisations.

Second, the injection of political heat into housing. This might not have boosted the housing programme but it may have avoided even worse results than were achieved.

Third, a more enlightened public about the complexities of the housing problem should make the introduction of radical solutions more acceptable. Paradoxically, although this roused public opinion has been created largely in protest at the mediocre achievements of politicians in the past, if offers them their best opportunities from now on. Politicians who really want to get results know how to use public opinion to that end.

By 1970 Shelter was a national institution. It had raised over £3 million, it had 350 local Shelter groups, and helped to rehouse 6,000 families. It had made housing the major domestic political issue of the late Sixties. And it had provided a vehicle for the idealism of a considerable number of younger people. It had also shown that a charity could be highly effective as a spokesman for the cause, and an advocate on policies and expenditure priorities. It had demonstrated the importance of professionalism. It had pioneered a number of new techniques – the more hard-hitting advertising, the periodical reports with reinforcing advertising and direct mail, the barnstorming of local areas, the use of dynamic campaign newspapers and professional, integrated design, and the realisation of the full potential of public meetings.

The Shelter of my directorship has been criticised since for being unsophisticated in its political objectives. But housing policies by the end of the 1960s were not that unsound – there was a mix of new building with rehabilitation, security of tenure for unfurniushed tenants, proposals for extending rent subsidies to the private sector, discussion of the concept of neighbourhood rehabilitation, and we were much more humane in our approach to the homeless. The different strategies of the political parties guaranteed that a debate would continue on housing policies, and there were plenty of academics producing books and reports on housing finance, and other detailed policy issues. There is no question in my mind, therefore, that Shelter's priority should have been exactly what it was – to convey the nature of the housing problem to the majority of the population, to campaign for greater priority for housing for social as well as compassionate reasons, and to put so much steam into the issue, that no party could afford to do other than commit itself to keeping housing at the top of its agenda.

Sequel

Over 13 years have passed since I left the Directorship of Shelter. The organisation has changed dramatically in that time. One reason for this is that the system of financing the rehabilitation of older property reduced the need for an injection of charitable money. While Shelter still contributes to housing operations, a higher percentage of its expenditure is on education and on housing aid and advice. Over the years the campaign has become much more involved in the intricacies of housing finance, the workings of the Rent Act, council housing policies, and the like, and has produced some superb research reports on these subjects.

Unfortunately, after a considerable improvement in housebuilding, rehabilitation, and approaches to the homeless in the seventies, the housing problem has begun to steadily worsen in the early 1980s, not helped by the policies of the Thatcher Administration. Shelter now finds itself faced with statistics that in many cases are worse than when we launched our campaign based on the theme 'a national emergency' in 1966. Then, for instance, there were roughly 150,000 on local authority waiting lists in London – now there are well over 200,000. Shelter foresees a major housing crisis in the late 1980s with families once more split up or living in one room, with a high proportion of older housing deteriorating rapidly and families unable to spend any money on maintenance.

Shelter celebrated its fifteenth anniversary on December 1, 1981, and its present director, Neil MacIntosh, for whom I have unlimited admiration, kindly invited me to deliver a lecture to mark the occasion. We decided to extend this to a series of appearances in other major cities, and Neil and I were able to resurrect the old barnstorming approach once more. The idea of a re-look at the problem after 15 years by the first director and the current director of Shelter captured the imagination of the media. *The Times* devoted almost a full-page to a substantial extract from my lecture, illustrated with photographs.

Fifteen years after the launch of Shelter, we had come the full circle. On our trip round the country Neil said to me there was no question in his mind that Shelter would once more have to put its emphasis on housing need, and the need for greater priority for housing, rather than involve itself in too much detailed policy debate. We were on the verge of a major crisis, an emergency. We had to publicise the problem of the hidden homeless.

Did this signal the failure of the Shelter of my days, or for that matter Neil's day? No, why should it? Shelter is not *responsible* for tackling Britain's housing problem – it is merely an advocate, a participant to a small extent, and ultimately, like everybody else, a spectator on the performance of the public authority and private industry.

The question is not 'Has Shelter failed?' but rather 'What would the state of Britain's housing be if Shelter had not been there?'

What I found exciting about what Neil was saying was that 15 years after the launch of Shelter, the anger was still there, and the determination to fight was still there. In other words, Shelter has not failed in the number one requirement of a pressure group faced with a major problem . . . it still has perseverance.

6 CLEAR
– A PRESSURE GROUP
SUCCESS STORY

ON SUNDAY, 24 January 1982, a news story appeared in *The Observer*. It stated that a campaign for lead-free petrol was to be launched the following day – 'the biggest environmental campaign for years'. Although it said 'details are being kept secret', it contained just enough information to whet the appetite. The story was planted by me, a deliberate leak to convey to the rest of the media that they should take notice of a press conference that coming Monday. It was a mini-exercise in hype, but justified by events for this was the beginning of a pressure group campaign that was in 15 months to take on and defeat some of the most powerful multinational industries – the petroleum industry, the car manufacturers, the lead industry – and Ministers and civil servants and to achieve a spectacular victory with a reversal of national policy and a decision in principle to move to lead-free petrol.

In the course of the campaign almost all of the techniques outlined in this book were employed, and I tell this story not for glory but because I think it is both a useful illustration of how to run a single-issue campaign of this kind and hopefully a source of encouragement to others.

Let's start at the beginning – with the problem itself. Lead is a neurotoxin – a brain poison. Excessive exposure to lead can cause serious illness and even death. Up until fairly recently it was assumed that at everyday levels of exposure – i.e. at blood lead levels of 35 ug/dl (micrograms per decilitre) or less – no harm would be caused, and this has been the justification for its continued widespread use in paint and in water-piping, and, above all, in petrol. Recently, however, a number of scientists in different countries, including the United States, Great Britain, Australia, and Germany, have produced evidence to suggest that children could be adversely affected at much lower levels of exposure than previously realised, and are at risk of reduced IQ, learning difficulties because they are easily distracted or frustrated, and other behavioural problems at levels of 10–15 ug/dl or even less.

Now I must emphasise that the scientific world was and still is divided on the issue. There have been studies that reinforce the fears, and

Drive to end lead in petrol

A NEW drive to ban lead in petrol, is to be launched tomorrow. It promises to be the biggest environmental campaign for years, writes Geoffrey Lean.

Details are being kept secret, but the launch is thought to be supported by over 100 MPs of all parties and by most of the leading environmental groups.

Oil companies, car-makers and the lead industry are likely to be surprised at the political support secured by the organisers. It will put pressure on the Government to insist on lead-free petrol in the face of evidence that it damages children's brains.

The Government's medical advisers estimate that 'hundreds of thousands' of children are at risk. Other evidence suggests this may be a conservative estimate.

The anti-lead movement has until now been run from her home by Mrs Jill Runnette, a Wimbledon housewife, with part-time help and the backing of several academics.

After years of pressure by the movement, and a campaign in THE OBSERVER, the Government announced last May that it was reducing the maximum level of lead allowed in petrol by almost two-thirds from 0.40 to 0.15 grams per litre by 1985.

The reduction was unexpected because it followed a report by a Department of Health and Social Security committee that there was no convincing evidence that many children were harmed by lead and that little of the lead absorbed by people came from petrol.

The new campaign marks the re-emergence on the campaigning scene of Mr Des Wilson, the New Zealander who launched the housing pressure group, Shelter, 15 years ago.

Two important new studies are expected to be unveiled at tomorrow's launch, one adding to the evidence that even low levels of lead impair children's intelligence, and the other to show it is linked with still births.

The 'leak' published in The Observer *on 24 January 1982, prior to the launch of CLEAR*

studies that fail to confirm them. The issue increasingly became: could we ever achieve 'conclusive' evidence of harm? And, secondly, how many children had to be exposed to risk until the issue was scientifically settled? Those who believed that lead exposure at these lower levels did damage children, took the view that urgent action should be taken to reduce exposure. Those who were unconvinced about the dangers took the view that the necessary action did not justify the cost and inconvenience involved.

In the United States of America, the Environmental Protection Agency decided that the evidence of a *risk* to health represented sufficient grounds for action, and decided as far back as 1970 that it made sense to remove lead from petrol. There was an additional argument for this, namely, that they wished to introduce catalytic converters to cars to control other emissions and lead damages the converters. So for *both* reasons they ruled that all new cars coming on the market from 1975 should run on lead-free petrol, and that lead-free petrol should be available at all petrol stations. By now the United States is over 60 per cent lead-free and by the end of this decade it will be almost totally lead-free. Japan is now over 95 per cent lead-free. Australia has decided to introduce lead-free petrol from the mid-1980s, and many other countries are considering a similar step. Britain currently allows 0.40 grams per litre of lead in petrol, but plans to reduce to 0.15 grams per litre by 1985.

The Americans have also virtually banned lead in paint used in domestic circumstances – their maximum permitted level is 660 ppm (parts per million). In Britain, however, there are no controls whatsoever, although there is a voluntary understanding between the paint manufacturers and the authorities that there will be warning notices on all paint containing more than 5,000 ppm. The comparison is astonishing – in Britain the lead content of a tin of paint has to be over eight times that permitted in the United States before even a warning label is required!

Over the years tougher action has been taken in Britain over lead in water pipes, although there are still many old houses with leaded water pipes, and there is still some use of lead in solder.

Food can manufacturers in Britain announced in 1983 that as a result of the CLEAR campaign they were going to eliminate the use of lead in solder and in the manufacture of their product altogether.

But to return to lead in petrol, the position at the beginning of 1981 was that Britain was permitting 0.40 grams of lead per litre of petrol and the car manufacturers and the petroleum industry hoped that this would continue. There was, however, increasing concern about the health risk, much of it motivated by the Conservation Society which set up a special working party, and a small number of scientists, notably Dr Robert Stephens of the University of Birmingham and Professor Derek Bryce-Smith of the University of Reading. A report by a DHSS working party, chaired by Professor Patrick Lawther, had recommended a number of steps to reduce lead exposure but had fallen short of recommending lead-free petrol. The Minister concerned, Tom King, at the DoE, finally decided on the basis of the Lawther report and under the influence of pressure from the industries, to reject lead-free petrol, and in May 1981 he announced in the House of Commons a compromise measure, namely the reduction to 0.15 by the mid-1980s. Given the strength of the Conservative Administration, and the Lawther report, it looked as if the anti-lead lobby was defeated and the possibility of lead-free petrol in this century appeared to be virtually nil. It was hardly the best time to launch a major campaign for lead-free petrol, and yet this was the background to the launch of CLEAR.

At this point we introduce to the story Mr Godfrey Bradman. A wealthy chairman of a public company, Bradman had lived with his family in Chelsea. Always sensitive to any threat to the health of his children, he had become concerned by occasional articles he had read about the emission of lead from car exhausts, and especially about the heavy traffic in the vicinity of his home. He decided to explore the issue for himself, and went to considerable lengths, including meeting Lawther, and studying books on the subject. His conclusion was that the risk was too considerable to be ignored, and his first step was to move his family home out of the centre of London. Fortunately, Godfrey Bradman is not the kind of man to look after himself and his family and not care about anyone else. He began talking to members of the Conservation Society Working Party and others and offered to fund a fresh campaign. They advertised for a Director.

While this was happening I was employed as Deputy Editor of the *Illustrated London News*, and one of my responsibilities was to cover the affairs of the capital itself. I decided to explore the problems of pollution caused by heavy traffic. This led me to the lead question and I was directed to Bradman. He told me of his campaign and as we talked he convinced me that the problem warranted serious investigation, while I convinced him that his plans for a campaign in the 'corridors of power' were unrealistic, and that what was required was a major public campaign. It was to be the beginning of a close friendship and an effective working partnership. He persuaded me to meet his advisers who were at that time interviewing for the Director, and the end result was an invitation to me to run the campaign as its full-time chairman. I was still doubtful, however, and spent some time attempting to investigate the problem further. The more I looked at it the more it seemed to be a classic case of multinational industries with enormous economic and political power ruthlessly persisting with a potentially hazardous practice with complete indifference to its health effects, of the close relations between these industries and Whitehall so that the industrial point of view carries far greater clout than the concern of ordinary people, and of apathy and compromise instead of the kind of decisive action with a built-in bias towards the public that we should expect from the authorities we elect to protect public health. My research convinced me that there was an overwhelming case for the elimination of lead from petrol, and for measures to reduce lead in paint, and lead in water piping, because of the *risk* to children.

However, there was another point, and given the confusion over the health evidence, it was the one that finally convinced me that action should be taken. (The Royal Commission on Environmental Pollution was some two years later to give priority to the same point.) This was that lead was non-degradable. In other words, unlike many other environmental pollutants, it does not disappear eventually. It just builds up and builds up around us. We produce and add to that build-up over 3.5 million tonnes every year. Scientists have demonstrated that the lead in our bodies is already in the vicinity of 500 times higher than natural levels – that the industrial exploitation of lead has led to its widespread dissemination all over the globe so that it is in the air we breathe, in the dust the children pick up on their fingers, in the water we drink, and in our food. Even if it could be proved that children have so far not been damaged, and I doubt if that can be proved, it is clear that as more and more of this poison accumulates around us, we are building up for generations to come a legacy of pollution that will have devastating effects. There was, therefore, a long-term environmental case for action. The problem, however, was how to persuade a Government which prided itself on the 'resolute approach' to change its mind so soon after it had proudly announced what it believed to be an adequate measure. Another problem was how to overcome the resources of finance and influence of these big industries. From the start, I was convinced that there was no point in detailed argument and negotiation unless it took place from a background of overwhelming public concern. We had to politicise the issue.

We decided, therefore, on a major campaign on the health question. We would refuse to become involved in arguments with industry over the costs and technical problems of the introduction of lead-free petrol. We would simply rest our case on the fact that the Americans and the Japanese had conclusively proved that it could be done, and had done it without much additional cost or loss of energy resources. We would not allow industry to deflect the argument on to ground where they could be most effective and into territory where they controlled all of the information (or misinformation). We would argue our case on health and long-term environmental grounds alone; once the decision was taken we could involve ourselves, if necessary, in the secondary debate about how it should be done and at what cost.

This was a crucial initial decision, and throughout the 15 months of the campaign the industry tried to move us off our own ground and on to theirs, but we steadfastly refused to be drawn. I believe this policy was a key factor in our success. That decision taken, we moved to our objectives. I have explained fully (in 'A is for Aims' on pages 49–51) the importance of establishing clear and realistic objectives, and how we set about this exercise for CLEAR.

Once we had decided on the ground on which we would fight, and on our objectives, the next steps were to set up the campaign in structural and financial terms. Godfrey Bradman had been incredibly generous, making available a budget of over £100,000 to finance the launch and build-up of the campaign. Clearly few pressure groups have an advantage such as this, and I fully acknowledge that without it we could never have won as quickly as we did. I do believe we would still have achieved our objectives, but it would have taken longer and been much harder work. I have always taken the view, however, that no campaign should be dependent on only one source of income. Inevitably there is a vulnerability in that position. Therefore, I made it our aim to try to match the Bradman input with money from other sources – donations from the public, fund-raising events, contributions by other organisa- tions, grants by trusts for research, etc. I didn't achieve a 50:50 breakdown during the CLEAR campaign, but we did raise around 40 per cent of the total budget from other sources, some of it with Godfrey Bradman's help in terms of contacts or under-writing of appeals.

Finance, therefore, was not going to be a major problem in the early days, and the pre-launch period was used for research, the preparation of first-class print material, and the creation of the coalition. (The necessity and the techniques for each of these are described in Chapter 4.) We assembled filing cabinets of reports, studies, and books on lead pollution, and examined them carefully in order to demonstrate to ourselves the strength of the case, and be in a position to demonstrate it to others. We considered all of the arguments of the other side and established convincing answers. We slowly developed a solid scientific case based on the best studies, and on a relatively cautious interpretation of those studies. We were determined not to over-state the case, and in this respect we expected to compare favourably with some earlier campaigners and thus wrong-foot our opposition.

We decided to take advantage of Godfrey Bradman's generosity to produce print material of a much higher quality than would normally have been possible or necessary. The justification was that when we launched the campaign we could present our evidence in a highly impressive and professional manner in order to undermine the charge that we were just a bunch of cranks. We produced a first-class newspaper and handbook for publication at the time of the launch.

It was because of this need to destroy the image of being a small, emotional minority, that we set about building a coalition with other organisations, and compiling a list of supporters to give the campaign a substance that would make it difficult to brush aside lightly. We set up a charitable trust, and recruited such public figures as Dame Elizabeth Ackroyd, former director of the Consumer Council, trade unionist Clive Jenkins, conservationist Lord Avebury, Dr David Bellamy, Jonathan Miller, former Whitehall adviser Professor Christopher Foster, and influential journalist Sheila Black. Invitations for the launch were issued by eight national organisations. By that time we already had 130 Members of Parliament in support, for in order to achieve maximum political support from the start, we had circulated to every Member of

Parliament our objectives, together with a form for them to sign indicating their support. In addition, I went to see Dr David Owen, parliamentary leader of the SDP, and wrote to Liberal leader David Steel, and Labour leader Michael Foot, and all replied with supportive letters that we were able to quote at the launch of our campaign. We ultimately built the list of supporting MPs to well over 200 by writing a second time to those who had not replied to the first letter and even arranging for some MPs to collect signatures on our behalf.

So we came to January 1982, with the date of the launch fixed for Monday, January 25. It was in January that we received the Yellowlees letter and took the decision not to employ it at the opening press conference (see Y for Yellowlees). It did, however, enormously strengthen our confidence for it was useful to know that when we walked into the press conference on January 25 we had in our pockets a complete answer to those who might say that there was no high-level medical opinion behind the CLEAR case.

In addition to sending out invitations to the media for the press conference, we made a point of identifying those journalists who had written about the issue before, and giving them personal briefings in advance so that they would feel particularly involved and give it priority. In addition, we met with Geoffrey Lean of *The Observer*, who had been campaigning on the issue in *The Observer*'s columns for a couple of years. Geoffrey was naturally keen to publish an item on the Sunday before the launch, rather than follow the national newspapers some six days later. It is in circumstances like these where trust and understanding between a journalist and campaigner are essential. We decided it would be helpful to the campaign to have a small apparent 'leak' in *The Observer*, and provided Lean with just enough information for him to be able to build a story but not so much that journalists at the press conference the next day would feel that they had been cheated. Thus, Lean did not have the right to publish the fact that the three party leaders were supporting the campaign, or that the number of MPs involved was in fact approaching 140, or the precise objectives of the campaign, or the details of two additional studies we were publicising at the launch. He was, however, able to hint that there was considerable political support, and to say that two studies would be published. Thus, all sides were happy; we got the necessary build-up to our campaign; Lean got the exclusive story about the forthcoming launch of the campaign; and none of the media the following day felt that the story had been pre-empted.

The press conference took place in a building in Westminster Square at 11.00 am on Monday, January 25, and for an hour beforehand we were giving radio and television interviews. It was well-attended and the publicity was widespread. We were under way.

On the same day as the press conference we mailed to all Members of

Parliament, and to other organisations and influential parties, copies of the handbook and the newspaper.

Not only did we receive widespread news coverage, but also considerable support in leading articles, both in national and provincial newspapers. *The Guardian* in a leader stated 'When there is such widespread feeling in favour of a reform, and a cleaner air bonus at the end of it, the government can be accused of obstinacy – and worse – in selecting this question as one on which to dig in its heels'. *The Observer* stated that Ministers should 'insist that new cars sold by 1985 – or soon after – should use leadless fuel . . . unless overwhelming new evidence emerges to show that there is no danger to children. Their health, and their future contribution to the country must have priority over all other considerations'.

By now we had created a small, united and professional team to run the campaign. We had taken a small, top-floor office in a building near King's Cross, staffed by myself, and by two colleagues, Susan Dibb, administrator of the campaign, and Patricia Simms, who acted as research assistant/PA. Our two top volunteer helpers and advisers were Dr Robin Russell Jones and Dr Robert Stephens. The latter, as I have mentioned, had been campaigning on the issue for some time, and his speciality was the environmental build-up of lead. Robin Russell Jones, who like Godfrey Bradman had moved his family out of London because of the problem, had made an extensive study of the health evidence. Throughout the campaign these two were to advise and speak on these two subjects, leaving the politics to me.

Immediately after the London launch the three of us set off on a provincial tour, holding receptions and making presentations in Coventry, Birmingham, Manchester, Liverpool, Leeds, Newcastle, Bristol, Southampton, and Cardiff. These cities were chosen because they are media centres, each with television stations covering the surrounding counties. The aim of the provincial tours was to achieve widespread publicity throughout the country at local level, meet local environmental health officers and others and inform them of our activities, and to build up local support and identify people who could represent the campaign at local level. (See B for Barnstorming on pages 54–55.)

While we were on the tour, we watched closely what was happening in the national media, where the petroleum industry and car manufacturers were trying to fight back, either with scare stories about the cost of lead-free petrol, or claims that there was no health hazard. On February 3 we were in Liverpool and it was there that we decided the time was coming to play our trump card – the Yellowlees letter. (The full story of the leak of the Yellowlees letter has been told in Y for Yellowlees on pages 131–5.) The impact was beyond my wildest dreams. *The Times* news story, and my article opposite the leader page,

Secret letter reveals risk to children of lead in petrol

By George Brock

A remarkable confidential letter written by the Government's leading medical adviser to several Whitehall chiefs last year reveals for the first time his fears about the dangers to children's health from lead in petrol.

Sir Henry Yellowlees, Chief Medical Officer at the Department of Health and Social Security, gave a warning in the letter that "there is a strong likelihood that lead in petrol is permanently reducing the IQ of many of our children".

The letter, which has been passed to *The Times* by the campaign for lead-free air (CLEAR), discloses fears which have been voiced in Whitehall while the Government's official announcements on the subject have been considerably more neutral. Contacted over the weekend, Sir Henry declined to comment.

"There is no doubt", the letter says, "that the simplest and quickest way of reducing general population exposure to lead is by reducing sharply or by entirely eliminating lead in petrol." Sir Henry adds that "some hundreds of thousands of children" are affected by the risk.

The letter, which Sir Henry describes as "an unusual step", was written at the height of the battle in Whitehall last year over whether lead in petrol should be reduced, or even completely removed.

Liquid lead is added to petrol to boost the octane rating and to improve its efficiency; governments have progressively reduced the maximum permitted levels over the past decade. Two months after Sir Henry's letter was written, the Government announced that the maximum level was to be reduced by 1985 from 0.40 grams per litre to 0.15 grams.

It was a sharper reduction than the one favoured by the Treasury and the Department of Energy, who had argued that such a change would add several pence to the price of a gallon of petrol and had pressed for a small cut of 0.40 to 0.35 grams per litre. But the announcement was attacked by critics who said that the Government should have gone further and declared an intention to eliminate lead completely. Whitehall sources said last night that Sir Henry's views were well known at the time of the Government's decision and had been one of several factors affecting the outcome.

Sir Henry's letter makes it clear he was no longer willing to accept the conclusions of the Lawther Report, a study prepared by a DHSS working party and published in 1980, which challenged the evidence linking lead and brain damage.

In an appendix to his letter he lists fresh evidence which is "accumulating all the time —and it always points in the same direction as the existing evidence, so that the health and stronger."

He describes research being carried out at an EEC laboratory at Ispro in Italy: "Evidence just arrived at my Department indicates that petrol lead may contribute on average about 27 per cent of total blood lead in adults, from all sources (including food), and about 40 per cent of total blood lead in children".

This conclusion does not yet appear to have been accepted by Ministers. Mr Giles Shaw, Under-Secretary at the Department of the Environment in charge of the lead pollution programme, said in a letter to Mr Ernie Roberts, Labour MP for Hackney, North and Stoke Newington, two months ago that petrol lead contributed "less than 10 per cent on average" of blood lead.

Mr Des Wilson, chairman of CLEAR, said last night : "If the Yellowlees letter had been made public at the time, the Government could not possibly have taken the decision that it did." Mr Jeff Rooker, Labour MP for Birmingham, Perry Barr, said last night that he intended to ask whether the decision on lead levels had been taken with the benefit of Sir Henry's assessment.

The lead level set for British petrol by the end of 1985 will bring Britain into line with other EEC countries, but anti-lead campaigners are still pressing the Government to follow the initiative of Japan, the Soviet Union, Australia and the United States, which have all taken steps to eliminate lead entirely.

All Australian cars sold after 1985 will run on lead-free petrol.

Text of letter, page 2
Des Wilson, page 8

The front page news story in The Times *that revealed the now-famous Yellowlees letter*

set the rest of the media off, and that night the *Evening Standard* published a leader supporting the campaign. By Tuesday, the matter was on the floor of the House of Commons and the Prime Minister herself was faced with the issue by both David Steel and Michael Foot. Up to this point the CLEAR campaign had been well-received; after the publication of the Yellowlees letter it became a genuinely popular cause, with letters of support and money flooding in, and almost 100 per cent media backing. The number of MPs who had signed up as supporters increased dramatically.

It was crucial to maintain the momentum. Back in 1981 Bradman had commissioned the City firm of Coopers and Lybrand to look at the issue and I had for some time had their report. Its value was not only the view that it would have been possible to introduce lead-free petrol, but also the company's reputation – no-one could possibly describe such a reputable company as emotive. Nevertheless, and perhaps injudiciously from the company's point of view, the authors of the report had actually stated that not to take every reasonable precaution would be 'criminal'. So a few days after the publication of the Yellowlees letter, I called a small press conference in my office for just five newspapers, and a representative of the PA, and briefed them on the Coopers and Lybrand report and gave them a copy. Reports appeared in all the main national newspapers and all over the country and once more lead-free petrol was in the news.

What was happening was a bandwagon effect: first the launch of the campaign, then the Yellowlees letter, then the Coopers and Lybrand report – the impression was of an irresistible force building up. We worked hard to maintain this momentum. The next step was to persuade a Conservative Member of the European Parliament, Stanley Johnson, who was on the European Parliament Environmental Committee, to table a motion calling for lead-free petrol and the CLEAR objectives. The publication of this, and the suggestion that the issue would now become a European one, attracted another round of publicity. About this time we took our full-page ad in *The Observer*, and this not only raised money and developed our list of supporters still further, but also led to several radio and television producers and other journalists deciding they wanted to take a closer look at the issue. Thus we achieved even more publicity.

While all this was going on, we had commissioned the MORI organisation to conduct an opinion poll (see O for Opinion Polls on pages 99–102) and when Bob Worcester, the Chairman of MORI, telephoned me, he said even he could hardly believe the results. 'They are some of the most decisive figures I have ever seen,' he told me. And indeed they were – nine out of ten people wanted lead out of petrol, and 77 per cent said they wanted action even if petrol prices went up by 'a few pence per gallon'. (See O for Opinion Polls on pages 99–102 for details of the arrangement we made for its publication in *The Observer*.) That Saturday night I was in the centre of London and, knowing *The Observer* could be purchased at that time, I picked one up. I quickly looked at the front page and could see no report on our opinion poll. I looked at the other news pages and it wasn't there either. I could hardly believe it. Had we been let down? I looked back at the front page and then realised why I had missed it – it was the *front page lead* and even I had not expected that. I had not even looked at the main headline on the front page. By now BBC Radio was leading its news with the story from *The Observer*, and all the national newspapers ran results of the poll the following Monday. *The Observer* leader said 'The poll . . . vindicates the campaign's objectives and pays tribute to the skill with which it is being conducted. . . . The one substantial question for the government to resolve is whether society is prepared to accept some inconvenience to the car industry and a few more pence on a gallon of petrol to protect its children. After today's poll there can be no further doubt that it is, and the government should hesitate no longer.' *The Guardian* also ran a leader in support. *The Daily Telegraph* headed its story with the fact that the government was 'losing the argument'.

We had now succeeded in maintaining the momentum for over six weeks and both the industries and the government must have wondered how long we could sustain it. It was an issue that concerned me as well. However, a campaign can create its own luck, and the bandwagon effect had been such that it almost developed its own momentum. We were given a boost by the disclosure that the Board of Science of the British Medical Association had voiced its concern: 'The Board believes that all sources of lead pollution should be eliminated wherever possible'. Then we received another leak – this time a British Petroleum internal briefing document that actually disclosed that oil companies had secretly recommended lead-free petrol a year earlier and their offer had been declined by the authorities. We were also helped by the staggering incompetence of our main opponents, the Associated Octel Company, who persisted in getting different members of the staff to write letters to *The Financial Times* and *The Guardian* raising the issue and presenting their case. This simply set up opportunities for us to reply, and thus they helped sustain the debate and controversy.

At this point it is worth pausing to examine how the opposition reacted to our campaign. Perhaps their biggest blunder occurred before the campaign was even launched. In early November 1981 we wrote to ten leading British oil companies stating that we were 'concerned about the growing body of evidence of a serious health hazard arising from the use of lead in petrol' and seeking further clarification of the individual companies' position, and the answers to a number of technical questions. We also requested that the companies meet a deputation to discuss the issue further. Had they been well advised, they would have answered the questions honestly, even knowing that the answers would be unsatisfactory, and would have received a deputation. It was no secret that a campaign was planned, and this offered them the opportunity to make acquaintance with the campaigners, to seek to achieve some dialogue or minimal common ground, or at least communicate their point of view. Instead, not one of the companies would answer the questions or meet the deputation; every one of the ten companies wrote an almost identical letter saying that we would be answered by the UK Petroleum Industry Association. The Association took ten weeks to reply and their answer was a public relations brush-off.

This was a disastrous error for the petroleum industry, for throughout our campaign we were able to demonstrate that we had attempted to establish a dialogue and to hear the industrial case, and been denied adequate answers or an audience. This, together with the unanswerable evidence that this response was orchestrated, strengthened our charges that the industry was only concerned to organise a cover-up. The petroleum industry did not help itself by its panicky claims of the high cost of lead-free petrol, often contradicted by other companies, and undoubtedly contradicted by the American and Japanese experience. Nor was it helped by the leak that showed it had recommended lead-free petrol and then for a year kept quiet about it.

On the whole, the petroleum industry tried to avoid the health debate altogether, claiming that this was not within their area of expertise. CLEAR replied that no manufacturer or producer had the right to adopt a position of neutrality on the safety of its product. As I wrote in *The Lead Scandal*, 'It has a responsibility to be fully involved, to explore the health risk it creates, and to enter the debate on it. If it does not, it is in effect saying that its concern is the making of money, and responsibility for the health of human beings belongs elsewhere. No individual, no company, can properly assume such a position.'

On the whole the petroleum industry was happy to leave the Associated Octel Company, manufacturers of the lead additives, to fight the battle on its behalf. Associated Octel's early response to CLEAR was to produce its own print material claiming there was no problem, and quoting all sorts of people out of context. For instance, the *British Medical Journal* had published a leader stating 'The BMJ believes there is a good case for removing lead from petrol; the metal is certainly toxic, and while the worldwide trend is towards lead-free petrol Britain would be wise to follow.' It then went on to say that it believed '. . . decisions on issues of this kind should be taken on the basis of reliable scientific evidence, not emotional propaganda'. Associated Octel frequently quoted these last words out of context, implying that the BMJ either had no view on the issue or opposed a ban on lead in petrol. The opposite was the case for it twice published leading articles supporting the elimination of lead from petrol.

In its print material, Associated Octel quoted a number of so-called scientists, most notably its medical officer for over 30 years, as authorities on lead and health, but failed to answer any of the four major studies on health risks that were the basis of the CLEAR campaign. In fact, it did not even refer to any of them or their authors in some of its brochures.

Associated Octel claimed to spend a fortune on 'objective research' into lead and health, but self-exposed these claims as untrue when it put a letter to workers on factory notice-boards stating that in answer to proposals for reductions of lead in petrol 'the company's activities over a wide field covering government departments, *research establishments*, contacts with MPs, etc., *to resist these proposals* have been known from time to time through our established consultative channels' (my italics). Associated Octel did its best to discover CLEAR's plans and when we were making a provincial tour it telephoned local television and radio stations seeking equal time. This, incidentally, we welcomed, because these encounters inevitably were beneficial to CLEAR rather than Associated Octel.

Associated Octel also organised a series of lunches at Locketts Restaurant in London at which it sought to persuade MPs over lunch of the weakness of our case. The company even took over one of the most expensive restaurants in Strasburg to wine and dine Euro-MPs.

All of the industries kept up the same series of charges: that our campaign was 'emotional'; that there was no evidence to link low level lead exposure with health; that the costs and technical difficulties would be too great. We countered these by saying that rather than being emotional, we were presenting scientific material in a scientific context coolly and factually; we countered their charge that there was no evidence by developing a slide show for audiences and detailed print material demonstrating the studies, their methodology and results; we countered the 'cost' argument with our own survey of petrol prices in America. We established that on the American experience petrol prices would increase by between one and two per cent in Britain if we moved to lead-free petrol.

In April we received a breakthrough in the scientific argument in the form of two major studies, both of them supportive of our position. The first, a massive study in the US, showed that by the time 55 per cent of the lead had been eliminated from petrol in America, blood lead levels across the country as a whole had fallen by 37 per cent. Statistical analysis of the studies, and interpretation by experts on behalf of the Environmental Protection Agency, led to the conclusion that the key factor in the reduction in blood-lead levels was the reduction in lead in petrol. This helped to demolish the case of the industries that petrol-lead was not the main contributor to body lead burdens. Our case in this respect was further boosted by the first results of an Italian study. This, took showed a clear relationship between petrol-lead and lead in blood. We worked hard to publicise these studies and achieved a major article in *The Sunday Times* and also news stories in other publications.

(It is, incidentally, worth noting that this is one of the benefits that pressure groups offer. Had CLEAR not existed, it is doubtful whether knowledge of these international studies would have ever been communicated in Britain. Assuming that the information was acquired by the British authorities at all, they would have had no incentive to publish it. The industries would not have published it. And thus it would never have been known.)

With the help of contacts within the Labour Party, we were able to place before Labour's NEC a powerful document on the effects of lead in petrol, and the NEC decided unanimously to support lead-free petrol. As the Falklands crisis was breaking, this was not picked up by political writers, but once more we were able to demonstrate how a pressure group can make sure that such initiatives do not go without notice. We tipped off friends in national newspapers and widespread publicity was achieved for the Labour decision.

By now the campaign had been going for nearly four months and we came to one of the main events on our campaign calendar – our three-day international symposium on lead and health. From the start we knew we would stand or fall on our ability to give respectability to the medical and scientific case, and this was our main throw. We had raised the money, including a £15,000 donation by a food company, to invite to Britain all of the scientists who had produced major studies on lead and health, and we now invited everyone concerned with the issue in Britain to come to a symposium to hear reports on the studies, and to cross-examine the researchers. We invited representatives of the different Ministries involved, all of the members of the Lawther Committee, environmental health officers, the scientific media, and advertised it widely, so that representatives of the petroleum industry, and Associated Octel, figured in the audience as well. We set the whole symposium up to the standards that would be expected of a high-quality scientific symposium. However, we still had to overcome the possible charge that the conference was loaded in support of our case. We therefore decided to seek a chairman about whom that charge could not possibly be made. The ideal candidate was Professor Michael Rutter, perhaps the leading child phychiatrist in the world, and a member of the Lawther Committee. To our surprise he accepted the invitation.

We had taken a substantial gamble. If, after hearing all the evidence, this distinguished scientist concluded there was no health hazard, it would be a major set-back and mean that all the money we had invested had been wasted. Thus we genuinely put the evidence on the line, trusting in the integrity of this respected scientist, but above all, trusting in the strength of our case. It is no exaggeration to say that when Rutter rose to his feet to summarise the conference we felt that he had it within his capacity at that moment to substantially boost our chances of success or set them back, perhaps beyond redemption. What happened is perhaps best independently described – by Geoffrey Lean in his article in *The Observer* the following Sunday:

Last week's call (for lead-free petrol) by Professor Michael Rutter, one of the world's leading child psychiatrists, has made a strong impact. Professor Rutter is a member of the Committee most respected in Whitehall and officials have frequently pointed to his signature on the Lawther report as showing that there is no need for a ban. His statement signals that the weight of medical opinion has now moved behind a ban. This is the result of a bold gamble by CLEAR. . . . It invited Professor Rutter to chair the symposium, not knowing whether he had changed his mind since signing the Lawther report, but confident that he would make up his mind on the evidence. To experts in the audience the meeting took on the atmosphere of a tribunal rather than a symposium, with Professor Rutter keenly questioning each speaker. By the end of the three day conference most were expecting a cautious and qualified endorsement of lead-free fuel. But after a thoughtful 5,000 word review of the evidence, Professor Rutter called trenchantly and unequivocally for immediate action.

He described the reduction announced by the Government last year as an unacceptable compromise without clear advantages and with definite disadvantages. He added 'The evidence suggests that the removal of lead from petrol would have a quite substantial effect in reducing lead pollution, and the costs are quite modest by any reasonable standard.'

In passing he demolished many of the basic arguments of the Lawther Committee's report. . . . His statement demolishes the entire platform on which the Government has stood. And, even worse for Ministers, it is not an isolated event. A substantial number of the Lawther Committee's members have now come to similar conclusions.

The Committee has split into hard-line opponents of a ban, many of whom failed even to reply to invitations to the symposium, and others who are moved towards recommending a ban. Five of the 12 members attended the meeting.

Unfortunately, the Falklands War was now under way and even the CLEAR campaign could not compete with that for editorial space. The symposium did not get the publicity it otherwise would have done, but nevertheless it had been a major set-back for all of our opponents, and we finally took a break and breather for the summer, more than content that we had won every battle in the war so far and were immeasurably strengthened by the experience.

Over the summer, we considered what we had achieved: First, from the small number of organisations declared as supporters at the beginning, we had experienced almost a landslide of support, so that in my book *The Lead Scandal* I was able to show the line-up after six months as follows:

Supporting lead in petrol	*Calling for a ban on lead in petrol*
DoE Minister Giles Shaw and his civil servants	The Labour Party
Health Minister Kenneth Clarke and his civil servants	The Liberal Party
Transport Minister Lynda Chalker and her civil servants	The Social Democratic Party
The petroleum industry	The Scottish National Party
The car manufacturers	The Ecology Party
The lead industry	Over 100 local authorities
Associated Octel	The National Consumer Council

Supporting lead in petrol

DoE Minister Giles Shaw and his civil servants

Health Minister Kenneth Clarke and his civil servants

Transport Minister Lynda Chalker and her civil servants

The petroleum industry

The car manufacturers

The lead industry

Associated Octel

Calling for a ban on lead in petrol

The Labour Party

The Liberal Party

The Social Democratic Party

The Scottish National Party

The Ecology Party

Over 100 local authorities

The National Consumer Council

The Consumers' Association

The National Society for Clean Air

The Institution of Environmental Health Officers

The Trades Union Congress (representing 11 million trade unionists)

The National Association of Health Authorities

The National Association of Head Teachers

The Inner London Education Authority

The National Association of Youth Clubs

The National Association of Women's Clubs

The Advisory Centre for Education

The Association of Directors of Social Services

The Association of Neighbourhood Councils

CALIP

The Association of Community Health Councils for England and Wales

The Cleaner London Campaign

The Conservation Society

Friends of the Earth

The Health Visitors Association

The London Amenity and Transport Association

The Pedestrians Association

The Spastics Society

Calling for a ban on lead in petrol
Transport 2000
The National Children's Centre
The Rambler's Association
The West Indian Standing
  Conference
200 Members of Parliament
Over 50 Members of the House
  of Lords
60% of GPs (*Doctor* magazine poll)
90% of British public (MORI poll)
The Times
The Observer
The Guardian
The London Evening Standard
Doctor magazine
World Medicine
New Scientist
The British Medical Journal

Second, all of the medical and scientific evidence that had emerged since the launch had been supportive of our case, and we had now drawn to our side such scientists as Rutter, and thus achieved genuine medical and scientific respectability.

Third, we had shown that this relatively narrow issue could remain in the forefront of attention month after month provided one had sufficient ideas for action, and worked hard enough to do it.

We were now a highly respectable cause, both in terms of acceptance of our argument, and in terms of our status, and the next step was to return with vigour in the Autumn and surprise both Ministers and the industries with our stamina on the issue – our ability to keep them on the defensive and to keep hitting until eventually they simply could not withstand the pressure. But how?

First, we decided on a number of fresh studies. We sent a detailed questionnaire to all environmental health officers on local authority monitoring practice. Second, we sent a van, manned by Friends of the Earth pollution consultant, Brian Price, and an assistant, to schools in cities around the country, to collect dust samples from playgrounds and pavements. This achieved widespread publicity wherever it went, while at the same time providing evidence of the relationship between lead emitted from car exhausts and lead in the vicinity of school buildings. Third, we raised the money from a trust to finance a study of lead in vegetables grown in allotments and gardens in London. The aim of the experience was to see whether the lead levels in vegetables in areas of higher traffic density was higher than the lead levels in outer suburbs.

Second, we planned a major assault on the party conferences. Fringe meetings were fixed for each, and material dispersed widely. As a member of the Liberal Party, I was able to move a resolution at the Assembly, with full television coverage and widespread publicity the following day. We launched our autumn campaign with a press conference attended by Gerald Kaufman, Shadow Cabinet Environmental Spokesman, who irrevocably committed Labour to a ban on lead. At the same press conference we unveiled our survey of local authorities showing that 85 per cent of those that had taken a policy decision on lead in petrol supported the drive to have it eliminated. We also published the results of our survey into monitoring.

About the same time Associated Octel demonstrated their extraordinary capacity to score own goals. They spent a small fortune on full-page ads in all of the major national newspapers presenting their case under the absurd heading 'The Health and Wealth of the Nation'. This proved totally counter-productive. First, it was so hopelessly inaccurate that it actually led to condemnation by the Advertising Standards Authority who upheld a considerable number of public complaints. Second, I was able to write to newspapers like *The Observer* and *The Sunday Times* and have letters published pointing out the errors and putting our alternative case. Third, it actually contributed to drawing widespread attention to the issue without achieving any credibility for Associated Octel. They had effectively spent over £100,000 giving us new issue-visibility and momentum that we possibly could not have achieved without them. With enemies like this, we thought, who needed friends?

We had worked to make sure that the TUC would also pass a resolution for lead-free petrol and this also achieved widespread publicity.

Undoubtedly the Autumn campaign came as a blow to the petroleum industry and the car manufacturing industry, who had hoped as a result of the summer break that we had lost momentum. I have been reliably told that the petroleum industry, who after all are the owners of Associated Octel, were furious at the latter's clumsy advertising campaign. We still, however, had one or two moves up our sleeve for the autumn, for we had been working hard to persuade the consumer bodies to launch a European campaign. Earlier in the year I had travelled to Brussels and met Tony Venables, of BEUC (European Bureau of Consumer Unions) and Hubert David, then Director of the European Environmental Bureau, and presented them with the evidence of harm by lead in petrol and the need for action. For the first time ever, these two organisations decided to launch a joint campaign across the whole of Europe on the issue, and I travelled to Brussels several times to help plan this campaign. It was decided to launch it in all the major European capitals on the same day, and I attended the main launch in Brussels, whilst one of the CLEAR Committee members went to the London launch. This once more achieved considerable publicity in Britain.

So came Christmas, and the New Year, and the campaign was one year old. We were aware that the Royal Commission on Environmental Pollution had decided to study the issue. This concerned us, because at least three members of the Commission had always been on the opposite side in the scientific debate. Furthermore, the Commission had indicated that they would not reopen the question of health damage explored by the Lawther Committee. We decided, therefore, there was a risk of a whitewash and that this should be anticipated in two ways: first, we should make clear in advance our concern about the Royal Commission so that if its conclusions were unsatisfactory, we could not be said to have condemned them after the event simply because they did not share our view; second, we would mount a sufficiently powerful campaign prior to publication of its report to balance any impact that a negative report might make.

(Given the ultimate conclusions of the Royal Commission, we clearly did it an injustice, although it has to be said that we have every reason to believe that the three people who we distrusted were in fact the main advocates of an alternative Commission conclusion. I believe our tactics were correct, with one exception. In my book, *The Lead Scandal*, due to be published shortly before the Royal Commission reported, I perhaps overstated our justification for anticipating a whitewash. At our press conference after the publication of the Royal Commission report, in the presence of its chairman, I made a point of saying how pleased I was to be able to admit I had been in error.)

The proceedings of our 1982 symposium were being published in March 1983 and I met Professor Rutter, who had co-edited the proceedings with Robin Russell Jones, to discuss his position, in the light of his conclusions at the symposium. He said he felt able to make a further intervention on the issue, provided it was in a suitably scientific setting, and we decided to stage a special lecture by him to mark the publication of the book. Rutter on that occasion pointedly, although not by name, criticised the over-stating of the health damage by Derek Bryce-Smith, but also made clear that this criticism did not in his view extend to CLEAR. He went on to argue even more forcibly that the evidence justified the elimination of lead from petrol.

Roger Ratcliffe, of *The Sunday Times*, another journalist with a splendid record on this particular issue, then persuaded Dr Richard Lansdown, another controversial scientist on the issue, to say that he felt the evidence now justified action, and *The Sunday Times* made the story of the conversion of Rutter and Lansdown their front page lead on March 6. The following day *The Times* published a letter signed by a number of leading politicians, scientists, and trade union leaders, and general secretaries of supporting organisations, calling for action.

However, we were now about to play the two cards provided by the research we had commissioned six months earlier. The first was the result of our survey of lead in dust outside schools all over the country. These were sufficiently high to achieve considerable national publicity, and even more at local level. Many local newspapers made it their front page headlines. The result was fresh uproar. A few days later we held a press conference to publish the result of the investigation into lead in vegetables by Dr Brian Davies of the University College, Wales. He had found that 40 per cent of land in inner London and 20 per cent in outer London was unsuitable for growing vegetables and we fielded at the same press conference the senior medical consultant for the Automobile Association, Dr James Bevan, who underlined the health risk. The lead-in-vegetables study caused another uproar. It was the front-page lead in London's *Evening Standard*.

There is no question that by this time it had become clear to senior people in the Conservative Administration that they were faced with a campaign of pressure they simply seemed unable to combat. The industries had virtually conceded defeat, and it was being acknowledged that whereas they could have withstood the scientific case that had been accumulated if it had not been reinforced by a pressure group, and they could have survived the activities of a pressure group if not supported by scientific evidence, the combination was unbeatable.

Now things began to move swiftly. Firstly, the Royal Commission concluded that it should recommend the elimination of lead from

The CLEAR lead-testing unit achieved massive publicity as the campaign moved to its climax

petrol, and this was reported to Tom King, now Secretary of State, and Giles Shaw, the junior Minister who had from the start handled the affair so badly from the Government's point of view. At the same time, influential people close to the Prime Minister were suggesting to her that with an election pending, it was foolish to be so isolated on the wrong side of an argument about the health of children. There is little question that Downing Street indicated to Tom King that a face-saving solution would be helpful, and that Tom King seized upon the Royal Commission report for that solution.

It is noteworthy that the previous report by the Royal Commission on Environmental Pollution on air pollution had to wait seven years for a governmental response, and the response was basically negative. Thus a Royal Commission report on its own was hardly likely to influence the Government; what made the difference was that the Government was actually looking for a way out of the corner into which Giles Shaw and some civil servants had backed it.

Geoffrey Lean of *The Observer* had been diligently exploring the activities of the Royal Commission and on April 3 reported that their report, to be published on April 18, would in fact come down on the side of CLEAR. By then the decision had probably been taken at Ministerial level to move to lead-free petrol and from CLEAR's point of view it was not a day too soon, because the campaign was about to face its first set-back. It had its origins in research commissioned two years previously on the links between low level lead exposure and health. Unfortunately the research had been given to scientists who were members of the Lawther Committee, or who were part of a group who had publicly consistently denied the strength of the evidence on the issue. CLEAR had consistently warned for over a year that this research would have no standing in the campaign's eyes. In fact it did identify an IQ deficit in children with higher lead levels, but attempted to show that there were other probable reasons, such as social class, for this.

The DoE, still at civil service level fighting their battle with CLEAR, took the unusual step of releasing their version of the evidence plus their interpretation of it. Once more the value of a pressure group was made apparent, because when CLEAR was telephoned by the newspapers, we were able to quickly react by condemning the way the material was being released to create the impression that the reports wholly supported the DoE view when they did not. As a result, the Government was angered to find headlines 'Government delivers verdict without releasing studies' in *The Guardian* and 'Lead reports cause fury' in *The Birmingham Post* with the stories largely dominated by our protest about the way the research was being manipulated by DoE public relations people.

The fact that at this point the already-taken Ministerial decision to move to lead-free petrol was restricted to Downing Street and Tom

King was reflected in the fact that on April 9 Lynda Chalker, junior Transport Minister, in the House of Commons, was still arguing that exhaust filters were the best way to move to lead-free petrol. However, on the weekend of April 16–17, the Government moved to make it clear that they were going to accept the Royal Commission's recommendations the following Monday. The fact that Mrs Thatcher was now personally involved was demonstrated by the breadth of the leaks and references such as that in the *Mail on Sunday* that 'the decision by Mrs Thatcher and other Ministers effectively steals some of Labour's political clothes', and in *The News of the World*, 'Premier Margaret Thatcher has decided to respond swiftly to a Royal Commission report'.

At 2.30 pm on Monday, April 18, Professor Richard Southwood, chairman of the Royal Commission on Environmental Pollution, duly published his report at a press conference and called for the elimination of lead from petrol. I was in the Strangers Gallery in the House of Commons at 3.30 pm that afternoon to hear Tom King accept that recommendation and announce that the Government would press for a European-wide ban on lead in petrol. 'Rout of stout party: Environmental Minister seen heading for the policy hills with the Royal Commission on Environmental Pollution and CLEAR, The Campaign for Lead-free Air in full pursuit' said *The Guardian* in a leader the

10 THE GUARDIAN

The long haul to get lead out of petrol

Rout of stout party: environment ministers seen heading with the Royal Commissital Pollution and Clear-Lead-free Air—in full p King, the Environment his statement yesterday debate about whether phased out of petrol that remains is the when. That is a welcome step forward argued before on so man the balance of likelihood lead emitted from car a rent a significant heal children, with consequ probably include lower i many propositions in the and beyond, the link is able. Though it is straig lish correlations, as re abundantly done, betwee blood lead levels, and l levels and intelligence, m not prove causality. At s the correlations become r sistent that presumption policy action, and that p passed. Britain already behind Japan and the U matter.

could be arranged in the circumstances. The Government, after the Lawther Report, did proceed to implement a new limit of 0.15 grammes of lead per litre by the end of 1983, compared with the old limit of 0.4 grammes. That was the speediest way to reduce blood lead level. The policy lacuna came because the lower limit still leaves lead at some quarter of the danger level, when we tolerate other toxins at no more than one tenth the danger level, and because, until now, no further action was contemplated.

The Environment team should now be

Cheer at lead ban in petrol

by David Utting

THE Government last night announced the advent of lead-free petrol — but failed to set a timetable for the change.

The move was hailed as "complete vindication" of an 18-month fight for the Campaign for Lead-Free Air to protect children from the effects of lead pollution.

Campaign chairman Mr Des Wilson said: "There can be no doubt that this is a triumph for the mobilised concern and determination of the parents of this country over the power of multi-national companies and the obstinacy of ministers and bureaucrats."

But oil and motor industry spokesmen said lead-free petrol would cost "a few pence more" at the pumps and would make new cars £50-£80 dearer and at least five per cent "thirstier" while slightly reducing engine performance.

Des Wilson

Tom King

The announcement came just one hour after the Royal Commission on Environmental Pollution pointed to the dangers of lead and called for a banning of lead additives by 1990 at the latest.

In a Commons statement, Environment Secretary Mr Tom King said there was no conclusive evidence that present lead levels in the environment damaged the health of children or adults in Bri-

tain. But he said the Government was committed to improving safety margins.

The Royal Commission also recommended that all motor vehicles should be redesigned to run on lead-free petrol from an early date.

"The Royal Commission estimates that the cost of this change be small in relation to likely gains in fuel efficiency over the

next few years," said Mr King.

But he insisted that the motor industry was organised on a European basis and that legislation on lead-free petrol would require EEC agreement.

The Government would be seeking to start negotiations with Britain's European partners as soon as possible. "We shall also, of course, discuss with the United Kingdom oil and motor industries a timetable for the introduction of unleaded petrol" he said.

Mr King added that lead levels in Britain were low and dropping. The Government had already acted two years ago by requiring lead levels in petrol of 0.15 grammes per litre by 1985.

But Opposition spokesman, Mr Gerald Kaufman, accused the Government of "far too leisurely" a response. There should have been an immediate change to lead-free petrol for new vehicles, he said.

Octel jobs threat
by Keith Ely

THE go-ahead for lead-free petrol could have major implications for Associated Octel which employs 120 at its plant in Anglesey.

The Ellesmere Port-based company is the UK's sole manufacturer of lead alkyls — the compound used for giving petrol its octane rating.

In a guarded response yesterday a spokesman said the firm would be making its own detailed study of the implications for the future.

"Octel believes the Government will continue to make its decision on this issue on the basis of reliable scientific evidence and evaluation and the company will continue to adopt a responsible attitude to the Government in its policies and legislation," he added.

The company has sai'd in the past that the alleged risks to general health remain unproved. It has also developed a filter which attaches to exhaust to trap lead particles but this has failed to attract much response from vehicle manufacturers.

Lead: put the ban in top gear

by Des Wilson

The Government decision to accept the advice of the Royal Commission on Environmental Pollution that lead should be phased out of petrol is very welcome. Equally important, the Government and the multi-national industries should learn the crucial lessons from this controversy.

The first is that people place a much higher priority on environmental protection than the authorities and industry realize. The Royal Commission took up the issue only because of public concern, though ministers initially treated this concern with arrogance and assumed that it would soon blow over. One of the real gains from the success of the campaign to eliminate lead from petrol is that environmental issues generally will now be placed higher on the political agenda.

The second lesson is that there are limits to the role of scientific research in policy making. It has become clear that the advice given early in 1981 by Whitehall's own Chief Medical Officer, Sir Henry Yellowlees, was prophetic – "Truly conclusive evidence may be unobtainable and it is therefore doubtful whether there is anything to be gained by deferring a decision until the results of further research become available."

The public have now demonstrated that they expect decisions to be taken on the basis of prudence, and where the evidence of risk is substantial, as in this case, they expect the necessary action and will pay the price.

That said, I do not believe the issue of lead-in-petrol is completely resolved. First, the Royal Commission says that lead-free

petrol should be available by 1990 at the latest. This really will not do. Either the Royal Commission's call for "a substantially greater safety margin for the population as a whole" is justified, or it is not. If it is, then a definite and earlier date should be fixed. To parents of babies born this year and next, 1990 and the promise of greater safety for the next generation of children is hardly satisfactory.

We do not want to see the petroleum or car manufacturing industry harmed any more than is necessary to make their products pollution-free. They must be given reasonable time to make the transition. But we are concerned that they will try to create all sorts of technical and economic obstacles to early action.

Already, their view of the costs and problems involved contrasts sharply with that of the Royal Commission. The Campaign for Lead-Free Air (Clear) does not have the benefit of its opponents' technical and propaganda resources, but nevertheless believes that those costs and difficulties were exaggerated. There is no question where the Royal Commission stands: "The most practical means of eliminating lead would marginally increase overall energy demand if other factors were assumed to remain constant. But by the time the changeover takes place, any such energy penalty, besides being small in absolute terms, would be complete continuing improvements in

and fuel economy. On a national basis it is highly improbable that removing lead would be reflected in any higher absolute expenditure and the impact on the individual motorist would be very small".

The Royal Commission recommends that ministers should call in the car manufacturing and oil industries to establish a timetable. Why cannot those whose endeavours have led to this decision also be involved? Why do these decisions always have to be left to the very people who have tried to postpone them and who, in this case, blundered in 1981 with the decision to proceed only to 0.15 grams per litre?

Third, while I accept that it makes sound sense to seek a Europe-wide initiative on this issue, and ministers should seek urgently to persuade our European partners to act together, Brussels has a remarkable capacity to delay action, and we cannot abdicate responsibility for the health of our children to others. We must press urgently for EEC-concerted action; if that does not come, we must proceed without it.

The ministers concerned will no doubt say they have committed themselves and we should trust them to act. They should recall that for 18 months they rejected our every argument, often distorted the evidence to their own advantage, and persistently claimed that their own policy was correct. They should not be surprised that scepticism remains about their determination to act with resolution.

The author is chairman of Clear and of Friends of

By Andrew Veitch, Medical Correspondent

The Government is to press for a European-wide ban on lead in petrol. Mr Tom King, the Environment Secretary, accepted the main recommendation of the Royal Commission on Environmental Pollution within an hour of its publication yesterday, and promised to negotiate a switch to lead-free fuel by 1990 at the latest.

Mr King refused to commit himself to unilateral action if his European initiative failed. However Euro-MPs of the right and left are already calling for a ban, and an EEC decision within 18 months is now a real possibility.

The Royal Commission recommended that by 1990 all new petrol-engined vehicles should be required to run on lead-free fuel. They called for immediate negotiations with the EEC and urgent discussions with the oil and motor industries.

No other toxic substance was distributed so widely and in such great concentrations. The

Commission's findings, Industry reaction, page 4; Leader comment, page 10; Parliament, page 25

Government's policy of reducing lead in petrol from 0.4 to 0.15 grams per litre in 1985

All new cars to take lead-free petrol within seven years

By Hugh Clayton, Environment Correspondent

All new cars will have to run on lead-free petrol by 1990, Mr Tom King, Secretary of State for the Environment, said yesterday. He was responding to a warning from the Royal Commission on Environmental Pollution that the amount of lead in the blood of the "general population" was too close to a potentially dangerous level.

Mr King's statement went further than any previous Government commitment. He said he would like new cars to be able to run on lead-free petrol before 1990, but there were two hurdles to cross before a date could be announced. One was to persuade the rest of the EEC to change Community rules to allow all member states to change to lead-free petrol, and the other was to agree with car manufacturers a date from which they could fit new models with appropriate engines.

At present petrol in the EEC must contain at least 0.15 grammes of lead per litre. The level to which British petrol will fall early in 1986. The present British level is 0.4 grammes per litre.

Existing engines can meet the 1986 low-lead requirement

but cannot run without lead-based anti-knock compound.

"I think this Royal Commission report has been valuable in cutting through a lot of the propaganda and a lot of the somewhat exaggerated claims of the various lobbyists on the various sides ", Mr King said later.

But Mr Gerald Kaufman, chief Opposition spokesman on the environment, said the Government's reaction to the Royal Commission was far too leisurely". A Labour administration would introduce lead-free petrol on a date of its choice, irrespective of the state of bargaining with the rest of the EEC.

Mr Des Wilson, chairman of the Campaign for Lead-Free Air (Clear), said: "It is a very exciting and even moving moment to find ourselves vindicated". But he demanded an immediate announcement from ministers of a definite early date for the introduction of lead-free petrol and a statement that opposition from the rest of the EEC would not delay its introduction in Britain.

He also wanted independent monitoring of the change to

prevent profiteering by industry.

The argument about lead in petrol overshadowed the commission's close investigation of all sources of lead, from pencils to beer. Mr King said he would comment later on its recommendations for removing lead from paint and drinking water.

Professor Richard Southwood, chairman of the Royal Commission, said it was important to reduce all forms of lead pollution to increase the safety margin between intake and the amount that could damage health.

The commission wanted quicker Government action to remove lead from piping, and was worried about an unresolved dispute between the Department of the Environment and the Water Research Centre over the phasing out of lead solder.

Professor Southwood said that concerted EEC action was necessary otherwise Continental lead pollution might "waft across the Channel", for example, in vegetables.

Continued on back page, col 3

THE TIMES

P.O. Box 7, 200 Gray's Inn Road, London WC1X 8EZ. Telephone: 01-837 1234

GOOD RIDDANCE TO LEAD

Nothing that can be said about lead has done more to give it a bad name than the supposed effect of even small quantities of [lead on the intel]ligence and [intel]l. Most of [the worst cam]paign for [the common]… [not]ably [from the self]… allow and ed environ- a significant children. It is campaign increasingly first charge singly con-

… environ connexion children's performance merely the accurate about of the sub- le measure- and beha- Other fac- IQ or social : similarly ilex pattern possible to 'eads.

mission on ution con- ion of this by saying, ccumulated te a causal the phys- ychometric cts of con- both. On

conclusively than the first. The children, not the lead, get the benefit of the doubt; and when would dare doubt it?

The report of the royal commission displays the extent of uncertainty surrounding the subject – uncertainty about the relative importance of different sources of lead pollution in the environment and of the different routes by which it approaches and enters the body, about the levels giving rise to poisoning or other harm, about the interpretation of the statistical evidence.

Constantly to stress the difficulties, the authors say, would be "an excessively negative approach". "Instead we have seen our task as making the best assessment from the existing information and drawing robust conclusions." One piece of the existing information impressed them, as well it might. The average blood lead concentration in the United Kingdom is one quarter of that at which unmistakable features of lead poisoning may occur. "We are not aware of any other toxin which is so widely distributed .... and which is also universally present at levels that exceed even one tenth of that at which clinical signs and symptoms may occur". The safety margin is precariously small in view of the chances of running into quite high local concentrations in the environment.

That, with the rest of its assessment, prompts the commission to open a general offensive against the practices through which man releases lead into the environment, from the most particular (boys with fishing rods closing split shot weights with their teeth) to the most general (emissions from the exhaust pipes of cars).

Petrol companies and motor manufacturers have been given a lot of stick in recent years, plumbers and water undertakings less stick than they deserve. Nearly half the houses in the country receive a water supply

that passes at some stage through lead piping. Where the water has the property of dissolving lead a person may receive more than half his uptake of lead from that source, which is more than twice as much as he is likely to get from lead in petrol.

The remedy is obvious, replace lead piping with one of the common and satisfactory substitutes. But it costs a bit, it requires action by householders, and it involves arguable decisions about apportionment of the expense. Instead of that there is a mixture of prominent grants, surveys by water boards, and additives to the water, all of which makes for small change. The Minister's practical enthusiasm for lead clearance should be judged by what he does about water pipes as well as what he does about petrol.

There is an already established trend in the industrialized world towards reduced lead content in petrol and ultimately lead-free petrol. Oil refiners and motor manufacturers are braced for further impetus in that direction coming from their governments, public opinion is expectant, and even motoring opinion, if that can be separated out, is becoming reconciled to the extra running and capital costs (which do not look too bad – part of the pain, according to the royal commission, coming not as extra fuel consumption but in the gentler form of fuel economy forgone).

The important thing now is to get the timing of this process right, which does not mean at the shortest possible time at all costs. The object is the avoidance not of certainties but of uncertain risks. It is therefore legitimate to weigh the economic costs of the innovation required and to balance that against speed of introduction. It is also right to seek as close a synchronization as possible among the major producers and markets. The commission looks to the landmark of all new cars built for lead-free petrol by the end of this decade. That is a reasonable target.

But where the advance of the subject may admit doubt the politics of the subject knows no such hesitation. It is now past the point where the onus of proof shifts from those who challenge current practices to those who would defend them. It is necessary to show [th]an environment [i]n to the risks [i]s necessary to [est]. And the [is] done no more

director of the Society of Motor Manufacturers and Traders, Mr Anthony Fraser, said that the industry would need five years to prepare for the new engines after a positive European decision. Lead-free petrol would cost an estimated 2p more a gallon at the pumps.

1990 deadline for lead-free petrol

Continued from page 1

The commission called for more research into lead in alcoholic drinks, but its main remaining concern was paint. Removal of paint containing lead by dry-sanding could be dangerous, the commission added. Contaminated dust could be inhaled or might settle in carpets. Although the yellow

paint used to make road markings outside schools did not contain enough lead to be dangerous, local councils should be forced to use paint with the lowest possible lead content.

The introduction of unleaded petrol is likely to add one or two pence to the cost of a gallon of petrol and mean a 5 per cent increase in fuel

consumption (Our Energy Correspondent writes).

The oil and motor industries both said yesterday that there would be no technical difficulty in switching to the manufacture of unleaded petrol by the proposed 1990 deadline.

But the Society of Motor Manufacturers and Traders said car prices could rise slightly following day. It was, said *The Times* in a leader, 'Good Riddance to Lead'.

We held our own press conference after Tom King, calling for the introduction of a definite date and saying that if there were delays in Europe, Britain should act unilaterally. But the battle on the principle was over. Of course, we did not have lead-free petrol, and CLEAR remains in being to fight for a definite and early date, to persuade other European countries to move to lead-free petrol as well, and to make sure that there is no sell-out. But the aim of the exercise was *a decision* – a decision by Ministers who did not want to take that decision, a decision in the face of Whitehall opposition, a decision in the face of the expenditure of vast resources by huge industries, a decision that was a reversal of an earlier Governmental decision two years earlier.

Was it because of the election? Perhaps that helped, but lead-free petrol would have been irrelevant in the election if CLEAR had not politicised the issue to the point where it was a factor. The Royal Commission's report was highly influential, but the Royal Commission only decided to look at the lead issue as a result of the CLEAR campaign, and earlier Royal Commission reports had to wait between two and seven years before notice was taken of them. Full credit had to be given to those in the Conservation Society and others who had worked on the issue before May 1981, but the fact is that the end result of their efforts had been a decision to reduce only to 0.15 grams per litre. CLEAR was, therefore, entitled to claim the decision as a result of its campaign, as a demonstration of the role and value of pressure groups when our institutions fail, and as reassurance that if people unite, contribute their money and their skills and their energies, and pursue their cause professionally with a sense of perspective, but with perseverance, they can triumph over considerable odds in protecting their interests.

Looking back over that 15 months one can see there were a number of crucial moments:

First, the publication of the Yellowlees letter in the early days added enormous authority to our case that there was a health hazard.

Second, the opinion poll with its extraordinary show of support, entitled CLEAR to say that it spoke for a huge constituency.

Third, the international symposium and the conversion of Professor Michael Rutter was a crucial psychological blow.

Fourth, the initiatives CLEAR took to dramatise the problem – the lead in dust survey outside schools, the lead in vegetables study, etc. – achieved colossal publicity and aroused enormous support.

Of all the activities we undertook, the tremendous effort we made to build up support from organisations, politicians, and local authorities, was perhaps the most valuable. However, I believe there are lessons for others in the way we determined realistic objectives, in the quality of our research linked to our determination to project our case with real authority, and in the way we refused to be diverted from our own campaign plan and our own battle-ground to that of our opponents.

The other side, particularly the industries, have their own version of events. Above all, they argued and would still argue that we exaggerated the health case and deliberately frightened people for no reason. It is, of course, true that we aroused concern all over the country about the health risk. But that was our task. It was precisely because the authorities refused to acknowledge it that we had to do this. I do not believe that people should be denied the knowledge of research and studies that indicate health problems. The people of Britain are adult and mature enough to consider the facts objectively and reach their own conclusions. Their instinctive human response was that they did not care whether the evidence was conclusive or not, for they could see that there were sufficient organisations and people of substance who were prepared to state that it was a risk, and they wanted action on the basis of risk. Not for them conclusive proof, achievable only by what would in effect have been experiment with their children.

I believe a number of other lessons can be learned from this campaign: The authorities have to learn that the people expect higher priority for environmental protection – that they rate the health of their children much more highly than the performance of their cars or the price of petrol. The industries have to learn that instead of trying to withstand the increasing concern for environmental protection, they would be far better to respond positively to it for if they do not they will end up being forced to act, often more expensively than if they had acted voluntarily. And hopefully the parents of this country have learned that when the democratic process fails them, when their institutions fail to respond, there is still hope – hope in the alternative ways of becoming involved – in voluntary organisations, charities and pressure groups, with a legitimate role in the democratic process and offering another way to exercise power.

References

1 Robert Benewick, contribution to *Knowledge and Belief in Politics*, Allen & Unwin, London, 1973.
2 Mick Hamer, contribution to *The Environmental Crisis*, Heinemann Educational Books, London, 1984.
3 Chris Rose, contribution to *The Environmental Crisis*, op. cit.
4 Francis Gladstone, *Charity, Law and Social Justice*, Bedford Square Press, London, 1982.
5 Frank Field, *Poverty and Politics*, Heinemann Educational Books, London, 1982.
6 Judith Cook and Chris Kaufman, *Portrait of a Poison – The 2, 4, 5-T Story*, Pluto Press, London, 1982.
7 Brian Martin, *Changing the Cogs*, FoE Australia, 1979.
8 Brian Martin, op. cit.
9 Denis MacShane, *Using the Media*, Pluto Press, London, 1979.

Further information

THERE ARE TWO organisations that can offer advice and a wide range of publications to assist pressure groups.

One is the National Council for Voluntary Organisations, 26 Bedford Square, London WC1B 3HU.

The other is The Volunteer Centre, 29 Lower Kings Road, Berkhampstead, Hertfordshire HP4 2AB.

An outstanding book on how to deal with the press, television, and radio is *Using the Media* by Dennis MacShane, published by Pluto Press and available in paperback for £3.95.

The following are the addresses of the main pressure groups Des Wilson refers to in this book.

CLEAR, 2 Northdown Street, London N1 9BG. Tel: 01-278 9686

Friends of the Earth, 377 City Road, London EC1. Tel: 01-837 0731

The 1984 Campaign for Freedom of Information, 2 Northdown Street, London N1 9BG. Tel: 01-278 9686

Shelter, the National Campaign for the Homeless, 157 Waterloo Road, London SE1. Tel: 01-633 9377.